POLICING SEX

This collection focuses attention on an important but academically neglected area of contemporary operational policing: the regulation of consensual sexual practices. Despite the high-level public visibility of, and debate about, policing in relation to violent and abusive sexual crimes (from child sexual abuse to adult rape) very little public or scholarly attention is paid to the policing of consensual sexual practices in contemporary societies. Whilst 'sexual life' is commonly understood to be a matter of 'private life' that is beyond formal social control, this book shows that policing is implicated in the regulation of a wide range of consensual sexual practices.

This book brings together a well-known and respected group of academics, from a range of disciplines, to explore the role of the police in shaping the boundaries of that aspect of our lives that we imagine to be most intimate and most our own. The volume presents a 'snapshot' of policing in respect of a number of diverse areas – such as public sex, pornography and sex work – and considers how sexual orientation structures police responses to them. The authors critically examine how policing is implicated in the social, moral and political landscape of sex and, contrary to the established rhetoric of politicians and criminal justice practitioners, continues to intervene in the private lives of citizens.

It is essential supplementary reading for courses in criminology, law, policing, sociology of deviance, gender and sexuality, and cultural studies.

Paul Johnson is Anniversary Reader in Sociology at the University of York, UK. His current research focuses on the relationship between law, sexuality and social control.

Derek Dalton is Senior Lecturer at the Flinders University Law School in Adelaide, Australia where he teaches in the Criminal Justice programme. His research interests cluster around the historic criminalization of homosexuality and contemporary issues surrounding the policing of sexual conduct in public.

POLICING SEX

Edited by Paul Johnson and Derek Dalton

Routledge
Taylor & Francis Group

LONDON AND NEW YORK

First published 2012
by Routledge
2 Park Square, Milton Park, Abingdon, Oxon, OX14 4RN

Simultaneously published in the USA and Canada
by Routledge
711 Third Avenue, New York, NY 10017

Routledge is an imprint of the Taylor & Francis Group, an informa business

British Library Cataloguing in Publication Data
A catalogue record for this book is available from the British Library

Library of Congress Cataloging-in-Publication Data
Policing sex / edited by Paul Johnson, Derek Dalton.
p. cm.
ISBN 978-0-415-66805-7 (hardback) – ISBN 978-0-415-66806-4 (paperback) –
ISBN 978-0-203-12073-6 (ebook) 1. Sex–Social aspects.
2. Social control. 3. Vice control. I. Johnson, Paul. II. Dalton, Derek.
HQ16.P648 2012
306.7–dc23
2011043842

ISBN: 978-0-415-66805-7 (hbk)
ISBN: 978-0-415-66806-4 (pbk)
ISBN: 978-0-203-12073-6 (ebk)

Typeset in Bembo
by Taylor & Francis Books

MIX
Paper from
responsible sources
FSC
www.fsc.org FSC® C004839

Printed and bound in Great Britain by
CPI Group (UK) Ltd, Croydon, CR0 4YY

CONTENTS

NOTES ON THE CONTRIBUTORS

Chris Ashford is Reader in Law and Society at the University of Sunderland, UK. A queer theorist, his research explores the regulation of 'bad' or illicit sex, focusing upon the phenomena of public sex, male for male sex work and barebacking. He has advised LGBT community and health groups, the NHS, police and the UK Parliament.

Derek Dalton is a Senior Lecturer at the Flinders University Law School in Adelaide, Australia where he teaches in the Criminal Justice programme. His research interests cluster around the historic criminalization of homosexuality and contemporary issues surrounding the policing of sexual conduct in public. He is also interested in cinematic representations of criminality, film classification law and dark tourism in places where crimes have occurred.

Paul Johnson is Anniversary Reader in Sociology at the University of York, UK. His current research focuses on the relationship between law, sexuality and social control.

Mary Laing is Lecturer in Criminology at Northumbria University, UK. Her research interests centre on the regulation of sex and sexualities with a specific focus on the sex industry. She is an academic board member of the UK Network of Sex Work Projects and has published in *Geoforum*, *Journal of Law and Society* and *Geography Compass*.

Dave McDonald is in the final stages of a PhD in Criminology at the University of Melbourne, Australia. His research explores social, legal and cultural representations of paedophilia. He has taught extensively at the University of Melbourne and La Trobe University, and in 2009 was awarded a prize at the University of Sydney Law School's postgraduate conference.

Leslie J. Moran is Professor in the School of Law at Birkbeck College, University of London, UK. He is Director of the Masters in Criminal Law and Criminal Justice programme. His current research interests are in hate crime, sexuality and the judiciary, and visual culture and justice.

Jo Moran-Ellis is a Senior Lecturer in the Department of Sociology at the University of Surrey, UK. Her research interests are primarily concerned with questions of competence, vulnerability and resilience in childhood. Her empirical work focuses on exploring these in the context of generational orderings and children's everyday lives.

Murray Perkins joined the British Board of Film Classification as a Film and Video Examiner in May 2000. In 2005 he became the Senior Examiner responsible for the 18 and R18 categories, consulting with the Metropolitan Police and the Crown Prosecution Service on obscenity and extreme pornography. Prior to coming to the UK, Murray worked for the New Zealand Office of Film and Literature Classification.

Antonia Quadara is Honorary Research Fellow in the School of Social and Political Sciences, University of Melbourne, Australia, where she completed the research upon which this article is based. She is also the Coordinator of the Australian Centre for the Study of Sexual Assault at the Australian Institute of Family Studies.

Teela Sanders is a Reader in Sociology at the School of Sociology and Social Policy, University of Leeds, UK. Her research focuses on the intersections between gender, regulation and the sex industry. Her monographs include *Sex Work: A risky business* (Willan Publishing, 2005) and *Paying for Pleasure: Men who buy sex* (Willan Publishing, 2008). With Kate Hardy, Sanders has completed a project funded by the Economic and Social Research Council on the lap-dancing industry, the findings of which will appear in *Flexible Workers: Labour, regulation and mobility in lap dancing* (Routledge, 2012).

André Smith is an Assistant Professor in the Department of Sociology at the University of Victoria, Australia. His research interests lie in understanding the biomedical regulation of vulnerable populations across a variety of health care settings. Recent publications include articles in the *Journal of Aging Studies*, *Dementia* and *Deviant Behavior*.

Kevin Walby is Assistant Professor in the Department of Sociology at the University of Victoria, Australia. He is co-editor of *Emotions Matter: A relational approach to emotions* with Alan Hunt and D. Spencer (University of Toronto Press, 2012) and is author of *Touching Encounters: Sex, work, and male-for-male Internet escorting* (University of Chicago Press, 2012).

INTRODUCTION

Paul Johnson and Derek Dalton

The inspiration for this book came from our interest in interrogating the long estab-lished and widely accepted idea that private and consensual sexual practices in con-temporary liberal, democratic societies are generally not subject to forms of policing. There is a persistent and, we believe, incorrect assumption in these societies that consensual sexual activities are beyond the scope of legal regulation and, as such, are free from social control by the police. Such an assumption is a common public 'story' that is repeatedly told in the nations that are the subject of this book. In Australia, Britain, Canada and the United States it is generally supposed that a 'turn to harm' (Fielding 2006) characterizes the criminal justice approach to sex and it has become increasingly accepted that any interference with 'sexual life' by the police responds to, and attempts to address, tangible harms that are being caused to victims (either to individual victims or to 'the public' more generally). It is further assumed that this approach to policing sex marks out these societies as distinct from other jurisdictions that seek to regulate sex in respect of 'traditional' or repressive forms of social morality. The recent and substantial media coverage in Britain of Uganda's now infamous 'Anti Homosexuality Bill' (Parliament of Uganda, Bill No. 18, 2009), for instance, expounded a general condemnation of the legal regulation of private male homo-sexual sexual practices while ignoring the fact that specific 'homosexual offences' existed in Britain until 2003.

The pervasive idea that the sexual life of consenting participants is long free from formal regulation has its roots in a cultural and legal approach to sex established by the *Report of the Committee on Homosexual Offences and Prostitution* (Home Office 1957). The 'Wolfenden Report' was forged within the furnace of a post-war debate in Britain about the role of the criminal law in regulating the consensual sexual behaviours of adults. It proposed the then contentious view – implicitly inspired by a Millian conception of individual liberty that was much propounded at the time by H.L.A. Hart (1963) – that, whilst it was appropriate for law to 'preserve public order and decency, to protect the citizen from what is offensive or injurious', it was not 'the function of the law to intervene in the private lives of citizens, or to seek to enforce any particular pattern of behaviour' (Home Office 1957: paras 13–14). This view is often imagined to be the blueprint that underpins the regulation of sex in the jurisdictions discussed throughout this volume. And it is a view that has achieved an almost hegemonic status among politicians (save for those who, rejecting it, would now be regarded as 'extreme') when they address the subject of sex. For example, in its most recent reform of sexual offences legislation in England and Wales, the UK government repeatedly asserted that its 'key guiding principle' was that 'the criminal law should not intrude unnecessarily into the private life of adults' and that '[a]pplying the principle of harm means that most consensual activity between adults in private should be their own affair, and not that of the criminal law' (Home Office 2000: para. 0.7).

A general acceptance that this view of regulation is 'true' means that, in contrast to high-profile public debates about policing in relation to violent and abusive sexual crimes (from child sexual abuse to adult rape), very little public or scholarly attention is paid to the policing of consensual sexual practices. We think this leads to making hidden the ways in which individuals experience forms of policing in respect of their mundane, ordinary and commonplace sexual lives. In commissioning these chapters and assembling this collection our motivation was not simply 'academic' but, rather, was driven by a concern to demonstrate, and to challenge, some of the ways in which policing impacts upon the real lives of individuals. As such, all of the authors in this volume contest the accepted story that policing does not intervene in private and consensual sexual life. Examining a wide range of sexual practices, and engaging with a broad canvas of regulation, the authors raise critical questions about the idea that 'harmless' sexual activities are free from social control.

Whilst this volume addresses a wide range of practices by different agents of social control that can be subsumed under the generic title 'policing', the primary focus is on the role of the public police. The book aims to show how operational policing, despite common-sense understandings to the contrary, is significantly involved in the regulation of the consensual sexual lives of individuals. The book demonstrates that ordinary sexual lives, far from being outside of the scope of police work, are still subject to various and significant forms of interventions. To show this, some of the authors in the book engage with police policy and practice directly in order to examine some of the ways in which operational police work impacts upon sex. These authors show how police work is directly implicated in fashioning the landscape of contemporary sexual politics and how it both challenges and sustains forms of social inequality and discrimination. Other authors examine the ways in which police practices themselves influence, underpin or respond to forms of regulation that are enacted by other agencies and individuals in the legal, welfare and medical sectors. Taken together, all of the chapters demonstrate some of the ways in which contemporary policing continues to target particular forms of sexual practices, or expressions of sexuality, and engage them in formal regulative scrutiny. In doing so, they show how policing plays a central role in reproducing 'archetypes of perversion' and contributes to common cultural conceptions of what is, and what is not, appropriate sexual conduct and experience in society.

Key themes

A number of themes and issues recur throughout the book and this demonstrates that, although there are wide variations in how regulation is enacted in different contexts and in respect of particular practices, policing sex revolves around some key concerns:

- *A question of morals:* Many of the authors demonstrate how the policing of sex in contemporary societies continues to be driven by moral (rather than harm-based) concerns. Johnson shows how policing is propelled by social morality, and Moran argues that policing is instrumental in the creation of a contemporary moral landscape of sex and sexuality which accords differential value to certain groups. Moral concerns are at the heart of Perkin's consideration of the censorship of 'sex works', and of McDonald's examination of how art is policed. Taken together, all of the chapters show the persistence of the role of police in enforcing forms of social morality and its impact upon individual lives.
- *The problem of consent:* Many of the authors challenge the commonplace characterization of certain practices as 'non-consensual' and question the regulation that flows from this. McDonald disputes claims about consent that underpinned the police intervention into a recent exhibition of photographs by the artist Bill Henson, Perkins outlines some of the issues encountered by experts who attempt to 'read off' consent from images in order to certify them as 'sex works', Moran-Ellis problematizes the argument that the exchange of images between teenagers via mobile telephones falls within legal definitions of sexual consent, and Quadara explores the ambiguous nature of consent in tabletop dancing venues where overt touching is prohibited but accidental and incidental forms of touching occur and are largely tolerated.
- *The private–public divide:* Many of the sexual practices detailed in the book take place outside of domestic homes but remain ostensibly private. Although there is a dominant and persistent view in society that sex outside the home is 'deviant' or 'perverse' and, as a consequence, should be policed, it remains the case that only certain forms of 'public sex' attract formal social control. Ashford, Dalton, and Walby and Smith discuss how particular forms of sexual behaviour, which take place in different public places, attract the attention of law enforcement agents. Laing, Quadara and Sanders challenge the idea that privacy puts consensual sex beyond formal social control by showing how sexual practices that take place on commercial private premises continue to attract intense forms of regulation. As such, all of these authors challenge the simple dichotomy between public and private that, following 'Wolfenden', is often said to underpin policing.
- *Technological change:* Rapid developments in information technologies have transformed the potential to both 'do' sex and to police it. Ashford highlights some of

the ways in which law enforcement agents use the Internet (through chat rooms and bulletin boards) as a form of intelligence, whilst Dalton, McDonald and Laing show how the Internet also provides a form of resistance to the regulation of sexual expression. Perkins provides an insight into the role of the police in regulating video representation. And Moran-Ellis shows how advancements in mobile telephone technologies have engendered increased regulation of consensual intimate expression.

- *Deviant types and cultural folk-devils:* Many of the authors remind us of the fact that the policing of sexuality evolves over time. Thirty odd years ago it would have been impossible to predict that the key targets of police scrutiny – like 'the flasher' or 'the nudist' – would fade into relative obscurity and be replaced by a new array of figures including 'the pole dancer' and 'the dogger'. The authors examine the extent to which new cultural forms and practices, such as pole dancing, dogging and commercial sex in general, represent new types of sex that have come to be regarded as deviant by the police. For example, Ashford and Dalton cast light on dogging as a new phenomenon that potentially turns police attention away from a traditional concern with male homosexual public sex. And Quadara, McDonald and Perkins touch upon the notion of the gaze and how certain forms of *looking* at sex are both encouraged and permitted (in the case of the pole dancing venues) or discouraged and disallowed (in the case of the gallery wall or the cinema screen).

Overview of the collection

We have deliberately commissioned a very heterogeneous collection of essays that, adopting different theoretical, methodological and disciplinary perspectives, provide diverse insights into the policing of sexual life. Taken together, our hope is that they provide a 'snapshot' of regulation across key areas of contemporary social life.

Part 1 focuses on the significant and far-reaching recent changes in the policing of sexuality in contemporary liberal societies.

Both Moran and Johnson explore some of the contradictions that have arisen in the policing of male same-sex sexuality in Britain and Australia since its decriminalization.

Moran explores the tension between the development of recognition politics in the English criminal justice system, which has enabled homosexuals to become regarded as 'good victims' of crime, and the tendency of the strategies and tactics of various agencies (including the police) to 'define down' and 'define out' crimes committed against them. He confronts the commonplace assumption that there has been a 'revolution' in police approaches to regulating same-sex sexual activity and places police policy within the broader complex of contemporary crime control. Moran shows that the political attempt to transform the social values associated with male same-sex sexuality may have made dramatic progress to achieve the goal of social justice for homosexuals, but it is a project that is neither complete nor one that has achieved stability. Contemporary policing policy does still focus particular attention on male same-sex sexuality, Moran argues, but there is a profound contradiction (and irony) in current approaches because it leaves gay men and lesbians particularly vulnerable to crime.

Johnson assesses the current landscape of policing sexuality in Australia through an analysis of the enforcement of moral law. He highlights the way in which discrimination can be produced by law that requires police officers to make moral judgements about particular sexual practices. Like Moran, Johnson explores a range of changes in policing that have taken place in respect of male same-sex sexuality. He shows how the police have attempted to respond to a range of competing social, cultural and legal demands regarding sexual orientation issues. Johnson demonstrates that male homosexual sex continues to attract police attention because of the way police officers respond to complaints from the public. As a result of this, the police are frequently labelled as 'homophobic' and said to 'over-police' gay men. Johnson examines how police officers struggle to deal with these competing moral demands.

Part 2 focuses on the issue of 'public' sex, challenging many of the assumptions that underpin the persistent regulation of various sexual practices.

Ashford turns his attention to the policing of consensual heterosexual sexual practices in Britain that take place outside of domestic homes. He views such policing as a state response to the challenges that public sex makes to both mononormative and heteronormative social relations. However, as Ashford notes, the work of the police in this area cannot be understood as straightforwardly repressive since policing operates in a complex web of competing and contradictory statutory law, public policy and community expectations. And the police themselves have recently attempted, albeit unsuccessfully, to escape from the burden of their mantle as 'moral guardians'. Ashford raises intriguing questions about the role of UK policing in sustaining normative heterosexuality.

The idea that policing serves to sustain the social construction of sex and sexuality in particular ways is considered by Walby and Smith through an analysis of contemporary surveillance techniques. They argue that the surveillance practices engaged in by law enforcement officials do not simply reflect, but actively reinscribe, dominant discourses of sexuality in society. Walby and Smith argue that police surveillance functions in respect of three long-standing binaries – public–private, gay–straight and risky–safe – that remain axiomatic to contemporary Canadian law enforcement tactics designed to capture men engaged in same-sex sexual acts. They consider how other forms of surveillance, such as surveillance medicine, utilize the same binaries in controlling male homosexual sex and show how these help to produce ideas about risky sexual subjects that justify police interventions. Walby and Smith argue that the surveillance of law enforcement officials produces, perpetuates and distorts understandings of sexuality, which pathologizes men who have sex with men.

Dalton examines male homosexual sex at 'beats' as a practice that has long attracted varying degrees of social animosity and police scrutiny. He traces the emergence of this problematic category of sexual practice that resists neat classification as public or private and illegal or legal. He explores how 'beat sex' is represented through legal discourse as disgusting, perverse and contaminating, and demonstrates how this legacy of disproval and disapprobation underpins police interest in regulating it. Dalton goes on to compare and contrast a range of strategies and initiatives that are employed to police 'beats', noting that, whilst some practices seem fair and reasonable, others involve dubious ethical and professional standards. Indeed, it is the particularly problematic tactic of entrapment that prompts Dalton to explore how gay men are using Internet sites to marshal and organize resistance to police attempts to foreclose on their desire in 'beat' spaces. Dalton concludes by contrasting 'beat' public sex with the phenomena of 'lovers' lane' and 'dogging', questioning why 'beat' spaces seem to attract disproportionate police attention compared to these other public sex 'problems'.

Part 3 focuses attention on the production and consumption of representations of sex and sexuality across various contexts and media. The authors consider how the classification of images as obscene, pornographic and abusive, allows their regulation in the art gallery, the video 'sex work' and the personal mobile telephone.

Perkins provides a rare and unique insight into the world of the censor. As Senior Examiner at the British Board of Film Classification (BBFC) with specific responsibility for the classification of 'sex works' (making him one of Britain's most influential censors of filmed pornography), Perkins shows how state censorship, even in the face of major technological changes that have enabled the easy possession and distribution of images, continues to fashion the contemporary visual landscape of sex. He demonstrates the ways in which the BBFC has, at times, attempted to restrict the availability of certain sexual imagery, only to find resistance to its decisions by those who produce sex works as well its own appeals committee. Negotiating a very dense network of individuals and agencies, the BBFC continues to collaborate with the police to regulate images deemed to be obscene. Perkins shows how the police have, at times, advised that particular representations of sexual activity should be censored in spite of their knowledge that some juries may be unlikely to regard such images as obscene; at other times, he notes how advice from the police has enabled the expansion of the availability of certain types of imagery. Perkins shows that censorship relies upon a range of 'expert' opinions, both legal and medical, to 'draw the line' that determines what is and what is not obscene and, in doing so, distinctions between 'morality' and 'harm' often become blurred.

Where to 'draw the line', and who is responsible for drawing it, is also central to McDonald's consideration of the regulation and censorship of images. McDonald examines how policing becomes implicated in public debates about what constitutes acceptable and 'artistic' representation of children. He shows how the labelling of particular artworks as 'obscene' is the outcome of the mobilization of dominant discourses about childhood and how this, in turn, influences the response of law enforcement agents. McDonald demonstrates how powerful 'folk' conceptions of paedophilia propel the police to assume particular standpoints, adopt specific enforcement positions and attempt to regulate images. In responding to hysterical calls for the censorship of 'perversion', law enforcement officials become bound up in defining sexual normativity in contemporary societies.

A similar concern with questions of childhood, pornography and sexual exploitation characterizes Moran-Ellis's analysis of the exchange of imagery by teenagers via mobile telephones. Moran-Ellis problematizes – in the first sociological examination of 'sexting' – many of the assumptions that pervade public discourse about this form of intimate practice. She shows, through an analysis of media and legal texts, how a range of actors, across multiple sites, are responsible for the social and legal 'translation' of a form of consensual and harmless intimate practice into a set of behaviours that seem to require regulation. Drawing on actor-network theory, Moran-Ellis argues that this multi-participant translation is vital in creating both an object and an offender that can be subject to social control. She highlights some of the ways in which regulation takes place, as well as demonstrating the ways in which it is resisted.

Part 4 examines the range of ways in which 'sexual services', most of which are legal and involve consenting adults, continue to be policed.

Sanders takes a broad look at the policing of prostitution in England and Wales and considers the inter-relationship between public policy and operational policing. Using a socio-historical framework, Sanders shows how policing strategies intersect with other forms of social control that originate in the welfare context. What is striking about her analysis is that she shows how recent developments in social and criminal justice policy have dramatically eroded the 'Wolfenden' settlement that characterized the policing of prostitution. Whilst 'public prostitution' continues to be subject to formal police regulation – and the introduction of Anti-Social Behaviour Orders now allow for those selling sex to receive custodial sentences for non-imprisonable offences – there has also been a heightened criminalization of 'indoor' work. Sanders argues that never before has the long-standing preoccupation with regulating female sexuality produced such intense policing of 'private' spheres. This increase in regulation, the result of a moral preoccupation with sex, problematizes assumptions that sex work is policed only when it produces tangible harm to victims.

Quadara's analysis of recent changes in the regulation of 'sexual services' in Victoria, Australia, utilizes an expansive definition of 'policing' to consider both the regulation of sex workers and their clients. Quadara focuses particular attention on an often-ignored aspect of such regulation: the ways in which it attempts to control men's desires and bodies. New law, she argues, reiterating long-standing heteronormative ideas about male sexuality, confers legal powers onto officials, such as fair trading inspectors, who are responsible for making discernments about real masturbation, simulated masturbation, real climax and simulated climax. Her analysis of this regulation of male sexuality in 'private' lap-dancing venues raises important questions about how this may necessitate forms of policing in 'public' spaces. Policing sex in this way, Quadara argues, ensures the naturalness of a 'phallogocentric order' and maintains a problematic cultural distinction between sex that can be 'paid for' and sex that is 'free'.

Laing focuses attention on the regulation of sex work in Canada through an analysis of federal law and local licensing arrangements. Using qualitative interview data from research with sex workers and law enforcement agents, she details the impact of law enforcement upon those who provide sexual services. She shows how, where licensing arrangements exist, particular forms of policing practices are engendered. Some licensed sex workers are supportive of police 'busts', Laing argues, because they serve to regulate the market and suppress competition. Other sex workers, Laing claims, attempt to negotiate with the police or resist incursions into their work. What Laing ultimately demonstrates is that whilst there is considerable variability in policing, both geographically and operationally, a constant police presence shapes the consensual activity of buying and selling sex. Policing, Laing concludes, is very much present in our bedrooms.

The aim of the book

Our overall aim in assembling this book was to demonstrate that policing, contrary to the spirit of the Wolfenden Report, continues to intervene in the private lives of citizens and, as a result, contributes to enforcing particular patterns of sexual behaviour in contemporary societies. We think that the collection achieves this aim, showing how policing is involved in the regulation of different sexual behaviours that can be characterized as private and consensual. Many of the authors demonstrate that such regulation is not intended as repressive and, as Moran argues, police services have made significant attempts to police in more 'democratic' and less intrusive ways. And, as the book shows, policing practices are often engendered not by the desire of the police themselves, but by the moral, social and legal concerns of a range of other actors (Hall et al. 1978). Nevertheless, policing (and, as many of the authors argue, legal regulation more generally) remains engaged with particular aspects of sexual life and particular types of sexual subjects. The result of this is that certain behaviours become singled out as deviant and, subject to a range of social controls, those individuals who participate in them are deprived of the promise that governments so often espouse: that their consensual sexual activity should be their own affair and not the business of the law.

Bibliography

Fielding, N.G. (2006) *Courting Violence: Offences against the person cases in court*. Oxford: Oxford University Press.

Hall, S., Critcher, C., Jefferson, T., Clarke, J.N. and Roberts, B. (1978) *Policing the Crisis: Mugging, the state and law and order*. London: Palgrave Macmillan.

Hart, H.L.A. (1963) *Law, Liberty and Morality*. Oxford: Oxford University Press.

Home Office (1957) *Report of the Committee on Homosexual Offences and Prostitution* (Cmnd 247). London: HMSO.

——(2000) *Setting the Boundaries: Reforming the law on sex offences*. London: HMSO.

Part 1

The contemporary landscape of policing sexuality

1

THE CHANGING LANDSCAPE OF POLICING MALE SEXUALITIES: A MINOR REVOLUTION?

Leslie J. Moran

I begin with two snapshots. The first is an extract from a police statement dated 25 August 1933. The statement is part of a file deposited at the United Kingdom's National Archives in London.[1] It is one of many files in the Archive's collections relating to the operations of London's Metropolitan Police Service.[2] The second comes from a guide produced in 2000 by the Association of Chief Police Officers (ACPO), an organization devoted to bringing together police service heads 'to share ideas and best practice, co-ordinate resources and help deliver effective policing which keeps the public safe' (ACPO undated).

First, the police statement:

> STATEMENT of _____, Police Constable,
> 528 'M' Division, who saith:
> At 11.15 pm, on the 24th August 1933, I was on duty in plain clothes, accompanied by P.C. 565 'M' Division_____, keeping observation on the public lavatory situated at the junction of Fair Street and Tooley Street, Bermondsey, in consequence of complaints having been received of indecent behaviour by male persons ... I entered the lavatory ... A short time later the prisoner, _____ entered the lavatory ... and he came round to the stall immediately on my right ... After a few minutes the prisoner made a half-turn towards me, stretched out his left arm and placed his left hand on my person and commenced rubbing it. I immediately took hold of his left arm, his left hand still being on my person. I said to him 'I am a Police Officer and I am going to take you into custody for indecently assaulting me'.
>
> *(MEPO 3/990, undated)*

This extract records part of a police operation in a public lavatory in London in 1933. It was conducted by two plain clothes officers based at Tower Bridge Police

Station. The full statement details an elaborate, intense encounter made up of gestures, movements and glances, between the police officers dressed in plain clothes and a number of other men late at night. My edit of the statement sets the scene and then moves to the recorded details of the devastating climax – 'his left hand on my person' – and its dreadful aftermath. The file records that the arrest led to a successful prosecution. The accused man was found guilty on two charges of indecency with another man, one an offence under the Offences Against the Person Act 1861 and another contrary to a London County Council By-Law.

The second snapshot comes from the 'Introduction' to the *ACPO Guidance on the Policing of Public Sexual Activity* (ACPO 2000). It begins:

> In 2000 the newly formed Association of Chief Police Officers (ACPO) Lesbian, Gay, Bisexual and Transgender (LGBT) Working Group identified a need for national guidance for responding to complaints from the public of men visiting public toilets and other public environments for the purpose either of engaging in sexual activity with other men there (cottaging) or elsewhere (cruising) …
>
> *(ACPO 2000)*

Despite the more generic focus of this document expressed in its title, 'policing public sexual activity', the preoccupation of the ACPO 'Guidance' is quickly revealed as male sexual activity and more specifically sexual activity between men. Several lines later the Guidance continues:

> … there needs to be a clear public acknowledgement that the reasons why men engage in public sexual activity are several and complex, in many cases reflecting personal experiences of homophobia. Thus, this model (sic) emphasises the value of building trust with local LGBT communities and engaging in consultation at all stages of the process
>
> *(ACPO 2000)*

Turning to the causes of the wrongdoing, there is some resistance in the Guidance to a one size fits all approach, though in the final instance one cause is highlighted: the existence of prejudice. This ACPO position, the Guidance explains, is one that seeks to engage communities and legitimate practices of policing. The objective is to ensure that, when taken, police action will be seen as 'fair, necessary and legitimate'. It goes on to say that if those who engage in public sexual activity themselves experience homophobic crime then, as victims of that crime, they will be supported by the police. The 'Introduction' concludes:

> Protecting lesbians, gay men, bisexuals and transgender people from homo-phobia … is a responsibility of the police and other statutory agencies acting in partnership …
>
> *(ACPO 2000)*

The Guidance then proceeds to set out 12 overarching principles to guide police when witnessing acts of, or responding to complaints about, sexual activity in a public place. It is followed by a detailed scheme outlining four stages of institutional decision-making applicable to policing this particular type of activity (see Chapter 3). The guidance has been widely adopted, making an appearance on police service websites throughout England and Wales.

Much separates these two snapshots. Time is one: almost 70 years. Another is the nature of the phenomenon portrayed. The first snapshot might be described as a description of a police response at a micro level. The second offers more of a macro-level response. The first extract is an after the event record detailing an actual police operation from the perspective of one officer involved. It tells us little about the police decision-making processes prior to the operation. The second is a national policy and a model operating procedure. It provides a framework for thinking about policing male public sexual activity. It purports to guide what ought to be done prior to and in the process of undertaking an operation. These two examples of police operations also have things in common. Both evidence an enduring interest in policing male sexual practices and a legal and institutional landscape devoted to their regulation. They are connected by an enduring attribution of disorder and insecurity to some consensual same-sex sexual activities. They share a point of departure: both are provoked by 'complaints' being received by the police. The objective of this chapter is to examine some of the factors that have generated the changes that separate these two connected snapshots. In part this will be pursued through an examination of the impact of recognition politics upon criminal law and criminal justice. It also involves a reflection on institutional changes affecting the crime control management of contemporary sexual order and disorder.

Recognition politics

Recognition politics is all about social injustice and struggles for social justice (Fraser 1995). It potentially touches on all social interactions. In the context of this chapter, the social justice in question is the individual and collective effects of the negative social and cultural values attached to particular sexual practices and their attribution to sexual identities by criminal law and criminal justice agencies. The history of criminalization demonstrates that the range of social interactions that might fall within these parameters is diverse (Moran 1996). The political project is one that seeks to transform the values attributed to these practices. In crude terms, it is an attempt to turn them from a negative to a positive; to give due respect to the subject of those practices and particular identities. In this case it is a political project that addresses the social injustice that flows from the multitude of negative associations connected to consensual same-sex erotic relations and to the formation of identity categories that have come to be closely associated with the political project of revalorizing those relations: 'Uranian', 'Invert', 'Homosexual', 'Gay', 'Lesbian' (Moran 1996; Weeks 1981).

Criminal law and the institutions of criminal justice have been and continue to be something of a preoccupation of a recognition politics concerned with male same-sex sexual practices. There are many reasons for this. The law administered by the police, and other criminal justice agencies more generally, has provided one context in which there has been a preoccupation with ideas about male sexuality and in which the negative values associated with male sexual practices with other men have been shaped, institutionalized and legitimated (Moran 1996; McGhee 2001). Certainly in England and Wales, the location of my particular study, women's sexuality in general and sexual relations between women in particular have been policed differently.[3] As part of the State machine that puts legal preoccupations with male sexuality as a threat to social order into practice, the police have played a key role in bringing the full weight of the law and, with it, the full force of the State's monopoly of violence to bear on the bodies of men.

Decriminalization of sexual relations between consenting male adults in private has often been and continues to be regarded as the essential first step in any campaign to address the social injustice embedded in the negative values associated with consensual same-sex desire that have long shaped and been given legitimate force in law and its institutions. But it is far from the end of the matter (McGhee 2001; Moran 1996). The gap between the Sexual Offences Act 1967, which introduced important but limited decriminalization of sexual relations between two consenting adults in private, and the Sexual Offences Act 2003, the most recent reform of sexual offences, was a period in which heroic campaigns were waged to reimagine the nature of sexual relations between men (Waites 2005). The eventual removal of several offences that were unique to male-on-male acts, in the 2003 Act, such as gross indecency, and indecency with a man, is one sign of that campaign's success (Johnson 2007).

Another dimension of the success of this campaign is to be found in section 2 of the Sexual Offences Act of 2003. That section creates a new offence, 'Assault by penetration'. It can be committed by men and women and the victim can be male or female. It criminalizes penetration 'with a part of his (sic) body or anything else' (Sexual Offences Act 2003, section 2 (1)(a)). The part of the body penetrated is the vagina and anus. Assault by penetration differs from rape as it is an act of unlawful violence that is not gender specific. The offence of rape, in section 1 of the 2003 Act, relates to the penetration of the vagina, anus or mouth of another person using a penis. A person convicted of that offence is liable to a penalty of imprisonment for life. The punishment for assault by penetration is the equivalent of that attached to the offence of rape.

Section 2 of the 2003 Act is relevant here as an example of the emergence of law that addresses men who have sex with other men and women who have sex with other women as 'good victims'. A 'good victim' is a subject whose experience of violence is recognized as a threat to good order. As a 'good victim' the subject gains access to all those criminal justice services that are dedicated to bringing disorder to an end. As a 'bad victim' the tables are turned against the one who calls for help. That call provokes a hostile intimate investigation into the subject's past behaviour and current practices in a search for disorderly conduct. A classic example of this economy of 'good' and 'bad' victim in a same sex context is the man who reports an act of violence against him during a public sex encounter with another man. The victim of violence here ends up being labelled the problem, being arrested. An example with a lesbian focus might be acts of sexual violence, rape, used to 'cure' the woman of her desires. As a 'bad victim' the lesbian would be construed as the 'cause' of the sexual violence (Rich 1980). The rise of political campaigns around 'homophobic hate crime', which in English law is violence motivated by hostility or violence that evidences hostility towards particular groups (Crime and Disorder Act 1998, section 28), is one example of recognition politics targeting and challenging the policies and practices that deny victims of violence access to the status of the 'good victim' and, as a result, access to safety and security (Moran and Skeggs 2004; Stanko and Curry 1997).

ACPO's Guidance on policing public sexual activity is shaped by the success of recognition politics as outlined above. Evidence of this is in ACPO's acknowledgement that:

> ... there is no doubt that men who engage in [public sexual activity] run a risk of falling victim to homophobic crime and the clear message needs to sent (sic) (and received and believed) that victims of such crimes will be supported by police.
>
> *(ACPO 2000)*

So engagement in what may well be criminal acts of consensual public sex does not necessarily preclude the same man being recognized as a victim of violence; the previously 'bad victim' must now, with regard to the violence he received, be treated as a 'good victim'. The words in brackets in the above quotation are of particular interest as they point to the ongoing cultural legacy of the impact of the status of 'bad victim' on the perceptions and expectations of men who have sex with other men. A survey of lesbian and gay expectations of discrimination by Stonewall captured evidence of the lingering effects of the role played by criminal justice agencies in producing and deploying discrimination. One in five lesbian and gay people reported an expectation that they would be treated worse than heterosexuals when reporting a crime to the police if their sexuality was know to the police. A quarter of lesbian and gay respondents expected they would be treated worse if they reported a homophobic crime. And expectations increased outside of London. Age was another factor. Lesbians and gay men over 50 reported higher expectations of discriminatory treatment (Hunt and Dick 2008: 11). Returning to the Guidance, the words in the brackets reflect this lingering expectation of discrimination. It is not enough for the police to send the message that any violence will be recognized; it calls for the police to make sure that the message is received and effective. The final sentence of the 'Introduction' nods towards the more general impact of successful campaigns to attach the label 'good victim' to 'lesbians, gay men, bisexuals and transgender people'. Protecting those people, the Guidance explains, 'is a responsibility of police and other statutory agencies acting in partnership' (ACPO 2000). These particular sexual subjects are recognized here as sexual citizens and as the potential beneficiaries of one of the fundamental aspects of the liberal myth of the social contract: safety and security delivered through the State's agencies of crime control (Phelan 2001).

Institutional change

The reference to 'police and other statutory agencies' in the closing lines of the ACPO Introduction brings into focus the second issue I want to address: the institutional dimensions of policing sexuality and changes to those institutions. Before going further I want to turn to some of David Garland's (1996) work and to his phrase 'the limits of the sovereign state'. It is a phrase Garland uses in a preliminary exploration of changes to criminal justice strategies occurring in Western liberal democracies that experience enduring levels of 'high crime'. In 'high crime' societies, he suggests, the perceived endurance of crime is generating a range of sometimes-contradictory responses and new developments. So, it generates a renewed commitment to using the state machine of criminal justice institutions to deal with crime. To name but a few changes, this may involve the removal of rules and procedures that are perceived to protect defendants, an increase in punishments, and the decline of reform-focused initiatives (Garland 2001). At the same time it gives rise to a recognition of the 'limit' of the power of those same agencies; to the inability of the state's traditional criminal justice institutions to meet the challenges of crime and to bring crime to an end. In response to this 'limit', crime control strategies are reoriented towards prevention, the containment of crime and the reduction of crime opportunities. My interest in Garland's analysis is limited to the insights it can facilitate with regard to contemporary strategies of crime control in the particular context of England and Wales. While all the strategies of change being generated in response to the recognition of the state's limits potentially have relevance for a study of policing sexuality, I confine myself to just two of them. The first is the rise of the multi-agency approach to crime control. The second is a strategy of 'defining down' crimes. What impact do these have on policing male sexual activity?

'Multi-agency' and other phrases such as 'partnership', 'inter-agency', 'activating communities' are all, Garland suggests, terms that refer to strategies and techniques of 'responsibilization' (Garland 1996: 452). This refers to contradictory institutional developments. On the one hand they institutionalize a 'limit' perspective, acknowledging that the traditional criminal justice agencies are not capable of, or are in themselves insufficient for, controlling crime. A turn to prevention of crime acknowledges that not all crime will be reported, successfully detected, prosecuted and punished. A focus on prevention also fits with an idea that those who commit crimes may not be reformable, so opportunities for crime have to be better managed and reduced. In institutional terms the strategic response is rather inconsistent. On the one hand the role of traditional criminal justice institutions appears to decline. Crime control prevention responsibilities become more diffuse involving many different state and non-state institutions, organizations and individuals. Multi-agency is a mechanism that allows responsibility for crime prevention to flow away from state criminal justice institutions to a wider range of state institutions and more importantly towards the civil society agencies and organizations that are drawn into the partnership web. At the same time that the crime control role of state agencies are recognized as being limited, there is a state-fostered growth in crime control strategies and practices by way of demands for new and ever closer engagement and cooperation: building and solidifying links between state and non-state agencies and organizations in their common pursuit of a shared crime prevention objective.

Let me give one example of a multi-institutional crime control network to illustrate the point in relation to policing male sexuality. It is from Brighton, a medium-sized city that has a sizeable LGBT community. The Brighton and Hove Crime and Disorder Reduction Partnership is made up of local criminal justice agencies, council services, several agencies with responsibilities for children, such as schools and child protection agencies, fire and health services, private sector agencies and organizations, such as local stores and businesses, and community and voluntary organizations, such as victim groups and faith groups. The Crime and Disorder Act 1998 introduced a statutory obligation to develop partnerships such as this to address crime and disorder. Section 6 of that Act requires these partnerships to produce crime reduction strategies. The Brighton & Hove Crime & Disorder Reduction Partnership is now into its second strategy that will cover the period 2011–14 (Brighton and Hove undated).

One of the community groups involved in the partnership was 'Spectrum'. Spectrum was the name of the lesbian, gay, bisexual and transgender forum. It was set up to assist and coordinate the realization of an LGBT community strategy. It was a forum dedicated to recognition politics, with a diverse policy agenda addressing a range of social justice objectives, including health, families, housing, education, culture, economic development and safety (The Associates 2001). The Crime and Disorder Partnership was one context in which it pursued these objectives and its 'safety portfolio' in particular. It was one of the 'Community and voluntary sector agencies' (Brighton and Hove undated) in that partnership. Other organizations under that banner were groups dealing with different aspects of the equality and social justice agenda: gender, race, ethnicity, disability, faith, age. Spectrum's existence and involvement in the crime control partnership was indicative of a major change resulting from the recognition politics described earlier, which involved the appearance of gay men, lesbians and bisexuals as active participants within policing organizations (McGhee 2005, 2010).[4]

One of the pages on the Partnership's website was dedicated to 'LGBT Hate Crime/Incidents'. While it is my primary focus here, this is not to suggest it was the only area of the partnership's activities that were of interest to Spectrum or the LGBT community more generally. The page contains the 'LGBT Strategic Action Plan 2008–2011' (Brighton and Hove 2008). The plan was formally networked, linked to a range of other policy initiatives, 'parallel plans', that related to housing, domestic violence, equality more generally and Spectrum's own raft of policies and plans. The plan identified 8 outcomes and 13 'agreed priority areas'. The outcomes clustered around three main themes: partnership working (sustaining, improving and further embedding partnership working); improving support for survivors of violence (hate crime and sexual assaults) in general and for particular groups such as victims of homophobic bullying in schools; and safety, a generic focus. All of this fell under a statement of 'performance indicators' by which the success of these initiatives was to be measured.

The only specific target was for a hate crime detection rate of 30 per cent by the end of 2010/11. Note, this was not a *conviction* rate. While this target did identify a key role for the police as a state agency of crime control, it was only one stage on the pathway to a successful conviction (a goal that is commonly associated with crime control). Some 30 per cent may well fall within the range of what can be achieved but it does also indicate that a 70 per cent failure is not in itself unacceptable. Building better working relationships to promote safety and supporting victims or 'survivors' fills up the gap left by the acknowledged 'limit of the sovereign state' to bring hate crime to either an end or to a determination of due punishment.

Turning now to the detail of the LGBT hate crime page, after a definition of 'hate crime' the focus turns to 'What you can do'. What follows is split into two sections: 'When you are on foot' and 'If you are a victim'. The former section contains the following advice:

> Act confidently; Go out or walk with friends or people you trust; Use a taxi – keep money for taxis; Try to use well-lit, busy roads; Stay alert – be aware of your surroundings; Have your keys in your hand when you reach home or your car; Avoid confrontational situations.

This list is not just about safety; it is about the self-management of safety. It is all about 'responsibilization'; making the individual responsible for his or her own safety. Under the title 'If you are a victim' the advice is less complicated: as well as urging victims to 'Make noise and shout for help' and 'Go to a safe place, as soon as possible' emphasis is placed on the need to 'report it immediately'. The reader is urged to report it in a variety of ways, via the police emergency number (999), by way of contact with other relevant authorities, or via third party reporting mechanisms. Some more detailed advice follows on how to preserve evidence. The preoccupation with reporting is not particularly surprising when so many community studies report that only a small percentage of homophobic violence is ever reported (Dick 2008). The call to report it via a multiplicity of agencies both seeks to enhance reporting but also mirrors the importance of multiple agencies. But reporting needs to be connected back to the limited role of the sovereign state expressed in the objective of a 30 per cent detection target.

One interesting feature of the Brighton & Hove Crime & Disorder Reduction Partnership website is the absence of direct reference to policing public sexual activity. It thus appears to be an aspect of policing male sexuality that has no place in crime control strategies in this location. But this is not quite the whole picture. The applicable policing policy relating to public sex – a summary of the ACPO Guidance – can be found on the website of Sussex Police. Following the Guidance, policing public male sexual activity is embedded in the relevant 'partnerships'. One of the principles adopted by Sussex Police, following the Guidance, flags the importance of crime prevention. In any intervention, it explains, any police response should be set within a duty to reduce crime and disorder and to enhance community safety. Other principles points to the importance of 'consultation with consultative groups' including LGBT and Crime and Disorder partners and the divisional Independent Advisory Groups (IAG) (Sussex Police undated).

Finally, I want to turn to the matter of 'defining down' or, in this case, strategies that might be better described as 'defining out' male sexuality from the crime control agenda. 'Defining down', Garland explains, refers to adaptations that effect a reduction in the level of demand placed upon criminal justice agencies (Garland 1996: 456). I have space only to mention a couple of strategies that have the effect of reducing the level of demand for policing male sexuality. The first is urban planning. One method is to remove locations where public sexual encounters might take place. For example, the public lavatory at the centre of the story of policing male sexuality that I used to open this chapter is no more.[5] Its closure is far from unique. It is an instance of what has been described as 'an alarming decline' in the number of public toilets in London (Blue Badge Tourist Guides 2005). Urban renovation is another method with the potential to achieve the same effect. Between September 2001 and January 2007 several central London Squares have been the subject of major restoration initiatives. At least one of those squares, Russell Square in Bloomsbury, was well known as a late night cruising ground for men that have sex with other men (Turner 2006). Funded by the National Lottery Heritage Fund, low-level bushes were stripped out and railings and gates were renovated and replaced. The result is a square that has been stripped of intimate locations and is closed after dark. One of the avowed aims of the renovation of this garden was said to be to deter men from using the square as a meeting place for sex (Anon 2005; Freeman 2001). In these examples the policing of male sexuality is defined down/out by urban design.

Another innovation that conjoins urban modification with new technologies is video surveillance (CCTV). Estimates vary as to the number of CCTV cameras in the UK, ranging from 4.2 million to 1.85 million (Lewis 2011; Anon 2011). Few of these cameras are owned or operated directly by the police. The vast majority are privately owned and operated but with public and quasi-public locations in view, such as leisure facilities, shopping malls, stores, galleries, bars and clubs and toilets. Gay venues are as likely to incorporate video surveillance into their fabric as straight venues. While the effects of video surveillance are difficult to determine they include the prevention of activity. But this is not their only effect; it may also lead to a displacement of activity to an apparently ever-diminishing number of locations that remain beyond the technological gaze. It may also enhance criminalization; the realist assumptions associated with camera technology (Tagg 1998) work to form CCTV images of male sexual practices as a potentially powerful form of 'evidence' (Biber 2007). Another effect is to exploit the aesthetic effects of visualization: turning male sexual practices into works of art (Biber and Dalton 2009) and the material for reality television (Doyle 2003; Mason 2003).

The ACPO Guidance embraces these and similar 'defining out' strategies. They are clustered in 'Stage 3' of a proposed 4 stage response. They come under the generic title of 'opportunity reduction'. One cluster of interventions focuses on environmental design and landscaping, including cutting back shrubbery and signage. Here aesthetics is harnessed to manage the disorderly potential of certain male sexual practices. Another cluster focuses on surveillance: lighting, 'guardians', such as park patrols or toilet attendants, and, last but not least, CCTV. These initiatives are all examples of strategies that seek to make public, or to make more public, particular practices of male sexuality in certain locations. A third cluster relates to the location itself: closure or timed restriction.

Conclusion

This review far from exhausts the differences that separate policing male sexuality in 1933 and the present. What it does do is to draw attention to some of the major political and institutional developments – the minor revolution – that need to be considered in any attempt to make sense of that gap and of the development of contemporary practices of policing consensual male-to-male sexual practices. If, in England and Wales, the political agenda that seeks to transform the values associated with male sexuality in a same-sex setting has made dramatic progress to achieve its goal of social justice, then it is a project that is neither complete nor one that has achieved stability. Men that have sex with men are no longer reducible to signs of disorder (see, however, Chapters 4 and 5). This male sexual subject now has the potential in crime control contexts to occupy the position of an officially recognized sexual citizen. The institutional presence of LGBT organizations within crime control strategies is both testament to the success of this recognition politics and a sign of the potential for ongoing injustice. However, the realization of that goal in the contemporary landscape of crime control initiatives produces a rather ironic effect. Just as it becomes legitimate to turn to the state for safety and security, many current crime control institutions and strategies emphasize the subject's own role in ensuring safety.

Notes

1 http://www.nationalarchives.gov.uk/default.htm (accessed 16 June 2011).
2 The file was closed to the public until 1993.
3 For example, the private realm of the family has played a significant role in policing women's sexuality. On lesbians and criminal justice see for example: Doan 1997; Dugan 2000; Hart 1994; Robson 1995. On gender and crime there is a large literature but, for example, see: Heidensen 2000, 2006; Naffine 1997; Smart 1977, 1989; Young 1990, 1995.
4 Another mode of appearance takes the form of self-identified gay, lesbian and bisexual people working as police officers (Burke 1993; Loftus 2008).
5 For a map showing the current location of public toilets in London see http://www.toiletmap.co.uk/ (accessed 28 May 2011).

Bibliography

ACPO (undated) *Welcome to ACPO*. Online. Available at http://www.acpo.police.uk/ (accessed 20 June 2011).
——(2000) *ACPO Guidance on the Policing of Public Sexual Activity*. Online. Available at http://www.met.police.uk/dcf/files/LGBTacpo.pdf (accessed 16 June 2011).
Anon (2005) *Hidden London: Russell Square*. Online. Available at http://www.hidden-london.com/russellsquare.html (accessed 22 June 2011).
——(2011) 'Big Brother is *Definitely* Watching You: Shocking study reveals UK has one CCTV for every 32 people', *Daily Mail*, 3 March. Online. Available at http://www.dailymail.co.uk/news/article-1362493/One-CCTV-camera-32-people-Big-Brother-Britain.html (accessed 29 June 2011).

The Associates (2001) *Count Me In: Brighton and Hove lesbian, gay, bisexual, transgender community strategy 2001–2006*. Online. Available at http://www.docstoc.com/docs/85539575/Count-Me-In (accessed 18 January 2011).

Biber, K. (2007) *Captive Images: Race, crime, photography*, Abingdon: Routledge-Cavendish.

——and Dalton, D. (2009) 'Making Art from Evidence: Secret sex and police surveillance in the tearoom', *Crime Media Culture*, 5(3): 243–67.

Blue Badge Tourist Guides (2005) *Public Toilets in London: Investigation by London Assembly*. Online. Available at http://www.blue-badge-guides.com/inconvenience.html (accessed 16 June 2011).

Brighton and Hove (undated) *Working to Keep You Safe in the City*. Online. Available at http://www.safeinthecity.info/ (accessed 22 June 2011).

——(2008) *LGBT Action Plan 2008–2011*. Online. Available at http://www.safeinthecity.info/files/LGBT%20Strategic%20Action%20Plan%202008-2011.pdf (accessed 21 June 2011).

Burke, M.E. (1993) *Coming Out of the Blue*, London: Cassell.

Dick, S. (2008) *Homophobic Hate Crime: The Gay British Crime Survey 2008*, London: Stonewall. Online. Available at http://www.stonewall.org.uk/documents/homophobic_hate_crime__final_report.pdf (accessed 29 June 2011).

Doan, L. (1997) 'Gross Indecency Between Women: Policing lesbians or policing lesbian police', *Social and Legal Studies*, 6(4): 533–46.

Doyle, A. (2003) *Arresting Images: Crime and policing in front of the television camera*, Toronto: Toronto University Press.

Dugan, L. (2000) *Sapphic Slashers*, Durham, NC: Duke University Press.

Fraser, N. (1995) 'From Redistribution to Recognition? Dilemmas of justice in "post-socialist" age', *New Left Review*, 212: 68–94.

Freeman, C. (2001) '£1.4 Revamp for Russell Square', *Evening Standard*, 9 August. Online. Available at http://www.thisislondon.co.uk/home/article-911526-14-revamp-for-russell-square.do (accessed 22 June 2011).

Garland, D. (1996) 'The Limits of the Sovereign State: Strategies of crime control in contemporary society', *British Journal of Criminology*, 36(4): 445–71.

——(2001) *The Culture of Crime Control: Crime and social order in contemporary society*, Oxford: Oxford University Press.

Hart, L. (1994) *Fatal Women*, Princeton, NJ: Princeton University Press.

Heidensen, F. (2000) *Sexual Politics and Social Control*, Milton Keynes: Open University.

——(2006) *Gender and Justice: New concepts and approaches*, Cullompton: Willan Press.

Hunt, R. and Dick, S. (2008) *Serves You Right: Lesbian and gay expectations of discrimination*, London: Stonewall.

Johnson, P. (2007) '"Ordinary Folk and Cottaging": Law, morality and public sex', *Journal of Law and Society*, 34(4): 520–43.

Lewis, P. (2011) 'You're Being Watched: There's one CCTV camera for every 32 people in UK', *Guardian*, 2 March. Online. Available at http://www.guardian.co.uk/uk/2011/mar/02/cctv-cameras-watching-surveillance (accessed 29 June 2011).

Loftus, B. (2008) 'Dominant Culture Interrupted: Recognition, resentment and the politics of change in an English police force', *British Journal of Criminology*, 48: 756–77.

McGhee, D. (2001) *Homosexuality, Law and Resistance*, London: Routledge.

——(2005) *Intolerant Britain: Hate, citizenship and difference*, Milton Keynes: Open University.

——(2010) 'From Hate Crime to "Prevent": Community safety and counter-terrorism', in N. Chakraborti (ed.) *Hate Crime: Concepts, policy, future directions*, Cullompton: Willan Press.

Mason, P. (2003) 'The Thin Blurred Line: Reality television and policing', in R. Tarling (ed.) *Selected Papers from the British Criminology Conference, Keele 2002*, Keele: British Society of Criminology. Online. Available at http://www.britsoccrim.org/volume5/003.pdf (accessed 17 July 2011).

MEPO 3/990 (undated) *Police Report*, Metropolitan Police, London: National Archives.

Moran, L.J. (1996) *The Homosexual(ity) of Law*, London: Routledge.

22 Leslie J. Moran

——and Skeggs, B. (2004) *Sexuality and the Politics of Violence and Safety*, London: Routledge.

Naffine, N. (1997) *Feminism and Criminology*, Cambridge: Polity.

Phelan, S. (2001) *Sexual Strangers: Gays, lesbians and the dilemmas of citizenship*, Philadelphia, PA: Temple University Press.

Rich, A. (1980) 'Compulsory Heterosexuality and Lesbian Existence', *Signs*, 5(4): 631–60.

Robson, R. (1995) 'Convictions: Theorizing lesbians and criminal justice', in D. Herman and C. Stychin (eds) *Legal Inversions: Lesbians, gay men, and the politics of law*, Philadelphia, PA: Temple University Press.

Smart, C. (1977) *Women, Crime and Criminology*, London: Routledge.

——(1989) *Feminism and the Power of Law*, London: Routledge.

Stanko, B. and Curry, P. (1997) 'Homophobic Violence and the Self at Risk', *Social and Legal Studies*, 6(4): 513–32.

Sussex Police (undated) *Public Sexual Activity: Sussex Police policy*. Online. Available at http://www.sussex.police.uk/about-us/information-rights/information-we-publish/current-force-policies/public-sexual-activity—sussex-police-policy (accessed 29 June 2011).

Tagg, J. (1998) *The Burden of Representation: Essays on photographies and histories*, Basingstoke: Macmillan.

Turner, M. (2006) 'Welcome to the Cruising Capital of the World', *The Observer*, 30 July 2006. Online. Available at http://www.guardian.co.uk/books/2006/jul/30/george michael.popandrock (accessed 22 June 2011).

Waites, M. (2005) *The Age of Consent: Young people, sexuality and citizenship*, Houndmills: Palgrave Macmillan.

Weeks, J. (1981) *Sex, Politics and Society: The regulation of sexuality since 1800*, London: Longman.

Young, A. (1990) *Femininity in Dissent*, London: Routledge.

——(1995) *Imagining Crime*, London: Sage.

2

THE ENFORCERS OF MORALITY?

Paul Johnson

Introduction

The relationship between sexuality, law and morality continues to prove fertile ground for debate. Half a century after the 'Wolfenden Report' (Home Office 1957) was published in the UK, the extent to which the criminal law should be used as a mechanism to protect or promote particular sexual moralities is still very much a 'live' issue. In the UK, at least, where a 'turn to harm' (Fielding 2006) is often said to now characterize the approach to law making, legislators continue to produce new statutes with the principal aim of prohibiting certain sexual behaviours in order to encourage a particular and preferred form of social morality. Recent examples of this are the criminalization of 'sexual activity in a public lavatory' and the possession of 'extreme pornographic material' where, in both cases, legislation was enacted in light of moral, rather than harm-based, concerns (Johnson 2007, 2010a).

What is missing from much contemporary debate about law and sexual morality is a consideration of the role of law enforcement. Law is – unless we accept command theories – never wholly self-enforcing but requires application by agents charged with its administration. Whilst law has a significant symbolic role in shaping the normative moral relations of contemporary societies, its power to do so is derived, in large part, from the existence of a system that enforces (or is perceived to enforce) it. Yet this vital aspect of law enforcement is strangely absent from much contemporary legal scholarship. Even legal positivists who, following Hart (1994), recognize that law expresses socially constructed and culturally relative values (rather than universal and natural ones) often fail to consider how, or by whom, moral law is actually enforced. An extreme, but persistent, assumption in much jurisprudence is that law formalizes social morality into rules that 'have a positive moral effect in that they cause a deposit of moral ideas in the mind' (Olivecrona 1971).

Yet any 'effect' that law has is significantly determined by the capacity for its enforcement. Devlin (1965) recognized that the most fundamental aspect of moral law, particularly in respect of sexual behaviours, was a system for enforcing it:

> The line that divides the criminal law from the moral is not determinable by the application of any clear-cut principle. It is like a line that divides land and sea, a coastline of irregularities and indentations. There are gaps and promontories, such as adultery and fornication, which the law has for centuries left substantially untouched. Adultery of the sort that breaks up marriage seems to me to be just as harmful to the social fabric as homosexuality and bigamy. The only ground for putting it outside the criminal law is that a law which made it a crime would be too difficult to enforce ... The boundary between the criminal law and moral law is fixed by balancing in the case of each particular crime the pros and cons of legal enforcement.
>
> *(Devlin 1965: 21–2)*

Whilst many now disagree with Devlin's assessment of which forms of sexual behaviour should be prohibited by law, his analysis of the way in which 'practical' aspects of enforcement determine the effect of moral law remains persuasive.

A focus on policing

As this book demonstrates, there are many agencies and individuals, both within and outside criminal justice systems, which can be said to enforce law in order to police sex. In this chapter my concern is with the public police and I focus, like Ashford and Dalton in this volume (Chapters 3 and 5), on the policing of consensual sexual activity in public places. The chapter draws upon previously published work (Johnson 2008, 2010b) in which I argue that laws relating to sexual activities in public places often encourage differential enforcement in respect of sexual orientation and, as a result, produces disproportionate social control of male homosexual conduct. Here, I investigate that proposition using data from an empirical study of the enforcement of law in Australia by the New South Wales (NSW) Police and, in particular, their negotiation of the 'sensitive issue' (NSW Police 2008) of policing 'beats' (those public locations, such as parks, beaches or public lavatories, where men meet to facilitate or engage in sexual activities).

The chapter draws upon data produced during a qualitative study conducted in New South Wales in August/September 2009. The study involved semi-structured interviews with a purposeful sample of 12 personnel from criminal justice agencies who are routinely involved with the policing of beats: 6 NSW police officers from the rank of superintendent to senior constable, all of whom are, or work closely with, Gay and Lesbian Liaison Officers (GLLOs) and 6 members of the 'Beats Working Group', an inter-agency forum that consists of representatives from health, law enforcement (including NSW Police, Park Rangers and NSW Attorney General's Department), local government, and gay and lesbian community organizations.

Using the data from the qualitative interviews, I show how the legal construction of public sex offences facilitates forms of police discretion that encourage the disproportionate social control of male homosexual conduct. Whilst selective enforcement of law on the basis of sexual orientation often produces the complaint that homosexual sex is 'over-policed' and that this expresses the institutional homophobia of the police (see Chapter 5), I argue that selective enforcement is the outcome of a more complex relationship between morally paternalistic statutory law and the contemporary demands of police work. Whilst it has been recognized that policing is influenced by officers' own conceptions of social morality (Reiner 2000; Westley 1970), and that officers 'drink regularly from the fount of morality and replenish their internal esprit de corps by invoking a larger virtue that their actions serve' (Herbert 1996: 815), what I demonstrate here is that officers' 'personal' morality is only one aspect that informs how they interpret and enforce moral law. Patterns of enforcement, I argue, are the result of how police officers negotiate a wide range of competing community, societal, organizational and personal moral demands when interpreting law.

The police interpretation of moral law

NSW Police officers can utilize a range of statutory law to enable the regulation of sexual activities in public places. All statutory provision is gender-neutral and, since the repeal of all male homosexual specific offences from the Crimes Act 1900 by the Crimes Amendment (Sexual Offences) Act 2003, there is no legal distinction between heterosexual and homosexual sexual activities in public or in private. The Summary Offences Act 1988, sections 4 and 5, is the law most frequently used by NSW Police in relation to sexual activity in public places. Section 4 prohibits 'offensive conduct' so that a person 'must not conduct himself or herself in an offensive manner in or near, or within view of hearing from, a public place or a school'. The test to determine whether any conduct is offensive is its capacity to 'wound the feelings, arouse anger, resentment, disgust or outrage in the mind of the reasonable person' (*Grivelis v Horsnell*, 1974, 8 SASR 43). The maximum penalty upon conviction of a section 4 offence is three months imprisonment. Section 5, a more serious offence, prohibits 'obscene exposure', so that a person 'shall not, in or within view from a public place or a school, wilfully and obscenely expose his or her person'. Whether exposure is 'wilful' is determined by an act being done 'deliberately and intentionally', rather than by 'accident or inadvertence', so that 'the mind of the person who does the act goes with it' (*R v Senior*, 1899, 1 QB 283). The interpretation of the word 'person' in the legislation remains undefined in Australian law and is not taken to mean, as in English law, 'penis' (*Evans v Ewels*, 1972, 2 All ER 22). The maximum penalty upon conviction of a section 5 offence is six months imprisonment.

Both sections 4 and 5, as legal instruments designed to enforce social morality, require police officers to make moral judgements about sexual conduct in relation to the standards of 'reasonable people' and 'community morality'. When sexual activities are classified in relation to ideas about the moral standards of 'reasonable' or 'respectable' people, homosexual acts have always been more vulnerable to classification as 'offensive' or 'obscene' because such standards of reasonableness and respectability have often been conceived in diametric opposition to homosexuality and, vice versa, homosexuality has often been regarded as a de facto infringer of a community's moral standards. Why certain forms of sexual conduct, and not others, become recognized as socially problematic and, in turn, as 'crime' is therefore the outcome of how sexual acts are understood in relation to socially dominant ideas, and moral evaluations of, sex and sexuality.

For instance, although section 4 potentially regulates *any* sexual activity in a public place that does not involve the display of genitals, officers are instructed to assess whether sexual acts are 'offensive' by determining their capacity to cause moral harm to an 'audience' who may witness them. To aid this assessment, NSW Police (2008) guidance suggests that officers consider the 'seriousness of the offences occurring in the location [and] the nature of the geographical location'. All of the criminal justice practitioners I interviewed stated that geographic location was central in adjudicating the 'seriousness' of the potential harm to 'the public'. One police officer, for example, made the distinction between sexual behaviour in a city public park and rural bush land to argue that sexual activity in a public park is easier to define as offensive because it takes place in a context where others are regularly expected to be. However, whilst the seriousness of offences is determined by an evaluation of the potential audience within different geographical locations, understandings of the relationship between geography and audience are informed by ideas about sexual orientation. For instance, in a consideration of kissing in a public place, one police officer stated that if two men were witnessed kissing in a public park at night, then this behaviour could be categorized as offensive because it could be deemed to be 'threatening' to those who witness it – something that would not be the case in relation to heterosexual conduct. The seriousness of offences, in this sense, is determined within a conceptual framework where male homosexual conduct is imagined as 'more' offensive to an audience (and this 'offended audience' is itself imagined as heterosexual).

That officers regard male homosexual acts in public places as having a greater capacity to be harmful to those who witness them is significantly influenced by culturally normative ideas about gender and sexuality. It is striking, for instance, that, when police officers are asked to account for why women are so infrequently charged with section 5 offences, they use cultural, rather than legal, understandings to explain this. All of the officers I interviewed explained the disproportionate focus on male conduct to stem from biological differences between male and female bodies, with one officer stating that 'it is difficult for a woman to commit [this offence] because it is difficult for a woman to show her genitals in public'. This understanding of bodies, which relies upon socially normative conceptions of female genitalia as essentially hidden and difficult to 'wilfully' display in public, provides the basis on which gender-neutral law comes to be enforced in a gendered way. Because this normative understanding of bodies underpins the offence categorization, it means that only displays of male genitalia are likely to be regarded as 'obscene'.

However, the point at which the display of male genitals in public places becomes regarded as obscene is subject to further culturally normative understandings about the display of bodies in public. It is not simply that the display of a penis in any public place will result in police officers classifying conduct as a section 5 offence. For instance, the officers I spoke to said that they would not use section 5 to deal with men urinating in a public place. Such behaviour does fall within the scope of the law, but officers felt it was rarely used because most men urinating in public were not 'deliberately' attempting to expose their penis to others. What constitutes 'deliberate' exposure is therefore subject to interpretation in respect of the context in which acts take place. For example, officers said that it would be uncommon to use section 5 in cases of public nakedness when a man deliberately exposed his genitals as part of some disorderly conduct. As in the case of urination in public, they said it would be more common to use section 4 to classify behaviour as offensive.

Where officers do encounter the deliberate display of genitals in the context of sexual activities, all of the criminal justice practitioners I interviewed stated that the decision to use either section 4 or 5 was significantly determined by the sexual orientation of those involved in the acts. All of the police officers argued that the use of section 5 in relation to heterosexual genital activities would be considered disproportionate by most officers; heterosexual sexual acts in public places are, they said, dealt with using either section 4 or, more commonly, through the issuing of 'move on directions' under section 197(c) of the Law Enforcement (Powers and Responsibilities) Act 2002. By contrast, in cases of genital sexual acts involving men, all of the officers I interviewed were unequivocal that the use of section 5 was potentially appropriate.

Policing for the community and responding to their complaints

Underpinning this interpretation of the law in respect of sexual acts in public places, officers argue, are the expectations of 'the community'. NSW Police (2008) state that the purpose of policing beats is to 'deter offensive behaviour' because of 'complaints' from 'residents or locals' and stress, through their publicly available and internal operational documents, that the source of, and desire for, the policing of beats is found in the community itself. In this sense, policing is officially imagined to be based on a model of community engagement and response within the tradition of neighbourhood policing where community concerns are seen as a vital element in defining and identifying the nature and presence of local problems. The NSW Police intranet informs its officers, for example, that it 'is often difficult to identify whether an area is a beat' and that beats are 'often identified by members of the public or members of certain occupations such as security guards and rangers who then contact police to report the matter'. As one officer explained, 'we are acting on the genuine concerns of the community' or, as another more prosaically put it, 'we don't go looking for it'.

When policing is understood to be a solution to community-identified problems, it means that any selective enforcement on the grounds of sexual orientation can be understood to be the outcome of community complaints rather than discriminatory policing. However, it is important to recognize that public complaints to the police about 'crime' in this area pose several problems. The most significant is that, as the Association of Chief Police Officers (ACPO) of England and Wales recognize, it 'is likely that the majority of complaints from members of the public are still likely to be about public sexual activity between men' (Metropolitan Police undated). ACPO recognize that complaints to the police cannot be seen to simply reflect a higher level of male homosexual public sex in a community but, rather, that disproportionate levels of complaints are shaped by and produced because of the broader social and moral relations of society. This is certainly a key concern of NSW Police. All of the officers and other criminal justice practitioners I spoke to were aware that complaints, across both urban and rural local area commands (LACs), largely relate to homosexual conduct and rarely to heterosexual sexual activities.

The nature of complaints about homosexual sexual activities in public received by the police suggests that complaints, as in relation to prostitution (Hubbard 1999; Sanders 2009), are often motivated by moral concerns. At one Sydney city centre LAC, for instance, complaints are regularly received from 'dog walkers' who report having seen 'homosexual activity' in public parks at night. These complaints, however, rarely relate to visible sexual acts witnessed by the complainants but, rather, to the congregation of men in a particular area. As one officer put it, complaints are frequently received about 'lots of parked cars with one bloke in each car'. Another frequent complaint to the police concerns 'littering' in areas where discarded condoms, underwear and other sexual paraphernalia are allegedly found. The police interpret these complaints as expressions of anxiety about behaviours perceived to be 'threatening' rather than as reports of visible sexual activities that could be legally classified as offensive or obscene. In other words, police are aware that complaints often express a culturally normative 'fear' about male homosexuals as predatory sexual 'monsters' or perverts (Warner 2000) rather than report instances of crime. This contrasts sharply with complaints regarding heterosexual public sex that, although infrequently received, overwhelmingly relate to concerns about the safety of those involved in activities and their vulnerability to crime.

Higher levels of public complaints lead to, as one officer put it, the 'inevitability' of higher levels of policing in relation to male homosexual activities. This officer saw the disproportionate policing of male homosexual sexual activity to be the outcome of a 'complaint driven' process that reflects the concerns of the wider community. Therefore, whilst officers are aware that higher levels of complaints are not necessarily based on any evidence that men are more frequently witnessed engaging in homosexual sexual activity in public places, they regard higher levels of policing as the inevitable outcome of the nature and scope of community policing. Many of the complaints received are often communicated to the police anonymously by telephone and, in the absence of any way of acquiring further intelligence, they invariably necessitate an operational response. Yet, officers do routinely consider complaints in relation to the motivations of the complainants. This was illustrated by one recent complaint that was received anonymously by telephone and conveyed by the regional dispatcher to officers in a rural LAC via their car radios. The officers received the complaint from the dispatcher in the following way: 'there are men having sex in the public toilets'. The officer I interviewed, who was on duty at the time the complaint was received, said that he immediately questioned the accuracy of the complainant's report and, in addition, whether it was 'beefed up' by the dispatcher. As was common with the other officers I interviewed, this officer questioned the validity of such complaints because of a tacit operational knowledge that sex between men in public toilets is highly likely to be discreet and largely invisible to the 'general public' – a view supported by Humphreys' (1970) ethnography of the interaction order of public sex encounters between men – and that complaints about such activity tend to be exaggerated.

Complaints in this area were regarded by those I interviewed as especially problematic because, reflecting the prejudices and biases of those making them, they often 'beef up' crime problems. Officers were concerned that complaints can (and do) become the foundations on which disproportionate policing activity is generated. Whilst one complaint about an area may result in one or more patrols by officers to a scene, more complaints may be regarded as the basis for sustained police presence. As one officer told me, complaints about beats result in 'ongoing complaints areas' becoming identified and these produce more frequent police attention. This officer felt that the identification of such areas produces an escalation in policing that is problematic: because officers know these areas have received complaints, he argued, it can 'prejudice their policing' and 'cloud their judgement'. This is because of a failure on the part of some police officers, he argued, to distinguish between the nature of the complaints received and the actual nature of the problem. Because complaints rarely relate to nudity or visible sexual activity, but rather to 'signs' that a beat exists, the moral offence that underpins the complaint may not relate to any tangible crime. In short, officers raised the concern that, whilst 'the community' has become seen as the essential driver in all criminal justice matters (Garland 2001), expressions of 'problems' by members of a community need thorough, ongoing and formally guided analysis by the police.

Community morality and the role of discretion

It is because of the nature of complaints in this area that officers' use of discretion is highly significant. As criminal justice practitioners in Sydney told me, if an officer encounters a 'guy and girl in Hyde Park' having sex they will most often say 'piss off', or 'get a room', and move them on and make no formal record of the incident. For officers, the use of discretion in this way is justified by what they see as their responsibility to make decisions that reflect 'community morality' and uphold 'community standards'. It is common for academics to question whether, as the 'lens' through which community norms are filtered, police officers refract a particular conservative, sectarian or authoritarian set of standards (Reiner 2000) or reflect a common set of social values and beliefs (Waddington 1999) in their approach to the enforcement of the law. Some have argued that police officers must be seen as moral agents who, when enforcing the law, do not simply detect crime but actively conceive and construct it (Cohen 2002; Hall et al. 1978; Young 1971), and previous research in this area has shown that police officers do actively 'uncover' homosexual conduct – and therefore make visible behaviour that would otherwise go unseen by 'the public' – on the basis that *they* find it morally offensive or obscene (Desroches 1991; Moran 1996 and Chapter 1). However, it would be wrong to reduce the 'moral arbitration' of police officers in this area to the level of the 'psychological' or cognitive processes of individual officers (Mason 2007) or see it as an effect of 'police culture'. Rather, it is important to recognize how officers' discretion in relation to offence categorization is shaped by the broader normative community relations in which policing operates (Fielding 1988).

Understanding police discretion in relation to community norms is complex in this area of law enforcement. On the one hand, the officers I interviewed all said that the moral values of the 'general community' underpin policing in this area and that, in responding to this, a greater focus on male homosexual conduct was 'inevitable'. On the other hand, officers also said that changing social attitudes about the 'gay community' have resulted in policing approaches that do not simply criminalize beat users but also ensure their health and safety when they are themselves victims of crime. These ideas of community – of the 'general' and 'gay' communities – can be seen to create a number of tensions within policing that, in turn, produce different (and contradictory) police styles. Such tensions illuminate the more general problematic ideological notion of 'community' at the heart of 'community policing' (Findlay 2004). However, they also show how policing is a crucial nexus at which the needs and expectations of multiple and different communities meet and compete.

When police officers talk about the policing of public sex environments they do so in ways that imagine 'the interaction of police and all community members to reduce crime and the fear of crime through indigenous proactive programs' (Oliver 1998: 51). However, it is important to note the highly selective way in which a 'community' and its 'problems' become recognized and legitimated by the police. As Brogden and Nijhar argue, through the use of discretion 'the police determine the nature of the community, its problems and how such problems should be responded to' (Brogden and Nijhar 2005: 65). Given the competition between, what becomes framed as, the moral values of the 'gay' and 'general' communities, police discretion 'on the ground' is often an attempt to balance the demands of various interested community groups and individuals. As street-level bureaucrats (Lipsky 1980; Somerville 2009), the police therefore exert considerable influence in determining which moral values become privileged.

As I argued above, it is common for academic commentators to argue that the use of police discretion is influenced by the morality of individual police officers – what Reiner (2000) calls the 'working personality' of officers – and by 'police culture'. Whilst all those I spoke to said that police discretion does contribute to higher levels of formal control of male homosexual sex, they did not account for this as simply the result of the 'personalities' of individual officers or of police culture. Rather, they saw it as the outcome of the interaction between the individual 'values' of officers and the broader cultural and moral relations of the communities in which they work. For example, one officer said that his use of discretion in policing beats had 'changed dramatically' since joining NSW Police and accounted for this as the result of two main changes, in policing and in society: first, he saw the training that he undertook to become a GLLO as significant in altering his approach and, second, he felt that his time spent policing in a community where there was a high density of 'gay couples' had a significant impact upon his practice. 'This community was very accepting of gay couples', he told me, and there were 'older couples living with their life partners, with established businesses … ordinary people who just happen to be gay'.

The perceived impact of the 'gay community' upon policing beats, which was shared by all those I interviewed, is interesting for two main reasons: first, aligning the 'gay community' with 'beats' is problematic because many men who use beats will not identify as 'gay'; and, second, there is an implicit, normative, but empirically problematic, assumption that the 'gay community' is more tolerant of public sex than the 'general community'. Nevertheless, all of the criminal justice personnel I interviewed recognized broad change in the use of police discretion, resulting in a 'softer' approach to policing beats, to be the outcome of changes in 'community values' and a significant factor in this change was seen to be the greater visibility and presence of the 'gay community'.

Despite this change, those I interviewed saw competition between different community norms and values as central to policing in this area. One officer, for example, contrasted his experience of policing in Sydney with policing in a rural community where there were 'no visible gay groups' and where '90 per cent of the gay community is underground'. This LAC, he told me, comprised an 'old fashioned, old world Australian homophobic community'. He contrasted these two locations to make a point about the important relationship between law, policing and community: 'you have to be seen to be doing the job in relation to the law but also in relation to community opinion'. This officer found working in a 'homophobic community' frustrating because of the community expectation that policing should always uphold these values. All of the officers I spoke to expressed, in differing ways, the sentiment that they felt 'caught' between the expectations of the 'general community' and those of the 'gay community'.

The conception of tensions between different community values can be seen to have a significant impact upon police discretion in respect of section 4 and 5 offences. One officer, for example, described how a once standard surveillance practice designed to detect men engaged in sexual acts in public toilets – which involved officers looking under cubicle doors to count pairs of feet in order to determine whether there was more than one person in each cubicle – was regarded as antithetical to contemporary police work. When I asked him if officers still engaged in that practice he said 'you're damned if you do, and damned if you don't'. He went on to explain that, even when a complaint about offensive behaviour necessitated a duty to investigate, if he attended a scene and found no sexual acts being committed 'openly in public' then he felt there was no significant problem that demanded further investigation. But he added that the decision to not investigate further (by not looking under cubicle doors, or forcibly opening them) would not meet the expectation or gain approval from most members of the 'general public'. Another officer described how, following several complaints about litter, a high number of parked cars, and the destruction of the vegetation at a local beat, she organized a 'risk assessment' of all the local parks to determine the status of lighting and other aspects of the facilities. She was subsequently accused, she says, of harassing the gay community and asked 'how do you not know it was kids who destroyed the vegetation, or left condoms?' In line with NSW force policy, she also engaged in discussions with beat users as a method of discouraging the types of activity being complained about and was, she says, accused by others of 'encouraging gay sex' and 'sitting in a police car giving out condoms'. 'You can't win', she said.

Police discretion and 'habitus'

Because public sex offences are constructed through law that encourages a moral interpretation of behaviours (as 'offensive' or 'obscene'), the law engenders a 'strong' form of discretion. The law actively requires criminal justice practitioners to engage in moral arbitration around certain activities and this, inevitably, involves police officers making moral judgements. Police officers' moral reasoning in relation to different types of behaviour is a significant aspect in both the conceptual construction of 'crime' and the subsequent response to 'criminals'. As Punch argues, the police 'tend to divide people into "moral" categories, which generates powerful negative feelings about those involved … and leads to feelings of contempt if not hatred for criminals' (Punch 2009: 43). An implicit aspect of the moral categorization of all crime is, as Punch argues, how officers view certain behaviours as 'unsavoury and seedy' (2009: 43). In the case of public sex offences, the law makes these moral 'feelings' central and explicit. In one sense, because it is socially normative for male homosexual sexual acts in public places to be understood as 'disgusting' (Johnson 2007), it is unsurprising that individual officers disproportionately classify such behaviour as 'offensive' or 'obscene'. It is routine for male homosexual sexual acts in public places to be seen by police officers as 'other' to and 'outside' of normative conventions. One officer explained it like this: police officers, she said, are 'a part of the community at large' and 'this community at large cannot on the whole understand why anyone would want to be a beat user'. This officer explained encounters between police officers and beat users as a reflection of a broader moral tension between the 'community at large' and men who have sex at beats: when officers encounter sex at beats, she argues, it 'confronts their morality'.

A key aspect of the characterization of this 'confrontation' between moral values is that police officers are understood to occupy a particular standpoint in respect of sexual morality – the standpoint of 'ordinary' members of a community. What is significant about this standpoint is that it is not politically neutral, but is aligned with socially normative ideas about sex and sexuality. For instance, as one officer explained, in relation to sexual activities involving men in public toilets: 'all visible sexual behaviour is offensive because a reasonable person wouldn't do that'. These ideas, about what a reasonable person would and wouldn't do, are the basis on which police officers use their discretion to transform the abstract legal moralism of sections 4 and 5 into operational practice. It is for this reason that policing attracts the complaint that it 'intersects with the normalization of sexuality' (Walby 2009: 377).

However, police officers are not the passive instruments of 'heteronormative morality' but agents who are actively engaged in an ongoing moral evaluation, interpretation and classification of different behaviours. If, through their interpretation and enforcement of the law, police officers do reproduce the heteronormative morality of the 'general community' then this must not be seen as *inevitable* or *automatic* but, rather, as an *active* accomplishment of police work. 'Public morality' should therefore be seen as a dynamic resource that is used by police officers to reach judgements about the behaviours they police. Police discretion, in this sense, should be seen as the outcome of *individual* moral decisions made in relation to *socially dominant* ideas about particular types of conduct.

A way of understanding discretion in this area – as the product of both social norms and individual actions – is to see it as the outcome of 'habitus'. Habitus, Bourdieu and Wacquant (1992: 139) argue, is a 'structuring and structured structure' that 'engages in practices and in thoughts practical schemata of perception issued out of the embodiment … of social structures'. In other words, habitus is our embodiment of social relations and our expression of them through thoughts and actions. The concept of habitus is useful because it provides a way of understanding how individual actions, and the subjective perceptions that guide them, are shaped by the social and historical relations in which individuals are situated. Habitus is social relations inculcated into the body and manifest in the form of individual 'dispositions'. Such dispositions become felt and expressed as personal 'taste', in the form of 'aversion' or 'comfort' with particular ideas or events. The utility of this theoretical framework is its potential to explain how individualized 'feelings' about certain forms of sexual conduct, such as disgust, are the product of the social relations in which individuals are situated. This allows us to understand how broader normative relations fashion individual moral decision-making, rather than seeing it as the outcome of an individual 'psychological' process.

It is a sociological conceptualization of human agency that resonates strongly with police officers' own understandings of decision-making and discretion. For example, one officer described his own decision-making in relation to public sex offences as significantly influenced by his own 'background': 'as a police officer', he told me, you 'come across' instances of public sex 'now and again' and you tend to 'tolerate what you are used to'. He viewed his toleration of 'what you are used to' as the outcome of the process of 'growing up' and 'seeing certain types of behaviour as normal'. 'Young heterosexual couples having sex on the rocks by Sydney Harbour' is, he said, 'normal behaviour' and 'something that is part of young people growing up'. 'As a police officer', he said, when you see young heterosexual couples having sex in public places you respond by thinking 'it's just a young couple in the back of a car' and 'you tolerate what you as an individual could have said [about yourself] when you were younger: "that would be me"'.

For this officer, 'learned' conceptions about heterosexual conduct as 'normal' were understood to have a direct influence on shaping particular types of discretionary policing in relation to them. The police officers I interviewed were all very reflexive about the influence of heteronormative sexual morality on police decision-making and discretion. One officer described it as the relationship between 'what is in my mind, and the mind of the community' in order to explain how the 'mind' of the general community influences the 'minds' of police officers. This officer was critical of such an influence in relation to policing beats, stating that individual police officers too unproblematically translate normative social morality into police actions. The result of this, he said, is that when officers detect a heterosexual couple in a public toilet having sex they think 'they're just taking advantage of the privacy' and move them on saying 'on you go', but if it's a homosexual couple, 'well, God forbid'. It's our 'upbringing', he says, and our 'inbuilt' ideas about sexuality that make us 'fear what we don't understand' and then 'react against it'.

It is these 'built-in' ideas, and the 'reactions' that they produce, that NSW Police have been keen to address. Through the implementation of written guidelines and training, NSW Police can be seen to have engaged in addressing the habitus of individual officers in order to refashion their perceptions about beats. Nowhere is this more evident than in the use of specialist 'beats training'. Such training is not provided to all officers, as part of their standard constable training, but offered on a 'need' basis in LACs where there are identified 'problems' in policing in this area – most often this will be where beat users have made complaints against police officers and practices. One of the key aims of the training is, as the superintendent charged with running it told me, 'demystifying a beat for ordinary police officers'. The aim of 'demystification' is based on addressing, and changing, the *perceptions* of 'ordinary' officers about beat sex in an attempt to modify their police *practice*. Attempts to change police officers' perception are done in recognition that 'ordinary' perceptions about beats are problematic in contemporary police work. Whereas Chan (1996) views police training as 'rule tightening' designed to address problems in 'police habitus' that result from police culture, 'beat training' can be seen to actively confront the wider heteronormative social, cultural and political landscape in which police habitus are shaped.

Because of this, it was not without irony that those I interviewed said that they felt NSW Police policy was more 'liberal' in respect of male homosexual public sex than 'society at large'. They viewed this as a positive development, and argued that it showed awareness in the service that 'ordinary' social perception about beats was a hindrance to 'good policing'. Those I spoke to felt that it would be beneficial to include beat training as a part of standard constable training because, as one officer put it, the 'communities' that new officers 'come from' often shape their perception in ways that are in contradiction to official NSW Police policy. Many police officers come from 'closed communities', she told me, and they need to be given the 'tools to police professionally behaviours that they have not encountered before'. The key aspect of beat training is, she explained, to convey to officers the idea that 'you might be shocked by what you encounter at beats but the activity in question should elicit no greater response [than] to other [heterosexual] activities'. In other words, training is an attempt to address the 'ordinary' subjective 'feelings' that result from an embodiment of the values of these 'closed communities'.

Beat training can be seen as an attempt to problematize heteronormative social relations and the individual perceptions that depart from them. For those officers that I spoke to in rural LACs, this was regarded as particularly desirable. One officer felt that younger, inexperienced constables from rural communities should have access to this training. Because these constables often come from the communities in which they police, he told me, they 'grasp the community's values' but, because these can be 'narrow minded', it is 'not easy for them to gauge if the community is wrong'. He argued that policing needs to negotiate multiple sets of values – the values of the local community, of society and of the police service – and that it is important to be able to 'see outside' of small community norms. A key aim of beat training is to facilitate this broader vision: it aims to render the habitus of individual officers 'a fish out of water' (as Bourdieu often describes it) in order to 'make strange' those perceptions that, because they are shaped by the social relations in which they are situated, so often feel 'normal'.

Conclusion

The question of whether police officers enforce a 'homophobic morality' is obviously an important one. Yet, discussions about homophobia in 'law enforcement' tend towards emphasizing problems in policing rather than in law. The law in this area offers a wide space for moral decision-making and affords police officers a strong degree of discretion. Public sex law requires police officers to be 'moral arbiters' and demands enforcement in relation to the 'community standards' of 'reasonable people'. Recognizing that the standards of 'ordinary' (heterosexual) people often produce significant disadvantages for sexual minorities, beats training is significant in recognizing, and addressing, the way in which the 'ordinary' perceptions of police officers influences their use of discretion in ways that may discriminate against homosexual men. In addressing these subjective perceptions, NSW Police can be seen to have confronted the 'heteronormative habitus' of their officers. Yet, because heteronormativity is not specific to 'police habitus' (Chan 1996), but characterizes the cultural relations of contemporary Australian society more generally, it is important to recognize that the selective enforcement of the law to disproportionately criminalize male homosexual conduct as 'offensive' or 'obscene' does not result from a 'problem' in policing. Whilst 'police culture' plays a role in influencing officers' uses of discretion, the 'problem' of selective enforcement lies in the legislative framework that produces it. The law demands a form of enforcement that reflects the moral principles of 'ordinary' people and police officers, as proxy 'ordinary people', are the barometers through which the moral standards of the community are measured. If male homosexual sex, whether in public or in private, often 'offends' the majority of (heterosexual) people in society (Johnson 2005) police officers cannot be 'blamed' if they reiterate this heteronormative sentiment. To avoid discriminatory policing, therefore, what is needed is law that removes the need for police officers to make moral judgements about what 'reasonable' people find 'offensive' and 'obscene'.

Bibliography

Bourdieu, P. and Wacquant, L.J.D. (1992) *An Invitation to Reflexive Sociology*, Cambridge: Polity Press.

Brogden, M. and Nijhar, P. (2005) *Community Policing: National and international models and approaches*, Cullompton: Willan Publishing.

Chan, J. (1996) 'Changing Police Culture', *British Journal of Criminology*, 36(1): 109–34.

Cohen, S. (2002) *Folk Devils and Moral Panics: The creation of the Mods and Rockers* (3rd edition), London: Routledge.

Desroches, F. (1991) 'Tearoom Trade: A law enforcement problem', *Canadian Journal of Criminology*, 33(1): 1–21.

Devlin, P. (1965) *The Enforcement of Morality*, Oxford: Oxford University Press.

Fielding, N.G. (1988) 'Competence and Culture in the Police', *Sociology*, 22(1): 45–64.

——(2006) *Courting Violence: Offences against the person cases in court*, Oxford: Oxford University Press.

Findlay, M. (2004) *Introducing Policing: Challenges for police and Australian communities*, Oxford: Oxford University Press.

Garland, D. (2001) *The Culture of Control: Crime and social order in contemporary society*, Oxford: Oxford University Press.

Hall, S., Critcher, C., Jefferson, T. and Clarke, J.N. (1978) *Policing the Crisis: Mugging, the state and law and order*, London: Palgrave MacMillan.

Hart, H.L.A. (1994) *The Concept of Law*, Oxford: Oxford University Press.

Herbert, S. (1996) 'Morality in Law Enforcement: Chasing "bad guys" with the Los Angeles Police Department', *Law & Society Review*, 30(4): 799–818.

Home Office (1957) *Report of the Committee on Homosexual Offences and Prostitution* (Cmnd 247), London: HMSO.

Hubbard, P. (1999) *Sex and the City: Geographies of prostitution in the urban west*, Chichester: Ashgate.

Humphreys, L. (1970) *Tearoom Trade: A study of homosexual encounters in public places*, London: Duckworth.

Johnson, P. (2005) *Love, Heterosexuality and Society*, London: Routledge.

——(2007) 'Ordinary Folk and Cottaging: Law, morality and public sex', *Journal of Law and Society*, 34(4): 520–43.

——(2008) '"Crimes against morality": Law and public sex in Australia', *Alternative Law Journal*, 33(3).

——(2010a) 'Law, Morality and Disgust: The regulation of "extreme pornography" in England and Wales', *Social and Legal Studies*, 19(2): 147–64.

——(2010b) 'The Enforcement of Morality: Law, policing and sexuality in New South Wales', *Australian and New Zealand Journal of Criminology*, 43(3): 399–422.

Lipsky, M. (1980) *Street-level Bureaucracy: Dilemmas of the individual in public services*, New York: Russell Sage Foundation.

Mason, G. (2007) 'Hate Crime as Moral Category: Lessons from the Snowtown Case', *Australian and New Zealand Journal of Criminology*, 40(3): 249–71.

Metropolitan Police (undated) *ACPO Guidance on the Policing of Public Sexual Activity*. Online. Available at http://www.met.police.uk/dcf/files/LGBTacpo.pdf (accessed 3 September 2011).

Moran, L.J. (1996) *The Homosexual(ity) of Law*, London: Routledge.

NSW Police (2008) *Guidelines for the Effective Policing of Beats*, Sydney: NSW Police.

Olivecrona, K. (1971) *Law as Fact*, London: Steven & Sons.

Oliver, W. (1998) *Community-Oriented Policing: A systemic approach to policing*, Upper Saddle River, NJ: Prentice-Hall.

Punch, M. (2009) *Police Corruption: Deviance, accountability, and reform in policing*, Cullompton: Willan Publishing.

Reiner, R. (2000) *The Politics of the Police* (3rd edn), Oxford: Oxford University Press.

Sanders, T. (2009) 'Controlling the "Anti Sexual" City: Sexual citizenship and the disciplining of female street sex workers', *Criminology & Criminal Justice*, 9(4): 507–25.

Somerville, P. (2009) 'Understanding Community Policing', *Policing: An international journal of police strategies and management*, 32(2): 261–277.

Waddington, P.A.J. (1999) 'Police (Canteen) Subculture: An appreciation', *British Journal of Criminology*, 39(2): 286–308.

Walby, K. (2009) 'Ottawa's National Capital Commission Conservation Officers and the Policing of Public Park Sex', *Surveillance and Society*, 6(4): 367–79.

Warner, M. (2000) 'Zones of Privacy', in J. Butler, J. Guillory and K. Thomas (eds) *What's Left of Theory? New work on the politics of literary theory*, New York: Routledge.

Westley, W. (1970) *Violence and the Police: A sociological study of law, custom, and morality*, Cambridge, MA: MIT Press.

Young, J. (1971) *The Drugtakers*, London: Paladin.

Part 2
Policing 'public' sex

3

HETEROSEXUALITY, PUBLIC PLACES AND POLICING

Chris Ashford

Dogging – the practice of mixed-gender cruising in public spaces in or around motor vehicles – reflects a modern evolution of the historic 'lovers' lane', together with a recontextualization of the phenomenon of swinging. In contrast to the exclusively male constructions of cottaging/tearooms (sex in public toilets) or cruising (sex in open spaces), dogging encompasses women and involves heterosexual and bisexual behaviour. It can encompass a range of activities, including: exhibiting oneself, observing an individual or couple exhibiting, and sexual acts typically revolving around a male/female couple and other participators.

It is a phenomenon that has spawned erotic literature (Abby 2005; Davies 2008) and pornography, and garnered considerable media coverage (Hennelly 2010). Much of this coverage has cast dogging as a successfully exported quaint English activity (Sax 2008). In 2010, the *New York Times* reported on complaints from the residents of one Surrey village that had apparently become increasingly attractive to 'out-of-towners', not for its better-known picturesque scenery but for providing the location of a particularly active dogging ground. One resident told the newspaper how she had found a pink vibrator in bushes near the dogging location. 'I gave it to the police', she said. 'They said, "What should we do with it?" I said, "Put it in Lost Property"' (Lyall 2010). This stoical pragmatism is perhaps untypical of the challenges faced by the police in responding to public concern, enforcing the criminal law, and responding with some degree of sensitivity to consensual activity, albeit in a public place. As this chapter will explore, in a legal area best characterized as 'grey', the police must balance a range of competing agendas and demands when 'policing sex'.

The sexual iceberg

Smith and Smith (1970) have noted the challenge of exploring sexual activities that may be regarded as part of the 'sexual freedom movement' because of the 'iceberg nature' of the phenomena. Whilst dogging emerged as a visible sexual phenomenon in the early twenty-first century, it remains difficult to ascertain the extent to which the phenomenon has been revealed, and how much remains 'beneath the surface'.

However, dogging now forms part of the complex web of 'promiscuities' (see Samuels 2010) that pre-occupy academics, journalists, social commentators and – significantly for our purposes – lawmakers and law-enforcers. These promiscuities can be seen to challenge the heterosexual hegemony of monogamous heterosexual marriage and threaten the basis on which marriage continues to be socially and economically privileged within Western cultures (see VanEvery 1996: 4–41). Although the basic notion that one sexual partner is 'enough' for every married man and woman is central to the traditional idea of marriage, we also know that in a high percentage of marriages one or both partners look outside of that relationship for further sexual excitement (Cole and Spaniard 1974). As such, this suggests that dogging as a phenomenon should be regarded as far from surprising but, rather, reflective of 'authentic' or 'true' desire that may previously have been hidden.

Dogging necessitates the use of signals that enable someone driving into a car park or picnic location to convert from being a passing member of the public to being a 'dogger'. This can take the form of the flashing of brake lights to signify interest, or subtle moves from one's car to observing a couple in a car, to being invited to view, to touch or to interact. This is an example of how sexual interaction is dependent upon what have been termed 'undercover sex signals', the somatic behaviour between humans that indicates sexual desire/interest, including leaning towards an individual, licking one's lips or the casual brushing of an arm (Lowndes 2006: passim). Once again, therefore, dogging and the dogging spaces serve as a natural extension to 'authentic' sexual desire, and it is the authentic nature of this phenomenon that suggests a practice capable of sustaining itself (rather than being some 'sexual fad') by responding to the evolving challenges presented to it from policing.

One might assume, given the 'public' nature of this activity, the existence of far more literature exploring the dogging phenomenon than is currently available. While the public sex environments of the public toilet and cruising ground for men to have sex with other men is comparatively well documented (see Ashford 2006, 2007, and Johnson 2007), along with more commercial spaces such as the bathhouse (e.g. see Bedfellows 1996), dogging remains comparatively undocumented by academics, perhaps reflecting the wider reluctance to problematize heterosexual identities (Richardson 1996).

Defining dogging

The origins of the term 'dogging' are unclear, but the general consensus among journalists and academics appears to be that the term owes its origin to the veil of legitimacy that participants are imagined to rely on: 'I was just out walking my dog.' However, given that the participants have typically driven to the location, and are unlikely to have a dog with them, this seems a potentially flawed explanation. Alternatively, it may owe its origin to the act of dogging – to harass, follow and observe someone. It may even be a reflection of dogging as 'animalistic': an ephemeral and intense sexual encounter in which a dog might engage.

Bell (2006: 388) has observed that a dogging scene 'typically involves heterosexual singles and couples driving to secluded locations, and engaging in sexual acts in their cars or in a nearby open space' with other participants, observers or observer/participants, and can also take place in locations away from the initial 'pick-up'. Since Bell's observation, and a surge in dogging-themed pornography, the term has come to be applied to any public sex space involving heterosexual couples in the act of sex in a public location (without observers) which effectively returns to the 'lovers' lane' of heterosexual tradition. Yet this, I would suggest, reflects the commercial demands of pornography rather than a wider shift in practices among doggers.

Dogging sites typically include country parks, 'viewing' spots/areas (normally isolated beauty spots), picnic sites, nature reserves, woodland and historic sites (Byrne 2006). Crucially, these sites tend to be 'isolated', and yet also well-connected to transport links, and many are signposted by the brown-coloured tourist signs common across the UK (Byrne 2006). Significant levels of vegetation or woodland in close proximity to the car park are seen as a desirable characteristic in order to maintain some degree of concealment, so that visitors who enter the site cannot be viewed from a nearby road. The presence of a ranger or warden is, perhaps unsurprisingly, viewed as a barrier to a successful heterosexual public sex environment (PSE) (Byrne 2006).

Dogging encounters are increasingly arranged over the Internet to ensure that there is a greater chance of an encounter taking place, rather than an individual or couple sitting in an empty car park for hours on end. Once within a dogging space, couples typically indicate they want to be viewed by flashing the internal courtesy light of their car, and men may then gather around a vehicle, with outside access to a vehicle sometimes granted/invited by the lowering of a window or the opening of a door. More often than not, however, an evening of dogging could be characterized by sitting in a car at an isolated location, along with three or four other cars, all containing single male drivers, and then driving home a number of hours after having exchanged nothing more than a passing frustrated glance with a fellow dogger.

Nonetheless, dogging arguably represents Weeks' (1989: 219–20) notion of 'rampant promiscuity', in which sex operates in isolation and comprises 'sex for its own sake', that is, sex takes place in a public space and further serves to challenge the normative framework of sexuality in the contemporary. Warner (1999: 177) noted the expectation that '"you" have children, are at home and go to "public places" in order to shop' and that dogging serves as a direct challenge both to these normative conceptions of domesticity and also normative public space. In doing so, it unsurprisingly attracts a socio-legal response.

Collymore

In March 2004, high-profile former England footballer Stan Collymore was revealed by British tabloid newspaper, the *Sun*, to be a 'dogger'. In a front-page exposé they published a photograph of him in a PSE with undercover *Sun* reporters with whom he had exchanged various text messages and even showed around other dogging locations. The paper branded him a 'sleazeball', but the story firmly propelled dogging into the public consciousness and – despite the 'sleazy' labelling by the *Sun* – also highlighted that this was an activity that 'sexually desirable' individuals (rather than 'dirty old men') engaged in (Syson and Hagan 2004). Collymore had been subject to the sort of sting operation that was previously more typical of police 'agent provocateur' tactics in public conveniences (see Ashford 2006, 2007; Johnson 2007; and Chapters 1 and 5). The incident served to act as a public shaming for Collymore and represented a considerable shift in the publicity and exploration of dogging within the British media.

The reporting of the Collymore story, and the subsequent media outcry, was greeted with raised eyebrows by more liberal-minded sections of the British media. The *New Statesman* (2004) noted in an editorial, with heavy irony, that had it not been for this reporting, readers

> might have thought, as Mr Collymore apparently did, that 'dogging is just a bit of fun'. Now, they have learnt from Deidre, the *Sun's* agony aunt (or are they called sex counsellors now?), that 'it's dangerous and sordid sex with strangers … which damages lasting relationships and risks sexual health'.

The editorial went on to note the sharing of precise dogging location details in news stories describing how terrible dogging was – ironically, since this alerted people to these locations and presumably prompted an impromptu parade of doggers to the highlighted dogging spots.

Swingers

As a sexual practice, dogging represents an extension of 'swinging' into public spaces. Swinging, as with dogging, may be regarded as multi-partner sexual activity (see Bell 2004) that has become increasingly visible (Anon. 2002) in contemporary culture. The regular featuring of swingers' clubs, such as Sheffield's *La Chambre*, in television documentaries has helped to provide a visual conception of swinging and swingers, in a way that the private home-based swinging 'orgies' are less documented (see Sheppard 2005 for some insight).

Walshok (1971: 488) defined swinging as 'the agreement between husband and wife to have sexual relations with other people, but in contexts in which they both engage in such behaviour at the same time and usually in the same place'. Both swinging and dogging include single individuals as well as couples. These 'singles' are typically men, and this is reflected within the dogging environment, where a couple may put on a 'show' or invite further single players or other couples. In both spaces, single males generally outnumber couples, and although this can be regulated in commercial space (e.g. through 'couples only' evenings), it cannot be controlled in the same way in a dogging environment. The reluctance to publicly share information about dogging locations often reflects this as much as a desire to 'hide' the details from law enforcement or other disruptive elements. A poor single male to couples/female ratio can result in a dogging environment quickly ceasing to be viable.

It is perhaps easy therefore to regard 'dogging' as a less controlled 'outdoor' version of swinging. In many ways it is, but it does offer a very different sensory experience, and these distinctions are often the very reason for legal interest and regulation of the phenomenon.

Swingers clubs have served to provide a commercial space in which those couples and individuals with an interest in swinging can meet in a place that has designated rules about behaviour and provides an anonymous space. Couture (2008: 32) has noted that, compared to gay public sex spaces, the heterosexual space can be slower and a more difficult space to navigate, with a hierarchy that places the single man as inferior to the couple, who are in turn inferior to the (rare) single woman. This hierarchy reflects the supply and demand of the swinging environment and is inevitably also replicated in the dogging space.

The legal framework

English law pertaining to dogging is something of a grey area, and one that is in part currently under review by the Law Commission (2010). In terms of statutory offences, there is no specific 'dogging offence' but there are a number of provisions that can be applied. Section 66 of the Sexual Offences Act 2003 provides for 'exposure', stating that an offence exists where a person intentionally exposes their genitals and intends that someone will see them and be 'caused alarm or distress'. The offence can result in an imprisonment term of not more than six months or a fine, or a combination of the two. However, for doggers, the 'exposure' of one's genitals in a PSE is not intended to produce alarm or distress, and as such this statutory offence is arguably limited in terms of successful application to the dogging environment. Moreover, one can draw a clear distinction between the 'flasher', who exposes themselves at a passer-by to cause distress, and the dogging encounter, which is a consensual public sex experience.

Along with section 66, the Sexual Offences Act 2003 also provides for the offence of 'voyeurism' in section 67. This offence relates to a person who, for the purposes of seeking sexual gratification, observes someone performing a 'private act' and knows that the other person does not consent to being observed. Once again, we can perhaps draw a distinction between an individual who might be spying upon someone against their consent and someone participating in a dogging encounter where the observation of a couple engaged in sexual activity is consensual. A consensual dogging encounter, therefore, arguably falls beyond the scope of this provision. This section also contains similar penalties to section 66 and also encompasses non-consensual voyeuristic video recording.

The final statutory provision that can be applied to this area is the Public Order Act 1986. Sections 4a and 5 of this act address offences which cause harassment, alarm or distress. Section 4a is designed to address more serious and persistent behaviour whilst section 5 is designed for less serious offences and anti-social behaviour – and thus the more likely provision that dogging would be addressed under. It is a defence under this section if the person 'had no reason to believe that there was any person within hearing or sight who was likely to be caused harassment, alarm or distress'. Here the statutory framework presents significant ambiguity for doggers. By virtue of being in a public place, there is arguably the possibility that someone may come along and see or hear something they find alarming or distressing. Thus, a rural picnic recreation spot is, by day, likely to find visitors using the spot for picnicking and leisure. However, it is unlikely that people will visit the same location at 4 am for such activities and thus a dogger could conceivably argue that, at such a time, they had no reason to believe that someone would come within hearing or sight of a dogging encounter. A further complication arises, however, in that a police officer can be the very person to be caused alarm or distress. This remains a question of fact to be determined in each individual case.

In addition to these statutory provisions, the common law provides the additional offence of 'outraging public decency'. This requires that an offence must be committed 'in public', although this does not need to be public property, rather a space that can be viewed by the public (see *R v Bunyan*, 1844, 1 Cox CC 74 and *R v Knuller*, 1973, AC 435). The offence also requires that the act is capable of being witnessed by more than one person (as distinct from *actually* being viewed by more than one person). Dogging would therefore fall within this common law offence, operating as an activity that is designed to take place in public and as being capable of being viewed by multiple players.

Although 'disgust' forms an integral part of judicial understanding of 'outrage', it focuses upon the possibility that someone could be outraged rather than that someone was outraged. In *R v Mayling* (1963, 2 QB 717) it was held that it was sufficient if one person saw an act, whether or not they were disgusted. Finally, the offence of outraging public decency is generally regarded as being a strict liability offence – that is to say, not requiring any intent on the part of the dogger to disgust or be 'indecent' – making this a very attractive legal option for the police, and a much more complex offence for the public to understand.

Policing strategies

Current Association of Chief Police Officers (ACPO) guidance on the policing of PSEs stems from 2000, and makes reference to cottaging and cruising, but not dogging. Its emphasis on working with LGBT groups also suggests that the original focus of the document was upon same-sex public encounters (see Chapter 1). Nonetheless, the document also sets out the approach that police forces should take to the policing of all public sex encounters. Following the receipt of a complaint, it has to be investigated. If it appears a genuine complaint, then a process of 'scanning and analysis' should take place, working with local groups and partnerships to explore if other complaints have been made, together with an examination of agency databases, CCTV and potentially the use of plain-clothed officers and further cameras. If it is then determined that the complaint is more than an isolated incident, a 'stepped response' will take place (ACPO undated).

This involves three stages. Step one is to 'inform, dissuade', through the use of health outreach workers, posters, media and LGBT networks. This can be seen in operation by Northumbria Police, who utilized the BBC in 2009 to notify the public (and would-be doggers) that a 'dogging hotspot' would be policed (BBC 2009). It named the road that would be policed and stated that 'anyone caught having sex in the area is being warned that action will be taken against them'. No indication of complaints by the public is provided, but Northumbria Police did state that 'we have seen an increase in the number of men attending this area ... for the purposes of meeting for sex'. As if the threat of prosecution was not enough to deter people, a police inspector is quoted as stating 'our patrols will be taking the registration of any vehicle suspiciously parked in the area and the owners of these vehicles may be subject to a home visit by one of our officers'. This suggests that, whilst an individual might not be caught 'dogging', the presence of a vehicle in a dogging location could result in the police visiting them at home. The police also indicated that dogging websites would be used to further notify doggers of the planned action.

Bell (2006) has noted that the presence of these reports, particularly in the local media, has served to inform potential doggers of locations, and the availability of these local news reports on news websites enables the knowledge of these locations to be shared beyond local borders. However, it should be noted that whilst a report of a dogging PSE in a national newspaper informs doggers that it remains illicit and an activity of interest to the police, the presence of such reports in the local media also ensures that doggers become acutely aware that the police are engaged in surveillance in their communities. Rather than being hypothetical, the possibility of police intervention in their lives becomes recast as a real and tangible possibility.

ACPO's 'step two' involves 'situational crime and disorder prevention measures' leading to the closure of facilities, access control, signage, landscaping, cutting back shrubbery, CCTV use and longer-term environmental design. This approach can be seen in operation in 2010, when local councillors decided to close a café and lay-by between Guildford and Farnham because the lay-by was being utilized by doggers and it was seen as being too close to a school and village. On this occasion, the police worked together with schoolteachers and the council to obtain closure. The café owner (who one might imagine would be aware of such action during the day if it really did pose a 'threat' to the school) objected to the decision, essentially on economic grounds, noting that it would result in the loss of four full-time and two part-time members of staff, and the closure of his business (Hall 2010). (The café ultimately stayed open with various measures proposed to restrict access to the site: BBC 2011)

The third step is described as 'preventative patrolling' in which uniformed policing takes place in a location. The appearance of 'Plod' may be the first time that a dogger encounters the police, when a marked car sweeps into a darkened car park, and catches doggers in their headlights.

The ACPO policy also specifically addresses the issue of agent provocateur tactics, historically a source of controversy in the policing of cottages and cruising locations (Ashford 2006, 2007; Johnson 2007; Moran 1996; and see Chapters 1 and 5), stating that the policy does not 'allow the use of plain clothes officers for any purpose other than information gathering in the scanning and analysis stage'.

In 2008, ACPO appeared to be considering new guidance on policing PSEs, when a draft document was leaked to *Jane's Police Review* magazine. It was, in many ways, an extraordinary document since it recognized that 'previous methods of policing

PSEs have adversely affected the relationship between the police and communities' and that 'previous methods of policing PSEs have discouraged users from reporting crime to the police' (ACPO 2008: 8). The document shifted the focus from seeking to stop people from engaging in public sex (although that remained a police function in this document) to protecting users of PSEs, recognizing that serious assaults and robberies were being conducted against users of PSEs, and PSE users were reluctant to report the offences. This in turn was said to be encouraging criminals to commit offences in PSEs, knowing that the crime was unlikely to be reported by the victim. The document stated that 'in the absence of specific complaints, crime prevention and public safety for all users should be the key priority for policing PSEs'. If enacted, this would have represented a dramatic shift in policy, and represented the most thoughtful, research-based response by the police to the policing of PSEs to date.

The document also recognized dogging for the first time, providing two links for dogging websites to aid 'profiling', along with one cruising/cottaging website, serving to also publicly recognize the way these sites were now being used by the police to obtain details about PSE locations.

The document echoed the 2000 advice in recommending the commencement of operational activities following receipt of a complaint, moving to 'scanning and analysis', but then differed in suggesting a five-step response rather than the previous three-step approach. However, in reality these stages mirrored the 2000 documentation, simply adding the steps of 'enforcement' at step four and 'assess' at step five, both of which formed part of the earlier ACPO advice.

Whilst the tone of the document was therefore significantly different, the policing approach in response to complaints remained the same. However, the document caused a media outcry on its release, resulting in it ultimately being withdrawn by ACPO – on the basis that consultations were still being carried out.

Mike Cunningham, the then Deputy Chief Constable of Lancashire Police, and author of the report, added to the controversy by stating to the media that:

> In any event it is not for the police to take the role of moral arbiter, the police role is to ensure that any complaints are dealt with fairly and professionally and that where individuals are engaged in lawful activity they may do so safely.
>
> (Independent 2008)

It was this rejection of 'moral arbiter' coupled with the more 'understanding' tone of other statements that led to the universal reporting of the report as 'turning a blind eye to public sex'. The then Shadow Home Secretary, Dominic Grieve described the report as 'unacceptable' (BBC 2008).

Crucially, the report never advocated 'turning a blind eye'; rather it advocated applying the law as it stands, which does mean that public sex can be legally acceptable in some circumstances, dependent upon interpretations of the common law and application of the statutory provisions discussed earlier. This nuanced position was evidently too complex for both politicians and the media, but it means the police continue to operate in the midst of some legal confusion.

To compound this, although the draft guidance was withdrawn, at least one police force, Kent Police (2010), redesigned their local policy on PSE in light of the draft ACPO framework – and continues to operate under that policy framework. Kent Police's policy includes a sample poster they have used in PSEs with the logo 'You said, We did' in the top corner, highlighting a response to public concern. The poster then features three boxes of text. The largest block of text states 'extra officers are on patrol in this area … ' the second: ' … to deal with criminal damage, littering and other unacceptable behaviour'. Whilst the behaviour in question is public sex activities, a euphemism is deployed which continues to privatize the acts. The poster concludes with 'when caught, you could be fined or face prosecution'. Although the police appear confident people *will* be caught, even they seem uncertain about whether any penalty with follow.

Virtual spaces and virtual policing

This confusion about the approaches of the police, and the reaction of doggers to it, is increasingly apparent in the context of the 'information society'. Specifically, the emergence of 'cybersex' and the Internet has positioned the web as a mediator for public sex encounters (Weeks 2011: 37). As such, the Internet has enabled the emergence of the 'cyber-cottage' (Ashford 2006; Mowlabocus 2010: 117), and created spaces for doggers to exchange information on locations and to advertise availability, increasing the likelihood of successful sexual encounters.

Reports of policing activity vary enormously in virtual environments but they are consistent in recognizing that the police have a regular presence in these spaces. Typically, it seems that people are questioned as to whether they are the vehicle's owner (and have their registration details checked), and often people are warned that illegal or sexual activity takes place in a particular location and they should be careful. This is supported by press releases from the police themselves, for instance this 2009 statement from Northumbria Police:

> Our officers will be conducting regular patrols and taking action against anyone commiting [sic] public sex acts in the area around [location deleted]. Our patrols will be taking the registration of any vehicles suspiciously parked in the area and the owners of these vehicles may be subject to a home visit by one of our officers.
>
> *(Northumbria Police 2009)*

Whether these comments by police officers are regarded as threatening, or are taken as a genuine warning issued in the interests of citizen safety, varies; but there is typically an air of 'resentment' regarding the police on dogging discussion boards. Comments often bemoan the attention of the police at the apparent expense of less attention to violent crimes and other 'safety' issues.

The police are typically cast as an irritant, moving people on, warning or leaving people feeling intimidated. There are also some online reports of the police sending letters to vehicles' registered home addresses, indicating that the vehicle has been seen in an area known for sexual activity, and asking the vehicle owners to contact the police if they have any information about this. Of course, where another household member is aware of the mail or opens it, difficult conversations may ensue if they had been unaware of their partner's dogging activity. Although reports of these specific letters are anecdotal, they do fit with the general stated strategies by the police (such as the Northumbria Police statement discussed earlier).

These approaches broadly align with the steps outlined within the ACPO guidance, and also reflect the concerns raised in the 2008 proposed policy document, that current strategies are failing in many respects and fostering a culture of distrust and disrespect.

Fear of attracting police attention to a PSE has previously been documented in the male-for-male cruising environment (e.g. see Gaissad 2005), in which some individuals would be excluded from spaces, and information regarding public sex environments is tightly controlled. Online discussion boards suggest this is increasingly the case in dogging environments, in which individuals who appear 'obvious' and who transgress the normative behaviour of the dogging ground are condemned. There is also a strong emphasis upon those who can access discussion boards and the danger that this may therefore present to the success of a dogging location if everybody knows about it. These concerns are well justified, given the specific provision of dogging websites in the 2008 ACPO guidance and the indication by the police in media reports that they monitor these Internet sites.

This is perhaps the central dilemma for doggers today. A fear of observation by law enforcement officials, and others who may want to disrupt the space (e.g. locals, journalists, young people sometimes characterized as 'scallies' and 'chavs') means that information must only be shared to trusted fellow doggers, and so relationships need to be built up. At the same time, this reduces the possibility of dogging locations being well-enough known to attract new players, and sufficient numbers of players to make a dogging location thrive, and therefore capable of fulfilling multiple-partner fantasies.

Similarly, the casual or curious dogger is likely to be deterred from the lengthy conversations. Young single men are likely to be distrusted, as potentially disruptive 'scallies' or 'chavs' seeking merely to know about a location so as to damage it (these labels introduce a further issue of 'class' and identity in this spaces: see more generally Jones 2011). Thus, locations become more middle-aged, and ever less attractive to the younger doggers who might have been attracted to these locations. As a result, doggers perhaps reflect the previous observation of swingers as 'uninterestingly normal' (Smith and Smith 1974), and the 'dull homebodies, with few interests, excluding watching television and reading the newspaper' (Bartell 1970).

Doggers also caution about avoiding visibility within the dogging environment as well as online. Smith (2010) has previously noted the online pleas to take litter home, and appropriate disposal of one's 'dogging kit' (e.g. condoms and tissues). For Smith, the act of 'cleaning up' reclaims privacy for the act of dogging. It is this litter that can ultimately form the basis for a complaint and provide the evidence for further investigation by the police and, thus, removing litter, not posting online details of dogging locations and observing rules of 'discretion' all serve to privatize the act of dogging.

Existing policing strategies appear to continue to disrupt dogging encounters, cause resentment among doggers and, as the 2008 ACPO draft guidance admitted, create less safe PSEs. If the goal of the police is to protect the public, the current strategy is failing in that aim.

Conclusion

Phillips has noted the potential for swingers and casual sex encounters to challenge mononormativity (Phillips 2010: 86). While queer theorists increasingly see homosexuality as an activity that is now battling with 'assimilation' – becoming 'recast' as a monogamous domestic relationship – monogamy has been seen as the starting point for a heterosexualist and heteronormative analysis. Casual sex can be seen to offer a radical challenge to traditional limitations created by a heterosexual identity. As Schofield (1976: 83) argues: 'If promiscuous sex were as inferior as the moralists would have us believe, the problem would not arise because no one would want to bother with it.' In one sense, the current policing of dogging therefore acts as state response to these challenges to mononormativity, suggesting that partnered couples can enjoy sex outside their state-sanctioned relationships, and can celebrate this in a very public way – through the use of dogging grounds/public sex environments.

Moreover, the literature relating to public sex has long been dominated by a focus upon the 'homosexual' or, more accurately, exclusive male encounters. At various points, this problematization of public sex as a 'gay' issue has meant that it has been seen as a part of a history of shame, and men that engage in such activities have been positioned as guilty of 'letting the side down', of clinging to anachronistic sexual practices and even as 'enemies of the gay movement' (Califia 2000: 14).

Dogging serves as an important counterpoint to these arguments, revealing that public sex serves as a radical recasting of sexuality. It exposes public sex as an activity borne from desire, rather than merely the necessity of historical shaming. Furthermore, if this is an activity in which 'straights' engage, then it raises questions about why public sex is increasingly a point of silence for a gay 'community' that traditionally celebrated public sex as pleasure. It may well be that, with the absence of historical and social baggage and the absence of the deep scars of AIDS (Muñoz 1996), doggers are today's public sex radicals who challenge policing and sexual control in equal measure.

The policing of this phenomenon therefore arguably reveals a preoccupation on the part of the state in regulating and limiting the sort of sex it deems to be undesirable. Califia (2002: 209) has noted that public sex represents 'straight people's ideas about what heterosexual men might do if they were free from the constraints of religion and marriage – and what women might do if being called a slut didn't make them vulnerable to shame, harassment, violence, and shunning'.

Although heterosexual public sex has its advocates (Easton and Hardy 2009), it continues to upset others. Doggers and the police must navigate a complex body of law whilst also seeking to negotiate compromise with the public and media. This negotiation places heterosexuality in the very difficulty that has confronted non-heterosexualities for some time, that of challenging normative sexualities. 'Insiders' are wrapping themselves in the cloak of deviancy and joining the historic ranks of queers, perverts and gays. The socio-legal radicalism of such behaviour should not be underestimated, and this perhaps explains the continued preoccupation of law and policing with public sex. Policing sex has rarely been more important to protecting the heteronormative power of the state.

Bibliography

Abby (2005) *Dogging: The novel*, London: Abby's Books.

ACPO (undated) *ACPO Guidance on the Policing of Public Sexual Activity*. Online. Available at http://www.met.police.uk/dcf/files/LGBTacpo.pdf (accessed 28 May 2011).

——(2008) *Guidance on Policing Public Sex Environments*, London: ACPO.

Anon. (2002) 'Taboo Lifting on Swinging?', *Contemporary Sexuality*, 36(8): 9.

Ashford, C. (2006) 'The Only Gay in the Village: Sexuality and the Net', *Information & Communications Technology Law*, 15(3) 275–89.

——(2007) 'Sexuality, Public Space and the Criminal Law: The cottaging phenomenon', *Journal of Criminal Law*, 71(6) 506–19.

Bartell, G.D. (1970) 'Group Sex Among the Mid-Americans', *The Journal of Sex Research*, 6(2) 113–30.

BBC (2008) 'Police Leniency Call on Park Sex'. Online. Available at http://news.bbc.co.uk/1/hi/england/lancashire/7674874.stm (accessed 28 May 2011).

——(2009) '"Dogging" Hotspot to be Policed'. Online. Available at http://news.bbc.co.uk/1/hi/england/wear/7878889.stm (accessed 28 May 2011).

——(2011) 'Plans to Curb Visitors to Outdoor Sex Lay-by in Surrey'. Online. Available at http://www.bbc.co.uk/news/uk-england-surrey-12732705 (accessed 28 May 2011).

Bedfellows, Dangerous (ed.) (1996) *Policing Public Sex*, Boston: South End Press.

Bell, D. (2004) 'Swinging', in J. Eadie (ed.) *Glossary of Sexuality*, London: Arnold.

——(2006) 'Bodies, Technologies, Spaces: On "dogging"', *Sexualities*, 9(4): 387–407.

Byrne, R. (2006) 'Beyond Lovers' Lane: The rise of illicit sexual leisure in countryside recreational space', *Leisure/Loisir*, 30(1) 73–85.

Califia, P. (2000) *Public Sex: The culture of radical sex* (2nd edn), San Francisco, CA: Cleis Press.

——(2002) *Speaking Sex to Power: The politics of queer sex*, San Francisco, CA: Cleis Press.

Cole, C.L. and Spaniard, G.B. (1974) 'Comarital Mate-Sharing and Family Stability', *The Journal of Sex Research*, 19(1) 21–31.

Couture, J. (2008) *Peek: Inside the private world of public sex*, New York: Routledge.

Davies, D. (2008) *The Isle of Dogs*, London: Serpent's Tail.

Easton, D. and Hardy, J.W. (2009) *The Ethical Slut: A practical guide to polyamory, open relationships and other adventures*, (2nd edn), Berkeley: Celestial Arts.

Gaissad, L. (2005) 'From Nightlife Conventions to Daytime Hidden Agendas: Dynamics of urban sexual territories in the South of France', *The Journal of Sex Research*, 42(1) 20–27.

Hall, M. (2010) 'Café and 'Dogging' Lay-by Set for Closure'. Online. Available at http://www.getsurrey.co.uk/news/s/2075956_cafe_and_dogging_layby_set_for_closure (accessed 28 May 2011).

Hennelly, S. (2010) 'Public Morality: The media construction of sex in public places', *Liverpool Law Review*, 31(1) 69–91.

Independent (2008) 'Police Should Turn Blind Eye to Public Sex', *Independent*, 16 October.

Johnson, P. (2007) 'Ordinary Folk and Cottaging: Law, morality, and public sex', *Journal of Law and Society*, 34(4) 520–43.

Jones, O. (2011) *Chavs: The demonization of the working class*, London: Verso.

Kent Police (2010) *M78 Managing Public Sex Environments*. Online. Available at http://www.kent.police.uk/about_us/policies/m/m078.html (accessed 28 May 2011).

Law Commission (2010) *Simplification of Criminal Law: Public nuisance and outraging public decency*, Consultation Paper No 193, London: HMSO.

Lowndes, L. (2006) *Undercover Sex Signals: A pickup guide for guys*, New York: Citadel Press.

Lyall, S. (2010) 'Here's the Pub, Church and Field for Public Sex', *New York Times*, 7 October.

Moran, L.J. (1996) *The Homosexual(ity) of Law*, London: Routledge.

Mowlabocus, S. (2010) *Gaydar Culture: Gay men, technology and embodiment in the digital age*, Farnham: Ashgate.

Muñoz, J.E. (1996) 'Ghosts of Public Sex: Utopian longings, queer memories', in Dangerous Bedfellows (ed.) *Policing Public Sex*, Boston, MA: South End Press.

New Statesman (2004) 'A Dogging Life', *New Statesman*, 8 March.

Northumbria Police (2009) 'Police Target Dogging Hotspot', Press Release, 9 February. Online. Available at http://www.northumbria.police.uk/news_and_events/media_centre/news_releases/details.asp?id=10434 (accessed 22 July 2011).

Phillips, S. (2010) 'There Were Three in the Bed: Discursive desire and the sex lives of swingers', in M. Barker and D. Langeridge (eds) *Understanding Non-Monogamies*, London: Routledge.

Richardson, D. (1996) 'Heterosexuality and Social Theory', in D. Richardson (ed.) *Theorising Sexuality: Telling it straight*, Buckingham: Open University Press.

Samuels, A. (2010) 'Promiscuities: Politics, imagination, spirituality and hypocrisy', in M. Barker and D. Langeridge (eds) *Understanding Non-Monogamies*, London: Routledge.

Sax, H. (2008) *Dogging: Guide für Outdoorsex*, Flensburg: Carl Stephenson Verlag.

Schofield, M. (1976) *Promiscuity*, London: Victor Gollancz.

Sheppard, S. (2005) *Sex Parties 101*, Los Angeles, CA: Alyson Books.

Smith, C. (2010) 'British Sexual Cultures', in M. Higgins, C. Smith and J. Storey (eds) *The Cambridge Companion to Modern British Culture*, Cambridge: Cambridge University Press.

Smith, J.R and Smith, L.G. (1970) 'Co-Marital Sex and the Sexual Freedom Movement', *The Journal of Sex Research*, 6(2) 131–42.

Smith, L.G. and Smith, J.R. (1974) 'Co-Marital Sex: The incorporation of extramarital sex into the marriage relationship', in J.R. Smith and L.G. Smith (eds) *Beyond Monogamy: Recent studies of sexual alternatives in marriage*, Baltimore, MD: John Hopkins University Press.

Syson, N. and Hagan, L. (2004) 'Collymore's Car Park Sex Shame', *The Sun*, 2 March.

VanEvery, J. (1996) 'Heterosexuality and Domestic Life', in D. Richardson (ed.) *Theorising Heterosexuality: Telling it straight*, Buckingham: Open University Press.

Walshok, M.L. (1971) 'The Emergence of Middle-Class Deviant Subcultures: The case of swingers', *Social Problems*, 18(4) 488–95.

Warner, M. (1999) *The Trouble with Normal: Sex, politics, and the ethics of queer life*, Cambridge, MA: Harvard University Press.

Weeks, J. (1989) *Sexuality and Its Discontents: Meanings, myths and modern sexualities*, London: Routledge.

——(2011) *The Languages of Sexuality*, Abingdon: Routledge.

4

SEX AND SEXUALITY UNDER SURVEILLANCE: LENSES AND BINARY FRAMES

Kevin Walby and André Smith

Introduction

The surveillance of sex and sexuality peers into the future as much as it gazes on the present. In the search for the so-called 'gay gene', for example, expert agencies and authorities become involved in the development of medical technologies to assess and predict the sexuality and sexual orientations of certain groups of people. This search for the 'gay gene' also satisfies the desire of some gay, lesbian, bisexual and trans (GLBT) individuals for social and political acknowledgement (see Brookey 2002). Genetics research on sexuality thus provides a powerful argument for gay rights, giving credence to the notion that homosexuality is an immutable characteristic deserving of legal status; however, it also presupposes a rigid dichotomy of gay versus straight (or homosexual versus heterosexual) and assumes that sexuality constitutes an innate, unchanging biological attribute. Such an essentialist understanding opens the door to the policing and monitoring of sexuality, as though sexuality indicated more than mere cultural categories for designating forms of sexual intimacy.[1] Ultimately, the medical search for the 'gay gene' represents an attempt to control sexuality through absolutist definitions that fail to comprehend diverse, socially nuanced forms of sexual conduct. If we posit that sexuality is socially produced and enacted instead of primordial, however, then we must turn our analytical attention to surveillance practices that seek to restrict and categorize sexuality. Indeed, these surveillance practices offer a window onto the ways that moral and political contestations of sex and sexuality are enacted and resisted. In this chapter, we cast a critical eye over the surveillance of sex and sexuality, analysing how the lenses through which policing agencies view sexuality and sexual practices reify sexual identities, often reinforcing the binary frames that demarcate such identities.

Current surveillance of sex and sexuality not only focuses on sexuality as a population attribute, but also voyeuristically gazes upon individual and public practices of sex.

The scholarly research contains many examples of the surveillance of sex in male-with-male bathhouses (see Bérubé 2003), as well as of male-with-male public sex in washrooms (see Johnson 2007; Dalton 2007; Edelman 1993) and in parks (see Walby 2009b). There also exist examples of surveillance agencies' preoccupation with consensual male-with-male sexual conduct in the private sphere (see Kinsman 1996: 148–96), especially before the 1957 'Wolfenden Report'[2] (Home Office 1957) and its impact on recasting the policing and surveillance of homosexuality to focus on the public sphere. This regulatory concern about sex and sexuality – especially whether they accord with social norms – intersects with the binary frames that typify certain discourses about sexuality.

In this chapter, we train attention on precisely this intersection between the regulation and discursive construction of sexuality, focusing on the surveillance of sex and sexuality, which follows organizational rules and tropes (see Johnson 2007; Dalton 2006). We argue that the lenses organizing surveillance work consist of three binary frames – public versus private, gay versus straight (or homosexual versus heterosexual) and risky versus safe – that have emerged through historical and material processes. Gayle Rubin (1993) similarly suggested that the lenses through which sex and sexuality become regulated are space, sexual identity and health. Our analysis builds on Rubin's model, showing how these three axiomatic lenses also configure public understandings of sex and sexuality, as well as organizing surveillance of the same. We stress a component of Rubin's (1993) argument that has not received adequate critical attention; these binary frames not only configure public understandings of sex and sexuality, but also facilitate the reinscription of sex through the work of surveillance and its associated activities of writing about, visualizing and depicting these practices, as in the police occurrence reports that we discuss below. Though they are socially constructed, the lenses through which sex and sexuality are viewed thus capture in their sights what they set out to secure (see Biber and Dalton 2009). These lenses do not simply magnify innate qualities of public or private, gay or straight, risky or safe, as if surveillance simply captures naturally occurring phenomena. Rather, these lenses reinscribe binary frames, thereby justifying surveillance carried out by policing agents and public health authorities. At the same time, medical surveillance conducted by public health authorities continually refines sexual risk categories that are in turn adopted as profiling tools of surveillance by policing agents.

In the first section of this chapter, we discuss historical examples that illuminate our conceptual approach to sex and sexuality and our argument about the binary frames of public–private, gay–straight and risky–safe. In the second section, we use contemporary empirical examples to explain how surveillance of sex and sexuality happens and how such surveillance intersects with the three axial binary frames. We also suggest that the desire of some GLBT people for acknowledgement sometimes increases their visibility and thus heightens the possibility of stigmatization. We conclude by returning to the conceptual issues highlighted in the introduction in order to reflect on their relevance for conjoining the sociology of surveillance and the sociology of sex and sexuality.

Surveillance of sex and sexuality in historical perspective

Kevin Haggerty (2009: 160) defines surveillance as 'the collection and analysis of information about populations in order to govern their activities'. This definition suggests that surveillance takes many forms and cannot be reduced to state-based monitoring or police control. Indeed, several historical examples of the surveillance of sex and sexuality bear out Haggerty's definition and elucidate the emergence of the binary frames (public–private, gay–straight, risky–safe) that govern current surveillance of sex and sexuality. Four key examples make clear the emergence and regulation of these frames: the sixteenth-century Florentine Office of the Night, which monitored and punished men engaged in male-with-male sex; the nineteenth-century medical examination of the intersex Herculine Barbin; the twentieth-century police surveillance of male-with-male sex in public washrooms; and the twenty-first-century police surveillance of cyberspace content relating to sex and sexuality.

The first example is the Office of the Night, active in Florence, Italy in the fifteenth and sixteenth centuries (Rocke 1996). In Florence and other Italian cities, male-with-male sex was tolerated (and routinely expected in some relationships) until the 1460s. Penalties for such behaviour were generally restricted to fines or banishment from the city. Male-with-male sex became a problem later in the fifteenth century due in part to social and economic issues: the men who were accused of such behaviour and prosecuted often did not live up to their familial obligations or the obligations associated with their government posts. The Office of the Night was the agency tasked with curbing this activity by monitoring what kind of sex men were engaging in and by punishing the men accused of engaging in illegitimate forms of sex. The Office used eavesdropping tactics that were effective in tracking city dwellers' activities. In the last decade of the fifteenth century, the number of convictions for sodomy increased concurrently with periods of epidemics that killed thousands. At this historical moment, men convicted of sodomy became popular scapegoats for religious authorities. Indeed, these authorities came to view sodomy 'as the act that most provoked the divine majesty's wrath' and 'the main reason nations were destroyed' (Rocke 1996: 231). Individuals accused of or caught engaging in male-with-male public sex suffered severe punishments, including death by burning at the stake. Men who engaged in more private male-with-male sex were also targeted for slightly less extreme punishment, such as forced labour on galleys at sea for life.

The example of the Office of the Night in Florence is significant for several reasons. First, it illustrates an early application of surveillance methodologies for the monitoring of sex. Second, it shows how understandings of sexuality intersected at an early historical moment with notions of public health and morality as religious authorities began to frame male-with-male sex as a 'risk factor' in triggering divine retribution in the form of pestilence and other epidemics. Third, it suggests that the binary frame of homosexual versus heterosexual was not yet established at this time, when there were no firmly defined categories designating male-with-male sex as inherently abnormal and when men who regularly engaged in male-with-male sex were also involved in sex with women and/or were married. This example thus implies that the binary frame of homosexual versus heterosexual sex developed later – namely in nineteenth century medical and psychiatric discourses, as Michel Foucault (1978a) describes.

Foucault (1978b) provides a pertinent historical example in his discussion of Herculine Barbin. Born in France in 1838, the intersex Barbin possessed a small vagina and internal testes and penis. Until age twenty, s/he lived as a woman but experienced ambiguous interests in both male and female partners. At one point, it became known that s/he was interested in sexual relations with women, and s/he became the object of surveillance by medical practitioners who discovered that s/he had internal, undescended male organs. These medical practitioners inspected and attempted to categorize Barbin as homosexual. Due to the pressures of this medical scrutiny, Barbin committed suicide. Foucault uses the example of Barbin to show how the surveillance of sex and sexuality attempts to sort the bodies and practices it investigates into a dichotomous framework of homosexual versus heterosexual. Foucault's (1978a) research is important in demonstrating when, how and under what conditions the discourses of sexuality emerged and in emphasizing the centrality of the body to these discourses as it was pried into and examined by practitioners of early medical science.

In addition to Rocke's and Foucault's analyses, Laud Humphreys' (1975) *Tearoom Trade* constitutes a key case study in the history on surveillance of sex and sexuality. To warn men engaged in male-with-male sexual practices of approaching police or other passers-by, Humphreys posed as a 'watch queen' in public washrooms where such activity occurred in the 1960s. As a researcher, Humphreys turned the tables on regulatory monitoring agents, himself monitoring surveillance agents, such as police, who sought to relegate these practices to the private sphere, assumed to be the home. In Humphreys' study, public opinion also increasingly associated male-with-male public sex with heightened concern about the risk of sexually transmitted diseases and the rise of public health; by the 1970s, then, the binary frame of risky versus safe began to shape regulatory and broader cultural understandings of male-with-male sex.

As Humphreys' study demonstrates, male-with-male sex in public not only affronts normative ideals of heterosexuality, but also challenges the idea that sex should occur in private by reclaiming certain public spaces (e.g. parks, beaches and washrooms) as amenable to sexual relations.[3] Defying normative framing of sex as private occurrences between a man and a woman, these forms of itinerant sex are always subject to intense surveillance and regulation (Bérubé 2003; Califia 1994). John Paul Ricco (2002) writes that the lure of sex between men in public involves anonymous sociality and itinerant encountering, and is therefore not governed by normative understandings of conduct, space use or fixed identity. The division between public and private is thus complicated when sexual practices violate this binary frame.

More recently, municipal and provincial/state police forces in Canada have created specialized surveillance units that focus on the surveillance of sex. These units are reminiscent of the 'vice squad', a policing unit made familiar to us via popular cultural representations and perhaps most famously associated with American cities of the 1920s, 1930s and 1940s. Vice squads were concerned not only with sex but also with gambling, drinking, drug taking, racketeering and other activities subject to moral regulation. The specialization and professionalization of vice units within police agencies are noteworthy because they represent an intensification of the regulation of sex. This intensification is nowhere more apparent than in the move, albeit slow, of policing agents to surveillance of cyberspace content related to sex and sexuality, specifically sex work and escorting websites. Policing agents pose as would-be clients through Internet chatting, trying to ensnare sex workers in entrapment scenarios. Municipal police also monitor websites (such as Squirt.org) where men chat with other men about organizing sexual encounters in public washrooms, parks or other public locations (Walby 2009b); this monitoring of online communications in such chat rooms in turn influences the locations of street-level enforcement work.

The trend toward online monitoring of sex relations is important for two reasons:

- it suggests that the organization of sex increasingly occurs via technologically mediated modes of communication; and
- it suggests that regulation and surveillance of sex increasingly occur via these same media.

The arrangement of sex work currently occurs much more frequently via the Internet than it does via a physical location, such as a stroll in the park or a visit to an escort agency. The same can be said about itinerant sex in parks, washrooms and other public spaces: such male-with-male public sex encounters are usually organized over the Internet. Because surveillance agents, by the very nature of their work, need to gather evidence in a voyeuristic fashion (see Johnson 2007; Dalton 2006), they have become adept in entering cyberspace to continue their monitoring activities (see Chapter 3). What is more, police officers engage in a kind of entrapment (called 'random virtue testing' in Canadian criminal law) by posing as clients and tempting escorts to write details about commercial sex exchanges that are used as evidence against them.

Sex and sexuality under the gaze

Walby's research on the trend toward online surveillance of sex and sexuality helps to explain how the work of online sex monitoring is organized and also to describe some of the stakes involved for individuals caught in the gaze of surveillance agents. Walby has explored the surveillance of male-with-male bathhouses in Ontario in the 1970s and 1980s (Walby 2009a), the work of conservation officers in monitoring male-with-male public sex in Canadian cities (Walby 2009b), and male-for-male escorts subjected to police monitoring and surveillance (Walby 2010). In this section, we discuss these three examples of surveillance of male-with-male sexual activities, showing how the reinscription of binary frames (public–private, gay–straight, risky–safe) occurs in both police occurrence reports and public responses to public sex – at the expense of more complex understandings of such practices for the men who engage in them.

In the 1970s and 1980s, camera technology for the surveillance of male-with-male bathhouses remained rudimentary. Cameras the size of pens were installed in several washrooms around the Greater Toronto Area (GTA) in the wake of gays' and lesbians' public struggle for human rights and increased recognition; at this time, gays and lesbians were harassed and targeted for surveillance. Ontario Provincial Police and municipal police forces monitored these GTA washrooms from adjacent rooms and gathered visual evidence in order to press charges of gross indecency under the Criminal Code of Canada. Police would often contact men identified in this way at their workplaces or arrest them when they returned home (see Walby 2009a). At the station, police would show them video evidence of their sexual relations with other men in a ploy to intimidate them into pleading guilty. In a world less hypermediated than today's, these men were often shocked to see themselves engaging in sexual relations that were deemed taboo (see also Biber and Dalton 2009). Several men charged with gross indecency committed suicide.

These gross indecency cases garnered intense media attention and prompted public outrage at the fact that men were having sex with men in public washrooms. Discourse about the riskiness of male-with-male sexual activity prevailed in both media coverage of the cases and public responses to them; indeed, these men were generally represented as vectors of disease. Public concern also focused on the potential for male-with-male sex to endanger the psychological well-being of children and youth who might inadvertently witness such sexual activity (see also Edelman 1993). In these cases, then, the activity of male-with-male sex was monitored through the lenses of public versus private, homosexual versus hetero-sexual and risky versus safe. These binary frames were reinscribed in media coverage of the trials that depicted these men as engaging in risky, taboo and inappropriate sex (see Desroches 1990).

A more recent example focuses on the surveillance of sex in Canadian cities by conservation officers. Although Canadians usually associate conservation officers with working in the wilderness to protect wildlife and prevent forest fires, their duties in and around cities also involve monitoring male-with-male public sex in parks.[4] In Ottawa, the National Capital Commission (NCC) monitors sexual activity between men in parks in several ways. For example, NCC conservation officers drive, walk or bike through parks, monitoring tree stands and bluffs for sexual activity between men. NCC officers also go online and monitor the chat rooms where men set up these encounters, writing occurrence reports about the details of the men's chat room conversations, as illustrated here: 'FYI primetime is around 12:00 … Timm Road seems to be their new favorite spot to have fun'; 'highly advertised on website … supposed to be highly active today!!! CO's heads up' (Walby 2009b: 373). Officers then stake out the public area designated as a meeting place and communicate what they learn to other conservation officers and to local policing and surveillance agencies. These communications serve to coordinate sweeping busts of men having sex with men in these parks. The following are examples of other narratives found in NCC officers' occurrence reports:

> 2009 05 25 – Rockcliffe Park – Observed three males engaging in sexual activity … went to intercept, two males ran away, caught one individual, explained regulations, issued ticket and expelled.

2009 06 06 – Riverside Old Dump brush area – While on foot patrol in the bush observed two males doing oral sex plus one male watching ... intercepted, explained regulations, issued tickets, expelled.

Walby's analysis of over one thousand occurrence reports makes apparent the considerable effort officers expend chasing men who have sexual relations in the parks. Such intense effort in expunging sexual acts from public spaces can lead to dwindling spaces for itinerant sex. Yet, as Chauncey (1994) discusses, the struggle between gay men who claim streets and parks as venues for public sex and police who regulate these same spaces produces an ongoing tug-of-war between sexual expression and social control.

This example of surveillance of sex in parks illustrates how the binary frames of public–private, gay–straight and risky–safe render the practice of male-with-male sex almost unintelligible in other terms, such as resistance or radicalism. NCC officers' regulation of male-with-male sex in parks encapsulates the normative notion that sex is meant to occur in the private sphere. The problematization of male-with-male sex in parks rests on the view that this kind of sex poses risks to others, especially to children who might witness sexual acts or find sexual paraphernalia left behind. For example, officers often make reports about condoms found in the parks that children could find. Public complaints accessed using access to information requests often identify potential risks posed to children by male-with-male sex. In both regulatory and public responses to male-with-male public sex, binary frames thus emphasize normativity at the expense of other interpretations of this sexual activity.

In the United States, the United Kingdom and Canada, men who sell sex to other men organize their encounters on special websites where they post profiles indicating the types of service they offer; they then arrange a price, a time and a place to meet over the phone (see Walby 2010). In interviews, escorts talked about intense police monitoring of the websites where they advertise and described attempts to entrap them during phone conversations between the would-be client – actually a surveillance agent – and the sex worker. As one escort put it:

I made a trip to Chicago. I only broke even on that trip, I did not turn a profit, I was only going to learn how to escort in the USA. It is a different game. I have not made any other trips ... I am afraid of the USA. It is different because you have to dance around on the phone and in your emails, you have to pretend you are offering a massage, you cannot answer blocked numbers. The police will set traps, they will do stings. If someone calls and says 'do you suck, do you fuck' ... you have to play dumb, assume that is a police officer trying to entrap you, say you do not talk about that over the phone.

Although escorts have strategies to determine whether a caller is a police officer, these strategies can be ineffective and arrests ensue, especially in the United States.

The binary frame of public versus private sex does not appear to apply to male-with-male commercial sex because it is consensual sex between adults that occurs in private. Indeed, escorts wonder why police monitor their work at all and feel unjustly targeted (Walby 2010). One explanation is that Internet use has pushed commercial male-with-male sex into the public domain of cyberspace. Because the Internet does not have built-in privacy safeguards and because it can be accessed by anyone with a computer, these websites can be considered part of the public sphere. Also, like female sex work, male sex work is associated with riskiness. Some public health researchers have argued that men who sell sex to men are sexually compulsive and are at greater risk of HIV infection or infection with another sexually transmitted disease (see Parsons et al. 2001). The case of male-with-male Internet sex work illustrates how the binary frames of public–private, gay–straight and risky–safe are not always apparent or deployed equally in the surveillance of sexual conduct. But the question of where these framing categories come from remains. Next, we explore surveillance medicine as one site where framing categories and discourses of sexuality are generated.

Proliferating sites: the case of surveillance medicine

In this section, we focus on the public health dimensions of sex, sexuality and surveillance, examining how the public health monitoring of sexual diseases and practices in a variety of populations perpetuates the binary frames of public–private, gay–straight and risky–safe. We build on Armstrong's (1995) argument about the emergence of 'surveillance medicine', a type of surveillance based on aggregate knowledge about populations and epidemiological techniques that 'dissolve the notion of the subject or a concrete individual, and put in its place a combinatory of factors, the factors of risk' (Castel 1991: 281). Through these techniques, surveillance medicine renders visible probabilities of risk for specific sexual behaviours (e.g. unprotected sex with multiple partners).

Surveillance medicine thus extends the gaze of public health agencies from the individual body to wider populations, as illustrated by massive national surveillance programmes to monitor rates of sexually transmitted diseases, including HIV/AIDS.[5] This type of surveillance involves systematic collection and analysis of data obtained from a range of sources, including physician reports, health records, laboratory results, community surveys and collection of body fluid samples (Thacker and Stroup 1994). Surveillance medicine indeed constitutes a precursor to other kinds of monitoring of sex, since it associates some sexual activities with specific risk profiles that surveillance agents can use to more easily target individuals. For example, epidemiological surveillance involves the reduction of sexualities to indicators of risk. In the case of male-with-male sex, this form of monitoring frames homosexual sex as being primarily associated with the spread of HIV/AIDS and other sexually transmitted diseases. The methodologies used to collect statistics on male-with-male sex also rest on a gay versus straight binary frame that reinscribes the notion that there are only two kinds of sexuality. Of course, sexuality is more complex and diverse than this classificatory scheme suggests.

Central to this surveillance activity are diagnostic categories that render measurements of sex and sexuality amenable to statistical manipulation. One of the first efforts to establish diagnostic categories dates back to the Kinsey reports, which produced findings on the frequency with which men and women participated in various types of sexual practices, including homosexual sex, extramarital sex and sadomasochism (Bullough 2004). American psychiatry also played a key role, transforming a host of sexual deviations (such as exhibitionism, paedophilia and voyeurism) into diagnosable psychopathologies. Homosexuality belonged to this list of disorders until 1973, when it was removed from psychiatric nosology under pressure from gay rights activists (Bayer 1981). These disorders are listed in the Diagnostic and Statistical Manual of Mental Disorders (DSM), which is published by the American Psychiatric Association (2000). The DSM serves as the main classification of mental disorders used by psychiatrists around the world to diagnose mental pathologies, including sexual deviations. The pathologization of these deviations further reinscribes sex and sexuality in binary frames: each disorder is defined by a list of categorical symptoms (present vs. absent symptom), which allow for expedient clinical diagnosis. These symptoms are then integrated into epidemiological measures to estimate the distribution of these disorders in the population.[6]

The aim of epidemiological tracking is to identify populations to be regulated by public health agencies on the basis of prevention and precaution (Castel 1991). For example, the treatment of sexual deviations with pharmacological drugs is well established and the subject of ongoing research that compares rates of success in treated and non-treated populations (see Greenberg and Bradford 1997). Interventions follow the neo-liberalist tenets of individualism and responsibility by appealing to individuals to self-regulate and voluntarily subjugate themselves to medical surveillance (e.g., blood tests, self-examinations). Pryce (2000) discusses the highly organized surveillance that public health agencies engage in, but also the kinds of self-regulation this can lead to amongst men who have sex with men. Pryce also criticizes the routine collection of bodily samples from men who have sex with men and the follow-up consultations that can be intrusive. French (2009) likewise demonstrates how public health agencies use metaphors of war and violent language to describe disease and HIV/AIDS, particularly within male-with-male sexual groups; this usage accords with the idea that the riskiness of male-with-male sex must be eradicated. This language of public health promotions perpetuates the binary frame of riskiness versus safe sex. In this way, surveillance medicine is fuelled by but also reinforces stories of the riskiness of male-with-male sex, resulting in the encoding of sexual practice in a language of risk, pathogen, threat and disease.

Surveillance medicine also extends the reach of public health agencies into the monitoring of sex education in schools. The proliferation of sex education programmes in schools has made children the target of surveillance over concerns about teenage pregnancy and sexually transmitted diseases. Education as a site of surveillance reflects public health discourses and the tracking of underage sexual practices as risk factors. For example, teenage pregnancy rates are often invoked to justify a range of interventions. Such interventions hide concerns with social order and the law; for example, teenage pregnancy often entails illegal underage sex. However, as Foucault (1978a) pointed out, the sexualization of boys and girls requires all the more surveillance directed toward it. Sex education is required, but at the same time raises questions about the sexualization of children, which necessitates control over what is said.

Surveillance of any talk about sexuality comes to be justified through worries about the risks posed to youth in even hearing about sex, let alone performing it. This logic engenders a parallel surveillance of sexual education practices. For example, Hayter et al. (2008) report on the state monitoring of teachers involved in sex education in classrooms in the United Kingdom: officials from the education board monitored the content of these teachers' lectures. School staff and administrators also conducted covert surveillance of nurses and sex educators who were talking about sex to students. Sexual education curricula are also the site of fierce political debates in the United States between liberal educators and religious conservatives, who decry such efforts as encouraging promiscuity and sexual deviation (see Irvine 2002).

Although surveillance medicine might not seem to regulate sex and sexuality in the same way as do policing agents, both surveillance medicine and police surveillance utilize similar categories in controlling sexual practices, particularly those involving male-with-male sex. These categories rest on binary frames that facilitate the identification of so-called risky populations and the implementation of regulatory interventions. Just as police and conservation officers monitor chat rooms to identify sites of public sex, health authorities monitor rates of infections and medical reports to identify individuals and groups that could pose a threat to public health. In both instances, ideas of risk justify the discretionary and often invasive acts of surveillance agents. Surveillance medicine also helps produce the trope of the risky sexual subject that justifies police intervention in non-medical arenas such as bathhouses, public washrooms and parks. These categories become a focal lens through which surveillance agents view men who have sex with men and public sex. When police make busts, when medical surveillance agents peer through their lenses, predetermined categories of risk are all too easily found, since they are embedded in the knowledge and practices that all forms of surveillance work entail.[7]

Conclusion: lenses, binary frames and distortion

Public versus private, gay versus straight, risky versus safe: these are the lenses and binary frames through which surveillance occurs. The concentration of each binary frame is not the same in all instances of surveillance. Sometimes surveillance focuses much more on one binary frame to the exclusion of the other two. Yet the other two are never far from view. Furthermore, surveillance is not about simply casting a gaze upon naturally occurring kinds of sex and sexuality. Rather, understandings of sex and sexuality as deviant and risky are in part produced by surveillance. Surveillance strategies rest on the idea that there are binary and mutually exclusive forms of sexual orientation, thus rendering all other possibilities and configurations less comprehensible. Not only do these binary frames structure public understandings of sex but they also reinscribe the objects of surveillance through dichotomous categories that divest sex of nuance.

The dividing line of public versus private rests on the presumption that sex and sexuality are improper practices or topics of discussion for the public sphere. The example of the monitoring of sex education in American and British classrooms suggests that even in the few instances when sex and sexuality are acknowledged in a public domain, they are highly scrutinized and monitored by public health and policing officials. The binary frame of gay versus straight, or homosexual versus heterosexual, assumes that sexuality can be split into two mutually exclusive categories. Such dualist discourse masks complexity, failing to acknowledge a diversity of sex practices and rendering other forms of pleasures wrong or nonsensical. The third binary frame is the risky versus safe opposition, which is often invoked to problematize male-with-male sexual activity and to justify epidemiological forms of surveillance that monitor the prevalence of sexually transmitted infections within primarily male-with-male sexual communities. These forms of surveillance contribute to the development of invasive public health interventions. Further, medical surveillance provides categories that surveillance and policing agents use in their work of monitoring and regulating sexual conduct.

Our analysis suggests that there can be a fruitful cross-over between the sociology of surveillance and the sociology of sexuality, insofar as both are concerned with categories and classifications that exclude nuance and diversity, assimilating sex to simplistic terms. We conclude by challenging the notion of sexuality as an attribute or a set of intrinsic features objectively detectable with surveillance devices. In this sense, the lenses and binary frames of surveillance constitute a primary means of distorting the complexity and fluidity that sex, touching and intimacy entail. As we have argued, these surveillance lenses and binary frames conceal as much as they reveal and they lead to a selective and pathologizing gaze. Rather than pertaining to individuals' primordial sexuality, the practices of sex we have discussed are inscribed according to discourses of sexuality, namely the primary binary frames of public–private, gay–straight and risky–safe. Surveillance produces, perpetuates and distorts understandings of sexuality along the lines of these dichotomous categories. Looking through these lenses and binary frames, surveillance and policing work to pathologize men who have sex with men and provide a distorted picture of their lives.

Acknowledgements

We thank the editors and Mary Elizabeth Leighton for their expertise.

Notes

1 Here, we distinguish sex from sexuality. Sex refers to erotic bodily practices, whereas sexuality consists of categories constructed through cultural and political discourses that render these practices intelligible (e.g. homosexual or heterosexual orientation).

2 The 1957 *Wolfenden Report*, influential in the UK and Australia, and also North America, simultaneously called for the withdrawal of regulation of sex in the private sphere and broader policing of public sex. This report facilitated the decriminalization of private 'homosexuality' in a 1969 amendment of the Criminal Code of Canada, but legitimated regulation of male-with-male sex in the public sphere.

3 The control of sexual relations between women in quasi-public spaces (e.g. 'the Pussy Palace' venue in Toronto) similarly challenges the normative ideal that sex should occur in the private sphere (Bain and Nash 2007).

4 The term 'public sex' belies the fact such sex often occurs in relative privacy, hidden from view behind bushes and in bluffs, for instance.

5 In the United States, the Center for Disease Control and Prevention (CDC) is the governmental agency that oversees the monitoring and prevention of HIV/AIDS through a specialized branch, the Division of HIV/AIDS Prevention (DHAP). In Canada, this role is assumed by the Public Health Agency of Canada.

6 A whole host of 'sexual deviations' are measured. Voyeurism is said to be the most common of these law-breaking sexual practices with a prevalence rate as high as 42 per cent where estimates for exhibitionism are much lower (4.1 per cent in men and 2.1 per cent in women) (Långström 2010). Paedophilia is described as 'a very severe public health problem of staggering proportions,' with up to 62 per cent of girls and 30 per cent of boys being victims (McDonald and Bradford 2000: 248).

7 There are many more examples of surveillance of sex. One example pertains to webcams. Koskela's (2004) argument is that the monitoring of oneself using a webcam and the broadcasting of that on the Internet can be a form of empowerment.

Bibliography

American Psychiatric Association (2000) *Diagnostic and Statistical Manual of Mental Disorders* (4th edn), Washington, DC.

Armstrong, D. (1995) 'The Rise of Surveillance Medicine', *Sociology of Health & Illness*, 17 (3): 393–404.

Bain, A. and Nash, C. (2007) 'The Toronto Women's Bathhouse Raid: Querying queer identities in the courtroom', *Antipode*, 39: 17–34.

Bayer, R. (1981) *Homosexuality and American Psychiatry*, New York: Basic Books.

Bérubé, A. (2003) 'The History of Gay Bathhouses', *Journal of Homosexuality*, 44: 33–53.

Biber, K. and Dalton, D. (2009) 'Making Art from Evidence: Secret sex and police surveillance in the tearoom', *Crime, Media, Culture*, 5: 243–67.

Brookey, R.A. (2002) *Reinventing the Male Homosexual: The rhetoric and power of the gay gene*, Bloomington, IN: Indiana University Press.

Bullough, V. (2004) 'Sex Will Never Be the Same: The contributions of Alfred C. Kinsey', *Archives of Sexual Behavior*, 33: 277–86.

Califia, P. (1994) *Public Sex: The culture of radical sex*, San Francisco, CA: Cleis Press.

Castel, R. (1991) 'From Dangerousness to Risk', in G. Burchell, C. Gordon and P. Miller (eds) *The Foucault Effect: Studies in governmentality*, Chicago, IL: University of Chicago Press.

Chauncey, G. (1994) *Gay New York: Gender, urban culture and the making of the gay male world, 1890–1940*, New York: Basic Books.

Dalton, D. (2006) 'Surveying Deviance, Figuring Disgust: Locating the homocriminal body in time and space', *Social & Legal Studies*, 15: 277–99.

——(2007) 'Policing Outlawed Desire: "Homocriminality" in beat spaces in Australia', *Law and Critique*, 18: 375–405.

Desroches, F. J. (1990) 'Tearoom Trade: A research update', *Qualitative Sociology*, 13: 39–61.

Edelman, L. (1993) 'Tearooms and Sympathy, or, The Epistemology of the Water Closet', in H. Abelove and D. Halperin (eds) *The Lesbian and Gay Studies Reader*, London: Routledge.

Foucault, M. (1978a) *The History of Sexuality*, Vol. 1, New York: Pantheon Books.

——(1978b) *Herculine Barbin: Being the recently discovered memoirs of a nineteenth century French hermaphrodite*, New York: Pantheon Books.

French, M. (2009) 'Woven of War-Time Fabrics: The globalization of public health surveillance', *Surveillance & Society*, 6: 101–15.

Greenberg, D.M. and Bradford, J.M.W. (1997) 'Treatment of the Paraphilic Disorders: A review of the role of the selective serotonin reuptake inhibitors', *Sexual Abuse*, 9: 349–61.

Haggerty, K. (2009) '"Ten Thousand Times Larger ... ": Anticipating the expansion of surveillance', in B. Goold and D. Neyland (eds) *New Directions in Surveillance and Privacy*, Cullompton: Willan.

Hayter, M., Percy, H., Massey, M. and Gregory, T. (2008) 'School Nurses and Sex Education: Surveillance and disciplinary practices in primary schools', *Journal of Advanced Nursing*, 61: 273–81.

Home Office (1957) *Report of the Committee on Homosexual Offences and Prostitution* (Cmnd 247), London: HMSO.

Humphreys, L. (1975) *Tearoom Trade: Impersonal sex in public places*, New York: Aldine de Gruyter.

Irvine, J. (2002) *Talk About Sex: The battles over sex education in the United States*. Berkeley, CA: University of California Press.

Johnson, P. (2007) 'Ordinary Folk and Cottaging: Law, morality and public sex', *Journal of Law and Society*, 34: 520–43.

Kinsman, G. (1996) *The Regulation of Desire: Homo and hetero sexualities*, Montreal: Black Rose Books.

Koskela, H. (2004) 'Webcams, TV Shows and Mobile Phones: Empowering exhibitionism', *Surveillance & Society*, 2(2/3): 199–215.

Långström, N. (2010) 'The DSM Diagnostic Criteria for Exhibitionism, Voyeurism and Frotteurism', *Archives of Sexual Behavior*, 39: 349–56.

McDonald, J. and Bradford, W. (2000) 'The Treatment of Sexual Deviation Using a Pharmacological Approach', *The Journal of Sex Research*, 37: 248–57.

Parsons, J.T., Bimbi, D.S. and Halkitis, P.N. (2001) 'Sexual Compulsivity among Gay/Bisexual Male Escorts Who Advertise on the Internet', *Sexual Addiction & Compulsivity*, 8: 101–12.

Pryce, A. (2000) 'Frequent Observation: Sexualities, self-surveillance, confession and the construction of the active patient', *Nursing Inquiry*, 7: 103–11.

Ricco, J. P. (2002) *The Logic of the Lure*, Chicago, IL: University of Chicago Press.

Rocke, M. (1996) *Forbidden Friendships: Homosexuality and male culture in Renaissance Florence*, New York: Oxford University Press.

Rubin, G. (1993) 'Thinking Sex: Notes for a radical theory of the politics of sexuality', in H. Abelove, M. Barale and D. Halperin (eds) *The Lesbian and Gay Studies Reader*, New York: Routledge.

Thacker, S. and Stroup, D. (1994) 'Future Directions for Comprehensive Public Health Surveillance and Health Information Systems in the United States', *American Journal of Epidemiology*, 140: 383–397.

Walby, K. (2009a) 'Surveillance of Male with Male Public Sex in Ontario, 1983–1994', in S. Hier and J. Greenberg (eds) *Surveillance: Power, problems and politics*, Vancouver: University of British Columbia Press.

——(2009b) '"He asked me if I was looking for fags ... "': Ottawa's National Capital Commission conservation officers and the policing of public park sex', *Surveillance & Society*, 6: 367–79.

——(2010) 'Interviews as Encounters: Issues of sexuality and reflexivity when men interview men about commercial same sex relations', *Qualitative Research*, 10: 639–57.

5

POLICING 'BEATS' IN AUSTRALIA

Derek Dalton

This chapter considers policing practices in relation to places where men meet to organize or have sex. In Australia, these spaces are known as 'beats'.[1] This chapter has four aims. First, my discussion seeks to trace the history of policing beat spaces in Australia and document why these spaces have attracted the attention and animosity of police. Second, this chapter seeks to provide a brief overview of some of the pressing issues that cluster around the policing of beats in contemporary Australia. Here I explore the extent to which the legacy of disgust and moral disapproval associated with past policing practices partly informs current police attitudes and practices. Third, this chapter seeks to briefly explore how men who use beats seek to resist police attempts to regulate their behaviour. It does so by exploring the emergence of the 'NSW Beats Project' – a grassroots Australian website that exists as a conduit through which beat users might be better informed about their rights in light of alleged police harassment, vigilante behaviour and hate-related crime associated with beats. Finally, this chapter concludes by ruminating on some of the pressing issues that will continue to cluster around the policing of beats in the future.

Beats: a history of police hostility to male sex in public

In Australia, the term 'beat' is used to refer to spaces where men gather to seek out or arrange casual sexual encounters with other men, irrespective of the sexual identity of participants. Beat users include homosexual men, bisexual men and heterosexual men who are closeted and/or married. Beats afford men a degree of privacy conducive to sexual intimacy (Carbery 1992: 132). Moore (1995: 328) has documented that beats have existed in Australia for well over one hundred years and that they have evolved in parks, secluded hinterlands, beaches, public shower-blocks and the like. However, the most common and notorious beats are those in public lavatory blocks in railway stations, parks and shopping malls. These public sex environments are found in just about every suburb in every city of Australia and many country towns (Swivel 1991: 237).

Beat spaces have a long and complicated history of attracting the attention and animosity of police. In Australia, some of the earliest arrests and criminal prosecutions for conduct at beats date back to the 1910s (Wotherspoon 1991: 66). Little is known about these matters as scant offence details have been preserved in court archives. Various historians of homosexual subculture note that the police were often aware of sexual conduct at beats and this period marks the start of police vigilance to the phenomenon of beats (French 1986; Wotherspoon 1991; Murdoch 2000; Carbery 1992).

By the 1930s and 1940s, police intensified their interest in beats and many prosecutions were brought for the crimes of gross indecency, wilful and obscene exposure, and public nuisance. As I have previously documented (Dalton 2006, 2007a), men having sex at beats were represented in criminological discourse of the time as posing a two-faceted threat to Australian society. First, homosexual men were believed to pollute other innocent (that is non-homosexual) men that they came into physical contact with. Youth were seen as being particularly susceptible to being 'converted' to homosexuality should they encounter a homosexual man at a beat (Dalton 2007a).[2] Second, once a man was polluted by exposure to homosexuality, it was imagined that a monstrous form of desire akin to vampirism propelled him to have homosexual sex. Such a subject, impelled by a *thirst* for sex, would trawl beats for sex and, in turn, pollute other men by introducing them to homosexual conduct (Dalton 2006). Given the alarmist discourse prevailing at the time that construed beats as spaces where moral and sexual contamination took place, state police forces across Australia turned their attention to policing beats.

A key trope that emerges in the early policing of beats is the notion that deviant men frequenting beats could pass as 'normal' heterosexual men. Newspaper reports in the tabloid press fuelled public anxiety that it was almost impossible to identify a homosexual 'pervert' until a criminal matter cast the light of the law on that individual's conduct. Here, the vigilant gaze of agents of the law was first heralded as a critical factor when policing homosexual offences, including beat crimes (Dalton 2006). Several well-publicized prosecutions of men for homosexual offences at beats, including that of a prominent newspaper editor in 1943, helped underwrite an impetus for police forces across Australia to devote resources and manpower to policing beats.

Newspaper reports of homosexual sex taking place at beats associated with public parks and public lavatories caused disgust and public outrage (Dalton 2006). The trope of homosexuals 'haunting' public space as the nemesis of public order, typified press accounts of homosexual conduct prior to the advent of gay liberation (French 1986; Murdoch 1998). Such was the attendant anxiety associated with homosexual offences in the 1940s and 1950s that this became the rationale behind agent provocateur policing initiatives that emerged during this period. Such policing practices typically involved plain-clothed (undercover) officers being deployed to various known beats in an attempt to apprehend homosexuals. It is hard to determine whether these policing initiatives arose organically within Australian police forces, or whether local police forces sought to emulate agent provocateur policing initiatives well established in the UK

(Moran 1996 and Chapter 1). The cities of Sydney and Melbourne saw the first recorded use of entrapment tactics. Officers would typically situate themselves at a beat or in its vicinity, wait for a man to expose himself or make a solicitous request and then arrest that individual.

The 1970s and 1980s saw an intensification of police interest and prosecutions for homosexual conduct in beat spaces (Dalton 2008: 102). It is appropriate to pause to consider what precisely it is about beats that so antagonizes the police and general public alike. The enactment of beat sex is invested with the potential to disgust, particularly when the beat space happens to be a public toilet. Maynard (1994) has detailed how sex between men links to prevailing legal discourses of the lavatory, representing 'toilet' sex as filthy, immoral and unsavoury. When gay sexual expression is located within these walls, the filth and dirt associated with the toilet attaches to the sex act itself. Indeed, as Berlant and Warner (1998: 560) have documented: 'in gay male culture, the principal scenes of criminal intimacy have been tearooms, streets, sex clubs and parks – a tropism toward the public toilet'.

Sexual behaviour in beats disturbs order because it circumvents rules, manners and expectations associated with these public spaces. Public conveniences are built and maintained for the purpose of enabling people to dispose of their bodily wastes. When these places become sites of sexual expression, this runs counter to the socially authorized use of these spaces. The disposal of wastes is a form of bodily *subtraction*. Gay sexual expression is a form of *addition* – the conjoining of bodies and the exchange of pleasure. These two differing equations coexist in a domain of tension. Yet both equations share a commonality. The disposal of waste and the expression of gay sexual desire in public are perceived as disgusting and repulsive activities. Indeed, as Miller (1997) has noted, disgust triggers powerful aversive responses in individuals. Where beats are concerned, such responses are often triggered by signs of desire. The visible presence of semen, glory holes, solicitous graffiti and the jettisoned accoutrements of gay sex (e.g. used condoms and wrappers, discarded tissues, empty packets of lubricant) have been identified as a spectacle that incites extreme disgust and revulsion (Dalton 2007b: 382) and helps explain why some public toilet beat spaces attract public scorn and disapprobation (Dalton 2004). The wider community is hostile to the existence of beats as evidenced by articles printed in local community newspapers complaining about the problem of dirty, clandestine, homosexual public sex (Dalton 2008: 103). Indeed, it has been the visible signs of beat activity, including the presence of men at beats, which has often attracted the attention of police.

As I have previously documented (Dalton 2007b: 380), in interviews conducted with men who had encounters with the police between 1964 and 1999, men seen near beats were often presumed by the police to be 'looking' for sex. Almost all of the respondents recounted experiences of police officers accusing them of misconduct and warning them away from the area. Men were typically threatened with arrest if they were found near the beat in the future. A common sentiment expressed by officers was that they did not want to *see* the men there again (Dalton 2007b: 381). The state of being 'there' – in or near a beat – transforms a place containing bodies into an imagined crime scene (Dalton 2007b: 379). Indeed, historically police have been well aware that beats are spaces where crimes of indecent public sex might be readily and routinely detected if they are vigilant in placing such spaces under surveillance (Dalton 2007b: 380).

In concluding this brief overview of the history of police hostility to beats in Australia, it is imperative to emphasize the role that duplicity and deception have played in policing initiatives linked to beats. For the agent provocateur entrapment tactics that emerged in the 1940s became a fixture in the regulative arsenal by the 1980s in many Australian police forces. Posing as gay men, police studied and mimicked their mannerisms and even dressed in ways that they thought would assist them to 'pass' as gay (Dalton 2002: 168). The police would then enter beat spaces and incite approaches from the men present. When men responded by touching the policeman's body, exposing themselves or making solicitous remarks, the elaborate legal charade would dissolve as the police would declare their true identity (often by brandishing a police badge) and executing an arrest (Dalton 2007b: 387). Hocquenghem (1978: 117) reminds us here that the police are complicit in voyeuristic practices of incitement: 'the phantasy of the cop is not some creation of the homosexual's deranged mind, but the reality of a deviant desiring operation on the part of the police and judiciary'.

Policing beats in contemporary times

Many of the issues that emerged in relation to the historic policing of beats endure in the present. I wish to compare and contrast the diverse approaches that police take to policing beats in contemporary times throughout Australia.

The first approach can be classified as evincing proactive crime prevention initiatives. Police patrol known beats to deter men from frequenting them and engaging in public sex acts and anti-social behaviour. These patrols are either conducted by uniformed police routinely patrolling their local district area in a marked police vehicle or by police in unmarked police vehicles. To complement such a deterrent purpose, the police may choose to promote and publicize that they are targeting anti-social behaviour at particular beats by disseminating advance notice of their operations in the gay and lesbian press (for a discussion of equivalent police practices in respect of heterosexual activities see Chapter 3).

Every police force/service in Australia deploys police to respond to complaints made by the public about suspicious behaviour or allegations of criminal misconduct in the vicinity of a beat. Indeed, as Johnson (Chapter 2) has documented, for the NSW police 'the source of, and desire for, the policing of beats is found in the community itself'. Johnson's examination of complaints about beats in NSW revealed that many police had a sophisticated understanding of the nature of complaints they received about beats. Many of the police officers he interviewed understood that complaints could be exaggerated and that this could lead to the problem of disproportionate policing of beats.

The second approach to policing beats is characterized by police employing tactics that carry the potential to instil distrust and resentment amongst the beat community. In part this is because there is a disjunction between the powers police are permitted to use and what actually happens in situ when police encounter men at beats. For example, in New South Wales, police guidelines stipulate that police cannot record personal details or take vehicle registration details simply because a man is in an area 'known' as a gay beat. Neither can they store and share this information using a database.[3] And police cannot explicitly inquire if a person is homosexual or demand to know their marital status. Such questions contravene anti-discrimination laws. And, yet, many men who have contacted a beats monitoring website (NSW Beat Project 2010) assert that police have, variously: harassed them about their purpose for being in public places; asked if they are homosexual; warned them to stay away from the area; and implied that their personal details would be recorded on a database. Policing beats is thus marked by activities that carry a strong message of intimidation. It has been reported that police sometimes search men for safe sex equipment (e.g. condoms, lubricants) to obtain evidence of intent to engage in sexual activity at a public space (NSW Beat Project 2010). Irrespective of the highly dubious legal value of such 'evidence', a legitimate public health concern is that beat users might stop carrying condoms and engage in risky unprotected sex as a result of police searches (NSW Beat Project 2010). This clearly undermines important strategies for the prevention of the spread of HIV/AIDS.

The third approach to policing beats entails rogue officers operating outside of police standards of conduct in their respective state or territory. Such an approach is marked by a mixture of homophobia, hostility and incivility. According to guidelines set out under the NSW Police Standards of Professionalism an officer must at all times treat everyone with respect, courtesy and fairness and respond to any incident in a professional and objective manner (NSW Police 2010). Unfortunately, this does not always happen. Rogue officers use inappropriate and homophobic language (including swearing) and express negative emotional responses towards men they encounter at beats. For example, an anonymous beat user said of his recent encounter with police that: 'I was made to feel disgusted about my behaviour; I was demeaned and looked upon as perverted' (NSW Beat Project 2010). Another beat user named 'Peter' told Radio 2SER on 11 November 2010 that:

> The police arrested me one night without charge. They threatened me with pepper spray, handcuffed me and claimed I was there [at the beat] for sex. They wouldn't listen when I repeatedly tried to tell them I was there to relax. I was afraid of them and they made a few smart-arse and personal insults before letting me go.
>
> *(Evans 2008)*

This is not a new phenomenon. I have previously documented homophobic sentiment and hostility as being a long-entrenched facet of police culture in relation to beats (Dalton 2002). Additionally, the shaming rituals beat users are subjected to such as being handcuffed, abused and derided as perverts are unfortunately not merely a vestige of a past homophobic police culture. Such behaviour is alleged to occasionally take place when men encounter unprofessional police at beats in contemporary times.

More disturbing than shaming rituals is the use of bribery and extortion. In an article devoted to beats in the Independent online news and current affairs site 'Crikey', academic lawyer Wayne Morgan spoke of the disturbing existence of police corruption in relation to beats. He stated: 'I know of circumstances where police at beats have told beat users: "Well, you give me something – usually money, but sometimes it's even sex – and we won't report you"' (Ting 2010). Whilst such incidents of bribery and extortion are no doubt rare, I uncovered allegations of sex being provided to police officers in exchange for their silence at beats in the city of Melbourne in the 1990s (Dalton 2002).

Another aspect of rogue policing is where officers police beats, not because of complaints, but as a 'sport'. This can entail officers using full beam headlights at beats at night to 'flush out' beat users, who then run. Officers give chase and apprehend, question and charge them (Johnson 2010: 418). The motivations for such unofficial, informal patrols include 'boredom', 'fun' and 'enjoyment' (Johnson 2010: 417). This type of policing is antithetical to NSW policy and thankfully is associated with aggressive and over-zealous individual officers operating on the margins of policing rather than the core of the NSW police (Johnson 2010: 417–19).

It must be stressed that the majority of police treat men at beats with respect and dignity and that the activities of a small percentage of rogue officers tarnish the reputation of otherwise largely ethical police forces/services throughout Australia. To the extent that reports continue to circulate about police incivility directed at beat users, one might question what is being done to intervene in and erode this culture of disrespect.

The existence of what can be loosely termed 'beat sensitivity' or 'awareness' training would seem to be a logical response to the problem of police incivility and hostility to beat users. Such training was pioneered in Melbourne in the State of Victoria in the 1980s under the auspices of a voluntary organization called the Police Lesbian & Gay Liaison Committee (Dalton 2002). Training initiatives target recruits or serving officers and provide them with an historical and cultural insight into why beats exist and who uses them. Sensitivity/awareness training humanizes beat users as ordinary men rather than as the archetypical perverts and deviants so entrenched in the police cultural psyche (Dalton 2006). The training reminds police that closeted and married men – not just gay men – use beats. The official place and prevalence of beat sensitivity training in the modern police landscape is somewhat difficult to gauge. New South Wales, Victoria and South Australia have adopted some aspects of sensitivity training in the past ten years. It is hoped that such programmes will continue to be implemented in the future as they provide a vital conduit through which individual officers might challenge preconceived moral judgements they have about beats that potentially underwrite homophobic behaviour. Indeed, Johnson has documented that the benefit of beat sensitivity training is that it carries the potential to demystify beat culture for ordinary police officers. And changes in police *perceptions* about beats can lead to changes in police *practice* (Johnson 2010: 415). An NSW police officer told Johnson that many police fear what they don't understand and then react against it (see Chapter 2).

The fourth approach to policing is shrouded in controversy and is very difficult to quantify as an official police practice in contemporary Australia. It appears from anecdotal accounts in the gay press that, when authorized by senior management, covert agent provocateur tactics are still occasionally employed. To the extent that agent provocateur tactics do exist, they do little to engender respect and cooperation within the beat community. Instead, they instil fear and mistrust. This is clearly counterproductive for all parties. Given that violence, assaults, robbery (Hennelly 2010) and tragically even murders occur in beat environments (Tomsen and George 1997; Mouzos and Thompson 2000), it is important that men frequenting these spaces perceive that the police are approachable and trustworthy.

One final aspect of policing beats in Australia warrants consideration. Private security firms and park rangers employed by local councils sometimes augment the role of police by conducting surveillance at beats. Such workers resort to summoning the police when suspicious or potentially illegal behaviour is detected. Indeed, the NSW Police intranet informs its officers that members of certain occupations such as security guards and rangers often identify beats and contact police (Johnson 2010: 408). This is not as unproblematic at it sounds. Some men in Sydney have recently alleged that council rangers have behaved in an aggressive manner, making derogatory and homophobic remarks (NSW Beats Project 2010). Any men oblivious to the existence of a beat who happen to be in a particular area are vulnerable to being subject to accusations and unwarranted aspersions by council rangers where such a climate of supplementary quasi-police vigilance exists. Supplementary policing measures here run the risk of getting out of hand. Walby's (2009: 367) study of the policing of parks by conservation officers in Ottawa, Canada, demonstrates the ramifications of supplementary policing initiatives: 'notions of so-called appropriate sexuality and space usage can be shaped and reinforced through policing and surveillance conducted by governance agents who have peace officer status.'

Walby (2009: 368) documented how the Ottawa conservation officers were so zealous in policing public sex in parks that they monitored online chat sites to try to identify cruising sites within the park to target for surveillance. Walby also explored how the issuing of 'occurrence reports' of allegations of public sex by park officers ultimately led to fines, charges and men being 'outed' to family and co-workers (Walby 2009: 374). Whilst Australian park and council rangers often work in more urban areas and do not have quasi-police powers like those invested in the Ottawa conservation officers, Walby's study offers a cautionary reminder of how park rangers help construct same-sex desiring men at large in parks as participating in 'abhorrent sexuality' (Walby 2009: 375).

Plural policing initiatives conducted by park or council rangers are not the limit of plural policing practices in relation to beats. In April 2010, Adelaide MP the Honourable Tom Koutsantonis issued an open letter to his West Torrens constituents, imploring them to help police the beat at Apex Park, West Beach. He urged residents: 'If you see drivers cruising suspiciously, I ask that you take down the number plate and description of the vehicle'. He stated that he would 'pass on this information to the local [police] Superintendent, so you can remain anonymous' (Crouch 2010). His request was met with both approval and condemnation from the public, as evident in postings on *Adelaide Now*'s online comment board. An article in a local newspaper entitled 'Tom Koutsantonis Accused of Inciting Hatred against Gays in Letter' (Wills 2010) emphasized that this particular beat was already a place where violent assaults had occurred.

This call to the public for help marks a very worrying turn in the policing of beats in Australia. It encourages the public to make uninformed judgements about the merits of men being in a public park and underwrites a witch hunt-like climate of hysteria where single men or men in groups unaccompanied by women must bear some sort of guilty stigma merely by being *there* – present in the park. Under this logic, men who wish to use the park for recreation and have no intention of seeking sex are constructed as harbouring criminal intentions. One can imagine the scenario of a single man parking his car and walking off to attend a family picnic being reported to the police for suspicious behaviour if a local citizen was to heed the Minister's advice. This is a disturbing situation and one that may fuel vigilantism and the likelihood of hate crimes taking place.

Resistance to policing initiatives: 'NSW Beat Project'

The NSW Beat Project is a grassroots movement that began as a series of picnics aimed at monitoring police harassment at beats in Sydney (Ting 2010). In 2008 a website was launched called the Sydney Beat Project. Two years later the site changed its name to the NSW Beat Project. Ting summarizes the project, writing: 'Initiated by beat users themselves in response to increased reports of police harassment, intimidation and mistreatment of men at beats across Sydney, it now monitors beats across NSW.'

The NSW Beat Project[4] describes itself as 'a peer based community network and online resource that is run by beat users for beat users' (NSW Beat Project 2010). It aims to:

- monitor and disseminate up-to-date information about police activity at beats throughout NSW;
- raise consciousness about police harassment, intimidation and mistreatment of men at beats;
- inform beat users about their rights and responsibilities;
- provide an independent reporting system to collect information on police behaviour at beats; and
- warn beat users about vigilante behaviour and incidents of hate-related crime against men at beats.

The NSW Beat Project has been controversial, attracting criticism from the LGBTI community and the wider public. Many of the claims made on the website have been dismissed as unsubstantiated opinion, but Johnson (2010: 418) found some operational officers who recognized them as having some legitimacy.

A key criticism is that the project draws public attention to an issue best left unexplored. As Potts has observed:

> [B]eat users don't have any sinister motives, however they are engaging in selfish behaviour with little regard for the communities in which they live ... [They] monopolise public spaces and facilities for purposes they were not intended for and take away the consent to be exposed to such behaviour from those who are there to use them for those intended purposes.
>
> *(cited in Ting 2010)*

This comment encapsulates the concerns of many in the LGBTI community who perceive the existence of beats as a sad anachronism that belongs in the dark and distant past when homosexuality was illegal and same-sex attracted men were forced to use them for furtive encounters. And, as Bell and Binnie (2004: 1815) have documented, many assimilationist gays perceive gay male public sex as an embarrassing problem that needs to be cleaned up.

Notwithstanding the fact that the project has its share of critics, the project coordinator Richard Capuano explains the impetus for starting the Beats Project [now NSW Beats Project]: 'We were concerned it would get back to the days when being a gay man was illegal, when police regularly harassed men at beats and used plain-clothed officers to entrap and charge men' (cited in Ting 2010). Indeed, it was the ever-present danger of encountering police that first led to same-sex attracted men adopting resistant strategies at beats to thwart police attempts to regulate their behaviour. In a qualitative study, I conducted interviews with 20 same-sex attracted men who had an encounter with police whilst visiting a beat between 1964 and 1999 (Dalton 2008). I discovered that they employed a variety of resistant tactics to prevent police from regulating their behaviour in beat spaces. These tactics were creative and ranged from: conducting risk analysis of the beat environment; passing as 'straight' (heterosexual) men to avoid or deflect suspicion; only using the beat to meet other men (having sex elsewhere); and being cautious about ascertaining whether other men were same-sex attracted before initiating any contact or offer of sex.

Moore (1995: 321) has identified a key attribute of the beat: 'The essential feature of a beat is that it must be a legitimate place to be seen, whether one is taking a stroll, sunbathing, walking the dog, or using public amenities.' Same-sex attracted men who employ resistant tactics at beats often exploit this notion of legitimacy. As one respondent noted in my study:

> Walking the dog is a good one. You know, you can tie it up to the tree and take off into the bushes. If you see anything happening you grab the dog and walk away. And then if the police approach you it appears as though you are just two people walking the dog.
>
> *(Dalton 2008: 111)*

I identified that very few men would ever admit their reason for being at a beat to police (Dalton 2008). A marked degree of subterfuge pervaded their resistant strategies. What is interesting about the NSW Beat Project is that the mode of resistance it entails is characterized by an unapologetic note of frankness and honesty. The Project states: 'Officers may ask you what you're doing in the area ... remain calm and be honest with them, they generally know what you are doing there' (NSW Beat Project 2010).

The Project also advises men not to flee from the police if challenged in a beat space, to be polite to officers and to try not to be intimidated by inappropriate comments. The Project defiantly advises beat users: 'DO NOT PANIC – You have every right to be in a public area at any hour of the day'. Queer theorists have done much to champion the notion that shame and fear have no role to play in the lives of same-sex attracted men in the modern era. The existence of the NSW Beat Project website marks an interesting turn in the mode of beat resistance that I identified in my earlier study (Dalton 2008). In providing advice to beat users about their lawful right to occupy public space and up-to-date warnings about police operations at particular beats, the Project provides support and tacit encouragement for a beat culture to continue to flourish throughout NSW.

The future of policing beats in Australia: a question of tolerance?

The existence of beats deeply polarizes the public. This fact is exemplified by a typically positive sentiment and, correspondingly, a typically negative sentiment expressed in an online comment board about the problem of a particular beat in South Australia:

> I lived near Apex Park for seven years and often went there with my young son. Gay men hung out there as long as I remember but were always very discreet and I felt quite safe. The place is clean and I have seen more condoms left by heterosexual couples at the beach near by ['Anna'].
>
> *(Wills 2010)*

> Get rid of them, their behaviour is disgusting ... the majority of people want these low lives gone. It's a public park not a gay park ['Andrew'].
>
> *(Wills 2010)*

The coexistence of these two differing community attitudes to beats – one of acceptance and tolerance, and one of hostility and intolerance – highlights the challenges police face in Australia. When it comes to policing beats, the police are caught between two imperatives. They must respond to public complaints about suspicious or illegal behaviour at beats that are underpinned by a prevailing heteronormative culture (Berlant and Warner 1998) that perceives homosexual sex in public spaces as, variously, disgusting, offensive, out of place and indefensible in the modern era where homosexuality has been decriminalized and gay bars and sex-on-site venues proliferate. The police are also called upon to protect gay men from potential violence in the form of hate-inspired crimes and vigilantism that often takes place in the vicinity of beats (see Chapter 1). Such vigilantism sometimes takes the shape of men outraged by beat activity resorting to violence by attacking gay men in what are often vicious and bloody assaults. To further complicate matters, Johnson (2010: 413) has documented that many NSW police officers feel they 'can't win' or are 'damned if they do, and damned if they don't' when policing beats. This is because they recognize their role in adjudicating different moral values when policing beats.

The history of policing beats demonstrates that it is impossible to entirely eradicate them from the landscape. When policing and local council initiatives (e.g. closing toilet blocks, installing single-use Exeloo^{TM} facilities,[5] removing shrubs in parkland[6]) manage to deter men from using particular public places as beats, other beats soon materialize as men lay claim to other locations. Indeed, new beats evolve over time, promoted by word of mouth and websites[7] that advertise their existence. Beat users also use Facebook to communicate with each other in Australia.[8] Thus the classic criminological concept of displacement occurs when beats are heavily policed. The 'problem' is moved on to other locations.

Beats seem likely to continue to provoke outrage, anger, frustration and disapprobation from those who would like to banish the spectre of male/male public sex both from the physical environment and the social imaginary. Notwithstanding the fact that many men merely use beat spaces to meet other men and have lawful non-public sex in homes (Gorman-Murray 2006), when men engage in public sex at beats, part of the attraction of this sex is that it entails immediate gratification, anonymity, a no-strings-attached encounter and the *frisson* of danger and excitement that comes with public sex (Edwards 1994).[9] It is this last factor – the presence of the police encapsulating the potential for surveillance and apprehension – that helps underwrite the allure of beat sex for many men. So police initiatives that seek to intimidate or warn off beat users may, paradoxically, be counterproductive.

Same-sex attracted men frequenting beats are not the only category of people who use public space for sexual purposes. 'Lovers' lanes' or 'dogging' public sex scenarios which involve heterosexual or bisexual couples do not provoke or antagonize the public and the police in the way that men having (or organizing to have) sex at beats do (see Chapter 3). The comments of two respondents to an online discussion board about beats illustrate this point:

> Here in Manly [Sydney] you'll find heterosexual teenagers shagging in parks and beach-front car parks on any given night of the week without any similar level of police scrutiny.
>
> *(cited in Ting 2010)*

> Not only do straight beats exist, they are advertised on numerous internet forums. As an avid power walker, I've witnessed it many times in parks and beaches around Sydney. The dogging craze ... was catching on here by about 2004 but it's simply never been targeted by police in the same way gay beats

have. This is a cultural issue within the police force. For decades plain clothed officers have run sting operations in public toilets and parks targeting gay men ... I challenge anyone to cite an example of a similar under cover sting being used to arrest heterosexual doggers. It just doesn't happen. There is undoubtedly a double standard here.

(cited in Ting 2010)

It remains to be seen whether the 'dogging' phenomenon will eventually attract as much public and police animosity as beats currently do. The phenomenon of hetero-sexual sex in public does not carry with it a long socio-historic stigma of being perverted, dirty and unnatural. Johnson (see Chapter 2) notes that criminal justice practitioners in Sydney told him that, in their experience, most police officers would typically tell heterosexual couples caught having sex to 'piss off' or 'get a room'. Of course, hetero-sexual public sex is not wholly tolerated in Australia and prosecutions occur every year, but beat spaces are those that continue to draw hostility and disapprobation from the public and police alike.

Ashford (2007: 518) argues that the criminalization of public sex 'has systematically failed to prevent the continued sexing of public space'. This failure explains why men will continue to 'do the beat'[10] and possibly encounter police patrolling their beat. The nature of the encounter they have with police is likely to vary greatly. As this chapter has outlined, police approaches to policing beat spaces vary significantly from highly visible proactive campaigns that pivot on a logic of deterrence to – at the other end of the spectrum – agent provocateur entrapment operations and other surreptitious tactics which marshal fear and intimidation against beat users. At the absolute worst end of the spectrum, some beat users have alleged that bribery and extortion have been employed by rogue officers. Policing initiatives linked to beats thus vary from best practice initiatives underpinned by sound criminological principles of deterrence and respect for all members of society, to practices like entrapment that are morally and ethically dubious. Indeed, the final practices – homophobic harassment, extortion and bribery – are not only illegal but redolent of a culture of corruption deplorable in any modern-day Australian police force or service.

This chapter has also highlighted that beat users are becoming more aware of their rights to unapologetically occupy and use beat space through grassroots initiatives such as the NSW Beat Project. This resource taps into a vein of resistance to police practices first identified by Dalton (2008). All over NSW, men are reporting police misconduct and/or notifying other men of the dangers of entrapment, heavy-handed police tactics and the activities of gay bashers at local beats. So, to the extent that the NSW Police Force is sending a message to beat users that *we are monitoring you*, the NSW Beat Project is responding with the message that *we beat users are monitoring you – the police*. This situation is advantageous but also problematic. The benefit of the NSW Beat Project resides in it monitoring beats and disseminating allegations of police mis-conduct and warning of the presence of gay bashers. Additionally, the Project helps raise awareness about policing initiatives (e.g. agent provocateur practices) that the public may disapprove of and lobby against. The NSW Beat Project is problematic in that its existence might exacerbate levels of police hostility to beats. Such a site could arguably be perceived as beat users thumbing their noses at the law. And, yet, an objective examination of the NSW Beat Project website reveals that it actually praises ethical police conduct and advocates that beat users cooperate with reasonable police requests at beats.

Writing about public spaces where men congregate to have sex with other men, the Canadian photographer Evergon (1997: 52) observed that 'Government and police forces are constantly trying to close down these areas through intimidation, limitation of access, and more recently, by gentrification. In this sense they are landscapes under siege – cultural battlegrounds.' Beats in contemporary Australia adhere to this formulation. They are landscapes under siege, subject to battles by those men who see them as legitimate places to pursue desire, and those who see them as a domain that deserves widespread public disgust and police action to eradicate what is construed as a public sex 'problem'. In the Netherlands, Amsterdam's Vondel Park has been set aside as a space where public sex is lawfully permitted (Walby 2009: 376). A similar scenario seems unimaginable in contemporary Australia. The existence of beats seems to antagonize some segments of the community who call upon the police to govern that which is essentially ungovernable. For male same-sex desire can manifest at any time in any beat space that affords such desire a space to be enacted. An interviewee in my beat study once remarked: 'Even the most innocuous toilet becomes a beat merely because of the presence of one same-sex attracted man' (Dalton 2007b: 385). Attempting to eradicate beat sex is futile. The police and public *wishing* for beat sex to go away is more akin to a *fantasy* underwritten by distaste for homosexual sex or any visible sign that it has been transacted in public.

The public and police may well have a low tolerance for beat sex, but, as this chapter has revealed, the men who use beats are becoming increasingly less tolerant of police attempts to regulate their behaviour and to force them to desist from using beats. They are using resources like the NSW Beat Project to stay informed and to register complaints about police harassment. They are contributing to a movement of unapologetic resistance. These competing forms of intolerance augur that the future of policing beats in Australia will be marked by continued clashes about the legitimacy of male same-sex desire in beat spaces.

On the notion of tolerance and acceptance, Walby (2009: 376) writes: 'While many men having sex with men learned how to safely engage in sex from the HIV/AIDS health panic of the 1980s and 1990s, heteronormative police and community associations have not learned to accept diverse sexualities.' The great challenge for police in Australia, and some members of the public, is to learn to accept beats. Is it really so 'harmful' that men engage in acts of consensual sexual pleasure in secluded spaces or behind toilet cubicle doors at beats? To the extent that the police fixate on the 'problem' of consensual male sex at beats, they will continue to leave themselves open to accusations of 'making crime' (Ericson 1981) out of what essentially, as Johnson (2007: 536) has described, are 'activities which would otherwise remain known only to those who engage in them'.

Notes

1 In the UK they are commonly referred to as 'cottages' and in the USA they are often historically referred to as 'tearooms'.
2 The paradox here is that this logic conflicts with the notion that beat sex is so depraved, disgusting and dirty that it could not be intrinsically appealing to anyone – an idea disseminated in newspaper discourse throughout the period (see Murdoch 2000).
3 Interestingly, the NSW police data system is called COPS.
4 It should be stressed that the NSW Beat Project does not receive Federal government funding and is not connected to the 'Anti-Violence Project' who currently chair the 'Beats Working Group' committee sanctioned and funded by government.
5 An Exeloo facility is a single-occupant toilet facility that has time limits applied to ensure that a person cannot loiter in such a facility.
6 For example, a well-known parkland beat in Adelaide – Apex Park – is periodically subjected to council-organized processes of removing scrub, bushes and other foliage. This is an attempt to deter use of the parkland as a beat by minimizing the availability of secluded space where beat users might gather.
7 For example, www.cruisinggays.com (accessed 28 May 2011).
8 For example, 'Gay Adelaide Beats' is a group 'aimed for all the guys that frequent beats around Adelaide'. The site advises that it 'gives information on happenings, NSW sites etc.'.
9 It is beyond the purview of this chapter to discuss precisely what constitutes 'public sex'. Australian criminal law varies from one jurisdiction to another, but recent cases suggest that any prosecutions that involve extraordinary measures to view an ostensibly private space (e.g. police peering through gaps in cubicle doors or under door partitions) are likely to fail to lead to a conviction.
10 To 'do the beat' is gay slang in Australia for men who set out to cruise in search of men for sex in public places.

Bibliography

Ashford, C. (2007) 'Sexuality, Public Space and the Criminal Law: The cottaging phenomenon', *Journal of Criminal Law*, 71(6) 506–19.
Bell, D. and Binnie, J. (2004) 'Authenticating Queer Space: Urbanism and governance', *Urban Studies*, 41(9): 1807–20.
Berlant, L. and Warner, M. (1998) 'Sex in Public', *Critical Inquiry*, 24(2): 547–66.
Carbery, G. (1992) 'Some Melbourne Beats: A "map" of a subculture from the 1930s to the 1950s', in R. Aldrich and G. Wotherspoon (eds) *Gay Perspectives: Essays in Australian gay culture*, Sydney: Department of Economic History, University of Sydney, 131–46.
Crouch, B. (2010) 'Koutsantonis Campaign Blunder', *Adelaide Now*. Online. Available at http://www.adelaidenow.com.au/news/south-australia/koutsantonis-campaign-blunder/story-e6frea83-1225837762273 (accessed 5 November 2010).
Dalton, D. (2002) 'Homocriminality: The legal and cultural imagination of gay male subjectivity', unpublished doctoral thesis, The University of Melbourne.
——(2004) 'Arresting Images/Fugitive Testimony: The resistant photography of Evergon', *Studies in Law, Politics, and Society – An Aesthetics of Law and Culture*, 34: 73–107.
——(2006) 'Surveying Deviance, Figuring Disgust: Locating the homocriminal body in time and space', *Social & Legal Studies*, 15(2): 277–99.
——(2007a) 'Genealogy of the Australian Homocriminal Subject: A study of two explanatory models of deviance', *Griffith Law Review*, 16(1): 83–106.
——(2007b) 'Policing Outlawed Desire: Homocriminality in beat spaces in Australia', *Law and Critique*, 19(1): 375–405.
——(2008) 'Gay Male Resistance in Beat Spaces in Australia: A study of "outlaw" desire', *The Australian Feminist Law Journal*, 28: 97–119.
Edwards, T. (1994) *Erotics and Politics: Gay male sexuality, masculinity and feminism*, London and New York: Routledge.

Ericson, R. (1981) *Making Crime: A study of detective work*, Toronto: Butterworths.

Evans, R. (2008) 'NSW Police: Hunting gay men at beats', *Green Left*, Issue 775.

Evergon (1997) 'The Ramboys: A bookless novel and manscapes: truck stops and lover's lanes', in Evergon and Will Stapp (ed.) *Evergon 1987–1997*, Bradford: National Museum of Photography, Film and Television.

French, R. (1986) *Gays Between the Broadsheets: Australian media references to homosexuality, 1948–1980*, Darlinghurst, NSW: Gay History Project.

Gorman-Murray, A. (2006) 'Homeboys: Uses of home by gay Australian men', *Social and Cultural Geography*, 7(1): 53–69.

Hennelly, S. (2010) 'Public Spaces, Public Morality: The media construction of sex in public places', *Liverpool Law Review*, 31: 69–91.

Hocquenghem, G. (1978) *Homosexual Desire*, London: Allison & Busby.

Johnson, P. (2007) '"Ordinary Folk and Cottaging": Law, morality and public sex', *Journal of Law and Society*, 34(4): 520–43.

——(2010) 'The Enforcement of Morality: Law, policing and sexuality in New South Wales', *The Australian and New Zealand Journal of Criminology*, 43(3): 399–422.

Maynard, S. (1994) 'Though a Hole in the Lavatory Wall: Homosexual subcultures, police surveillance, and the dialectics of discovery, Toronto, 1890–1930', *Journal of the History of Sexuality*, 5(2): 205–42.

Miller, W. (1997) *The Anatomy of Disgust*, Cambridge, MA: Harvard University Press.

Moore, C. (1995) 'Poofs in the Park: Documenting gay "beats" in Queensland, Australia', *GLQ*, 2: 319–39.

Moran, L.J. (1996) *The Homosexual(ity) of Law*, London: Routledge.

Mouzos, J. and Thompson, S. (2000) 'Gay-Hate Related Homicides: An overview of major findings in New South Wales', *Trends and Issues in Crime and Criminal Justice*, No. 155, Australian Institute of Criminology.

Murdoch, W. (1998) 'Disgusting Doings and Putrid Practices: Reporting homosexual men's lives in the *Melbourne Truth* during the First World War', in R. Aldrich and G. Wotherspoon (eds) *Gay and Lesbian Perspectives IV: Studies in Australian culture*, Sydney: Department of Economic History, University of Sydney.

——(2000) 'Homosexuality and the *Melbourne Truth*: An annotated listing, 1913–1945', in D. L. Phillips and G. Willett (eds) *Australia's Homosexual Histories: Gay and lesbian perspectives V*, Sydney: Australian Centre for Lesbian and Gay Research. Melbourne: Australian Lesbian and Gay Archives.

NSW Beat Project (2010) 'Online Network and Resource for the Beat Community'. Online. Available at http://www.beatproject.org.au/ (accessed 12 December 2010).

NSW Police (2010) 'New South Wales Police Standards of Professional Conduct'. Online. Available at http://www.police.nsw.gov.au/__data/assets/pdf_file/0009/87993/standards_of_professional_conduct.pdf (accessed 10 December 2010).

Swivel, M. (1991) 'Public Convenience, Public Nuisance: Criminological perspectives on the beat', *Current Issues in Criminal Justice*, 5: 237–49.

Ting, I. (2010) 'On the Beat: Debate on public sex dividing the gay community', *Crikey*. Online. Available at http:/www.crikey.com.au/2010/10/04/on-the-beat-debate-on-public-s-x-dividing-the-gay-community/ (accessed 4 November 2010).

Tomsen, S. and George, A. (1997) 'The Criminal Justice Response to Gay Killings: Research findings', *Current Issues in Criminal Justice*, 9(1): 56–70.

Walby, K. (2009) '"He Asked Me if I Was Looking for Fags … ": Ottawa's National Capital Commission conservation officers and the policing of public park sex', *Surveillance & Society* 6(4): 367–79.

Wills, D. (2010) 'Tom Koutsantonis Accused of Inciting Hatred Against Gays in Letter', *Adelaide Now*. Online. Available at http://www.adelaidenow.com.au/tom-koutsantonis-accused-of-inciting-hatred-against-gays-in-letter/story-e6frea6u-1225852756528 (accessed 5 November 2010).

Wotherspoon, G. (1991) *City of the Plain: History of a gay sub-culture*, Sydney: Hale & Iremonger.

Part 3
Policing 'pornography'

6

PORNOGRAPHY, POLICING AND CENSORSHIP

Murray Perkins

Introduction: the British Board of Film Classification

The British Board of Film Classification (BBFC) was established by the UK film industry in 1912 to provide uniform classifications for cinema films. Prior to this, films were classified by individual local authorities with varying results. One hundred years later, the BBFC continues to perform this function on behalf of local authorities in the UK. In 1984 the BBFC was designated by the UK government as the authority to classify video works under the Video Recordings Act 1984 (VRA). Approaching its centenary, the BBFC remains an independent, non-governmental body that is funded by fees charged to those who submit films and video works for classification.

While the BBFC is an independent body, in making its classification determinations it does not operate independently of the criminal law. Under the 'Letter of Designation', issued in accordance with the VRA, from the Secretary of State to the BBFC's Presidents, the BBFC is told: 'In undertaking your duties as designated authority, you will seek to ensure that works which infringe the criminal law are not classified.'

It is when dealing with 'pornographic' works that the BBFC finds its decisions most commonly influenced by the law. The BBFC defines pornographic works, or 'sex works', as 'works whose primary purpose is sexual arousal or stimulation'. This is consistent with the legal definition of pornography contained in the Criminal Justice and Immigration Act 2008 which states that: 'An image is "pornographic" if it is of such a nature that it must reasonably be assumed to have been produced solely or principally for the purpose of sexual arousal.'

The introduction of 'hardcore' at 'R18'

Under the BBFC's guidelines:

> Sex works containing only material which may be simulated are generally passed '18'. Sex works containing clear images of real sex, strong fetish material,

sexually explicit animated images, or other very strong sexual images will be confined to the 'R18' category. Material which is unacceptable in a sex work at 'R18' is also unacceptable in a sex work at '18'.

(BBFC 2009a: 29)

Works classified at 'R18' may only be shown to adults in specially licensed cinemas, or supplied to adults only in licensed sex shops. 'R18' video works, no matter the physical format on which they are recorded, may not be supplied by mail order.

Up until the late 1990s the BBFC routinely cut explicit images of sexual activity from submitted sex works – that is, images that explicitly show the mechanics of real sexual behaviour including penetration and oral sex. At the time, such material, commonly defined as 'hardcore' pornography, was considered likely to be found obscene under the Obscene Publications Act 1959 (OPA).

In 1997 the then Director of the BBFC, James Ferman, met with a Home Office minister and it was agreed to relax the BBFC position and allow brief hardcore images, excluding close-ups and depictions of ejaculation. This decision was taken without consulting the police or other enforcement agencies. But it was understood that such a move would improve the viability of the 'R18' classification and undermine what was then a thriving black-market trade in unclassified and stronger pornographic material that was being sold in unlicensed sex shops. At the time the BBFC was passing approximately 30 'R18' videos each year. In 1998, however, a UK distributor claiming an intention to distribute non-explicit 'softcore' versions of US hardcore titles was forwarded approximately 10 hardcore versions by the US company Sin City, apparently in error. HM Customs and Excise impounded the delivery. The distributor became aware that a film called *Pyramid* had been passed 'R18' by the BBFC for another distributor in a reduced hardcore version. The distributor queried this and learnt from the BBFC that it was now allowing tamer versions of hardcore titles at 'R18'. The distributor reported this to HM Customs and Excise and asked that their titles be released for BBFC consideration, but the request was refused. When the BBFC wrote to HM Customs and Excise, HM Customs and Excise alerted the Home Office of the BBFC's new position (Wingrove 1998: 17). The Home Secretary made it clear to the BBFC that it was operating in conflict with the standards employed by enforcement agencies, including the police who, like HM Customs and Excise, have a role in dealing with potentially obscene material. The Home Secretary obliged the BBFC to revert to its old position on 'R18' videos.

At this time a distributor had already been given an interim 'R18' certificate under the revised standards – that is, notification of the intended classification of a feature called *Makin' Whoopee!* The BBFC required that the distributor return the interim certificate, and cuts were written to remove the 'hardcore' sequences from the feature. When the distributor then refused to make the cuts that had been written, the BBFC rejected *Makin' Whoopee!*, refusing it a classification certificate altogether. As a result, the distributor took the BBFC to the Video Appeals Committee (VAC).

The VAC is an independent body constituted under section 4 (3) of the VRA to hear appeals from submitting companies against BBFC decisions. The distributor of

Makin' Whoopee! won its case against the BBFC decision to reject the feature. Specifically, the VAC did not accept that the video in question was likely to found obscene under the OPA. Although the BBFC was therefore required to pass *Makin' Whoopee!* at the original 'R18' without cuts, the BBFC was still obliged to follow the direction from the Home Secretary and maintain its old Guidelines on 'R18' sex works. In so doing, it also maintained a position consistent with enforcement agencies.

In 1999, there were seven hardcore sex works that the BBFC wrote cuts for, in line with the standards operating at the time, and in line with the standards understood to be in operation by the enforcement agencies: *Horny Catbabe*, *Nympho Nurse Nancy*, *T.V. Sex*, *Office Tart*, *Carnival International Version (Trailer)*, *Wet Nurse 2 Continental Version* and *Miss Nude International Continental Version*. When the two distributors of these films, Sheptonhurst Ltd and Prime Time Promotions, refused to make the required cuts, the seven features were refused certification and rejected. Again the BBFC was taken to the VAC. Having lost the argument at the last appeal, that the sexually explicit material in question was at risk of obscenity under the OPA, the BBFC this time relied on the argument that the material was potentially harmful. Specifically the BBFC argued that there was a risk of harm to potential underage viewers, persons under 18 years of age who cannot legally purchase '18' or 'R18' video works. Under the VRA, amended by the Criminal Justice and Public Order Act 1994, the BBFC is obliged to have special regard to the likelihood of works being viewed in the home, and to any harm that may be caused to potential viewers or, through their behaviour, to society by the manner in which the work deals with, in this case, human sexual activity.

The BBFC considered that making the works available for viewing in the home ran a risk of children gaining access to them. Although the BBFC produced expert evidence that the material could cause harm to children, the VAC found in favour of the distributors. The VAC suggested there might have been a different outcome had there been evidence that the potential harmful effects of this type of sexual material were affecting more than a small minority of children or that the effects were devastating if children did view the material. In short, the VAC concluded that the risk of harm was, on the evidence provided, insignificant. As a result, the BBFC sought a Judicial Review on grounds that the judgement was based on a definition of 'harm' that was an incorrect interpretation under the VRA. The High Court found against the BBFC.

Following the Judicial Review, a Home Office consultation paper was launched in respect of the regulation of 'R18' video works. Among other considerations it suggested changes to the VAC. In its response to the consultation paper, the BBFC did not accept the criticism directed at the VAC. Indeed, although the BBFC made some recommendations for change, the BBFC supported the VAC as both conscientious and responsible in its judgements (BBFC 2000a: 43).

The Judicial Review also coincided with the results of an extensive BBFC public consultation process, leading to new published guidelines in respect of the certification categories. The results of the consultation indicated, among other things, that the public was increasingly relaxed about sex on screen. As a part of this consultation process, in Citizen's Juries, the jurors concluded that anything legal should be permitted at 'R18'. While the nature of what was legal was not expanded upon, it is understood to have meant material that would not in itself be in breach of legislation, including, for example, the OPA or the Protection of Children Act 1978. So it may be supposed that fantasies or role-plays fictionalizing potentially illegal acts may have been acceptable to the jurors. However, with one representative comment being, 'why do they say you can't have semen on your face?' (Hanley 2000: 24), indicating the nature of activities being considered, it is quite probable that jurors may have thought twice about the acceptability of a credible adult role-play portraying incest or other abusive scenarios. It is an interpretation that is supported by a national sample in which only 13 per cent of respondents felt the BBFC's draft 'R18' guidelines were too strict (Hanley 2000: 24)

In 2000 the BBFC published its new 'R18' Guidelines to reflect the legal position resulting from the Judicial Review. In formulating the 'R18' Guidelines the BBFC considered the High Court judgement, the research findings, and it consulted with the Home Office and relevant enforcement authorities, including the Metropolitan Police Clubs and Vice Unit, the Crown Prosecution Service, and HM Customs and Excise. What was known as the Enforcement Sub-Group met at the Home Office. It was accepted by all parties that the Judicial Review left the BBFC with no option but to amend its guidelines. The intention for the BBFC was to understand what enforcement agencies were putting forward for prosecution and what, in their experience, was likely to lead to convictions. The Metropolitan Police Service was clear that the material the BBFC was proposing to pass would not pose a problem from their perspective. At the time there was a declining interest, even among provincial forces, to pursue material featuring consenting sex. Rather, there was a preference to concentrate on child pornography.

In July 2000, the new Guidelines came into force. At 'R18' these went further than the changes briefly made in 1997, allowing full 'hardcore' sexual representations without the previous limitations. It was intended that the new Guidelines would prevent further challenges by bringing the BBFC standards close to the line drawn by the criminal law.

While allowing the representation of full 'hardcore' sexual mechanics, the 2000 Guidelines still enforced limits on the nature of other material that could be passed at 'R18'. Guidelines then and now require, among other things, that all participants in sex works be adults; that the material not be in breach of the criminal law; that it not be likely to encourage an interest in sexually abusive activity, including paedophilia, rape or incest; that the activity be consensual, and that any form of physical restraint allows participants to indicate a withdrawal of consent; that it not involve the infliction of pain or lasting physical harm, with some allowance made for mild consensual behaviour; that there be no penetration with objects associated with violence or likely to cause physical harm; and that it not contain sexual threats, humiliation or abuse that does not form part of a clearly consenting role-playing game. Strong abuse, even if consensual, is unlikely to be acceptable. With these Guidelines in operation, by the end of 2000 the BBFC had passed 212 videos with 'R18' certificates. By 2003 the number rose to 1405, with 259 videos cut prior to certification. Over the next four years the number of videos classified at 'R18' decreased slightly year on year. In this time, year on year, the number of 'R18' videos that were cut increased (BBFC 2007: 39).

Cuts to remove dialogue, individual shots and in some cases entire scenes were made to scenarios with the potential to encourage an interest in abusive behaviour, for example: youthful-looking adult women portraying themselves as children; scenarios in which consent was ambiguous or where sexual activity was presented as non-consensual; activities with the potential to cause physical harm; and material tending to encourage strong abusive behaviour.

The Obscene Publications Act 1959

In 2000, as a result of the consultation with enforcement agencies at the meeting of the Enforcement Sub-Group at the Home Office, independent of specific considerations of harm under the VRA, the BBFC understood there to be a number of activities which, in the context of a sex work, would probably see a video put forward for prosecution under the OPA. It was noted by representation from the Metropolitan Police Clubs and Vice Unit that jury convictions could not always be relied upon for urolagnia (defined as urination during sexual activity, urination onto another person, urine being drunk or rubbed or poured or smeared onto any person) and 'fisting' (defined as penetration of the vagina or the anus by all five digits beyond the last knuckle). It was nevertheless accepted that these activities, among others, continue to be prosecuted and that there continue to be convictions. An understanding that urolagnia and 'fisting' remain likely to be found obscene was supported by the Home Office (BBFC 2000b). While in some cases the potential for physical harm may be a factor in determining possible obscenity, in other cases the activity could be consensual, legal to engage in and unlikely to be physically harmful. Nevertheless, when depicted in sex works submitted to the BBFC, some such activity would be cut on the understanding that current interpretation of the OPA meant that the material in question was likely to be found obscene.

Section 1 of the OPA, provides that:

> For the purposes of this Act an article shall be deemed to be obscene if its effect or (where the article comprises two or more distinct items) the effect of any one of its items is, if taken as a whole, such as to tend to deprave and corrupt persons who are likely, having regard to all relevant circumstances, to read, see or hear the matter contained or embodied in it.

The OPA provides for prosecution, under section 2, and forfeiture, under section 3, in order to penalize those publishing or seeking to publish obscene material; and to prevent obscene material from finding its way onto the market by seizing the material and through forfeiture of the material.

Section 4(1) of the OPA creates a defence of public good:

> a person shall not be convicted of an offence against section two of this Act, and an order for forfeiture shall not be made under the foregoing section, if it is

proved that publication of the article in question is justified as being for the public good on the ground that it is in the interests of science, literature, art or learning, or of other objects of general concern.

The question of whether or not material is 'obscene' is a question to be answered by a jury. However, in practice, in the absence of material being put in front of a jury, it is more common for material to be forfeited under section 3, with the understanding of obscenity based on past convictions.

Most commonly, cuts on the grounds of potential obscenity have been required to remove urolagnia and 'fisting'. Cuts which have been made on obscenity grounds have also included: the use of 'enemas', specifically where fluid, other than semen or lubricant used for lubrication, is expelled from the anus onto another person, where fluid expelled from the anus is drunk or rubbed or poured or smeared onto any person, or where fluid expelled from the anus is contaminated by faecal matter; 'blood sports', in this case the introduction of menstrual blood to sexual activity; 'roman showers', vomit being introduced to sexual activity; penetration with large dildos; wax dripping, specifically melted wax being dripped on the genitals or anus or wax being dripped onto a person in the context of a torture scenario; and sadomasochistic activity in which injuries are inflicted which are more than 'trifling' and 'transient'. Sight of urination alone, aside from the activities listed above, is not considered at risk of prosecution for obscenity and is passed in 'R18' sex works.

Urination vs. female ejaculation

In 2001 a video work was submitted to the BBFC entitled *More of What Women Want*. It was a US feature with a focus on sexual enhancement within relationships. It contained a scene featuring a woman introduced as 'one of the small percentage of women who squirts out a small amount of fluid through the urethra when she has an orgasm'. What follows is a sequence of vaginal penetration with fingers and masturbation, leading to sight of fluid being expelled from the woman's genitals. In this case the distributor of *More of What Women Want* requested an '18' classification believing that the explicit sexual detail in the feature was within an educational context and that it should therefore benefit from the BBFC's allowance for sex education works. The BBFC's Guidelines on sex education at '18' state: 'Where sex material genuinely seeks to inform and educate in matters such as human sexuality, safer sex and health, explicit images of sexual activity may be permitted.' While the BBFC accepted that elements in *More of What Women Want* were educational in intent, there were extended sequences of sexual activity that did not serve this purpose. The BBFC's policy on sex education is designed to prevent abuse by pornographic works and so allows only the minimum explicit sexual detail necessary to illustrate the educational point being made. As a consequence, *More of What Women Want* was not judged to be 'sex education' within the terms of the BBFC's Guidelines and policy, but rather a sex work. It is a distinction that meant the video was also considered far less likely to benefit from any public good defence under the

OPA. As a result, on grounds of obscenity, *More of What Women Want* was cut to remove a 5 second sequence in which a woman expels fluid from her genitals during sexual activity. It was then passed 'R18'.

On occasion the question of female ejaculation versus urination comes to the fore. When the BBFC changed its Guidelines on sex works at both 'R18' and '18', updating what was understood likely to be subject to prosecution for obscenity, it also took independent advice on potential physical harm and other considerations. The BBFC took advice on a range of sexual practices with a leading consultant physician in genito-urinary medicine. With regards to sequences in sex works submitted to the BBFC, purporting to be female ejaculation, the advice received was that the sequences seen thus far were urination. Because the BBFC consequently cut all similar examples of liquid being expelled from female genitals during sexual activity, or in combination with other proscribed activities, it was supposed that the BBFC denied the existence of, and discriminated against, female ejaculation.

In 2009 a sex work called *Women Love Porn* was submitted to the BBFC. It was, in almost all respects, a conventional and straightforward 'R18' submission, except for one sequence in which fluid is expelled from a woman's genitals immediately following oral sex, followed by a closer shot of more liquid being expelled from the same woman's genitals. In line with the BBFC's understanding of the interpretation of the OPA, a cut was written to remove the sequence in question. The distributor of *Women Love Porn* challenged the cut, arguing the sequence portrayed female ejaculation rather than urination, and should not therefore be considered obscene. The distributor made a formal request that the BBFC reconsider the sequence and pass it uncut.

The BBFC reconsidered the sequence and determined that the cut was consistent with current understanding of the interpretation of the OPA. While the BBFC was also conscious that the Crown Prosecution Service was in the process of updating its Guidance on the OPA, this had not been formalized and could not be taken into consideration.

In response to the reconsideration, the distributor was informed that the requirement to cut *Women Love Porn* was upheld. The formal response to the distributor went on:

> As the body charged with classifying video works under the Video Recordings Act 1984, we are obliged to seek to avoid classifying material which is in breach of the criminal law, including the Obscene Publications Act (OPA). Our advice from the enforcement agencies strongly indicates that, in a pornographic context, urination during sexual activity or onto another person as part of sexual activity is likely to render the material vulnerable to successful prosecution under the OPA.
>
> We note your assertion that the sequence features 'female ejaculation' rather than urination. The BBFC also note that the existence of 'female ejaculation' is a matter of debate in the medical profession, to quote one of the articles you submitted, 'controversy still exists around the "female prostate" and whether such a gland might be the source of fluid emitted during orgasm (ejaculation)'. In any case the issue for the BBFC is not whether 'female ejaculation' exists,

but whether the activity shown in the submitted video work is, or is not, urination, and, consequently, whether it is vulnerable to successful prosecution under the OPA. In coming to a judgement on these points the BBFC takes into account advice from the enforcement agencies and from a consultant in sexual health who had viewed a number of examples very similar to that shown in WOMEN LOVE PORN. We also note the conclusions of the *New Scientist* article which you cited: 'most pornography scenes that depict women ejaculating are indeed staged. Either the fluid is put into the vagina beforehand off-camera, or the actresses are simply urinating' (Moalem 2009).

If you wish to pursue this matter further, you can appeal to the independent Video Appeals Committee (details are on our website). Otherwise, please resubmit the work with the cut made as directed.

(BBFC 2009b)

In their response the distributor suggested obtaining chemical analysis of fluid expelled by the performer who featured in the DVD. But whether or not a performer was capable of expelling fluid other than urine could still not address the visual impression of the specific video representation in question, the conflicting medical opinion and the wider issue of potential obscenity with regard to fluid being expelled from female genitals during sexual activity. The BBFC added:

It isn't the case that the BBFC denies the existence of female ejaculation. With an understanding that female ejaculation remains a matter of debate within the medical profession, the BBFC's position is neutral.

…

We must judge what we see on-screen and what the on-screen activity appears to be, taking into account advice from enforcement agencies and medical expertise where relevant.

(BBFC 2009b)

The distributor of *Women Love Porn* declined to make the cut and indicated their intention to take the matter to the VAC. Before proceeding further, the BBFC reviewed its position in relation to the title in question, taking legal advice and consulting both the Crown Prosecution Service and the Metropolitan Police Service. To ensure that material passed by the BBFC is not at risk of containing content that may be subject to prosecution under the OPA, the BBFC had maintained a small gap between what it allows at 'R18' and what it understands the police will put forward for prosecution. In the case of *Women Love Porn* it became apparent from conversations with both the Crown Prosecution Service and the police that, while the content encroached on this gap, there was no realistic prospect that the work would be found obscene. Of particular importance was the requirement under the OPA that the work *taken as a whole* must tend to deprave and corrupt. In this case, the video work taken as a whole was ordinary 'R18' level content. It was also relevant that the manner of the fluid being expelled from genitals was at the lower end of the scale of such activity. It was not, for example, directly onto another person nor was the fluid drunk. It was given no other prominence in the feature. On the understanding that *Women Love Porn* was not realistically likely to be prosecuted for obscenity, the BBFC withdrew the cut and passed the feature 'R18'.

What the BBFC did was to narrow the small gap between what it would classify at 'R18' and what it understood would be likely to be prosecuted. It did so only after showing the sequence from *Women Love Porn* to the Metropolitan Police Service, along with similar material for confirmation of its position. While this clarified the BBFC's developing position, it did not resolve any unanswered questions about female ejaculation. Not least because examples of what purport to be female ejaculation and examples of urination are not easily distinguishable in the context of the average sex work, because the former is commonly simulated by the latter and because there is no indication that enforcement agencies will attempt to discern any distinction in the context of a sex work. The BBFC has, on a practical level, continued to treat examples of unintroduced fluid expelled from female genitals in the same way as it treats urination.

Liaison with enforcement agencies

Since 2000, the BBFC has met with the Metropolitan Police Service approximately once every 18 months to review examples from submitted sex works which raise questions of potential obscenity. It is necessary for the BBFC to understand the nature of material being put forward for prosecution and how content in submitted works compares. Meetings tend to take place either at the offices of the BBFC or the Metropolitan Police Service and most commonly include two representatives from both the BBFC and the police. While there is discussion of the occasionally curious details of specific activities – such as whether or not sliding down a playground slide that has been urinated upon constitutes smearing of urine onto a person – it is not the role of the BBFC to challenge what may or may not be put forward for prosecution. The BBFC uses its meetings with the Metropolitan Police Service to understand what is put forward for prosecution, and the result of these discussions continues to inform the line drawn by the BBFC.

In 2009 the Crown Prosecution Service (CPS) reviewed its Guidance on the OPA. As a part of this process the BBFC had the opportunity to consult on the range of activities that, if portrayed in a sex work, were at risk of prosecution for obscenity. In discussion with other agencies within the review process, including the police, it was apparent that the BBFC could probably relax its position on urolagnia, wax dripping and large dildos, subject to updating of the CPS's Guidance. It was also apparent that the precise nature of other material, considered material most commonly prosecuted, would be refined. 'Squish videos', for example, while not specifically added to the CPS's Guidance, were raised as a type of work that would likely be subject to prosecution. In this context 'squish videos', the crushing to death of small animals for sexual pleasure, were added to the

BBFC's own understanding of what would be refused certification on grounds of obscenity.

When the revised CPS Guidance was published in 2010, it included the following list of categories of material most commonly prosecuted: sexual act with an animal; realistic portrayals of rape; sadomasochistic material which goes beyond trifling and transient infliction of injury; torture with instruments; bondage (especially where gags are used with no apparent means of withdrawing consent); dismemberment or graphic mutilation; activities involving perversion or degradation (such as drinking urine, urination or vomiting onto the body, or excretion or use of excreta); fisting (CPS 2010). As anticipated, wax dripping and large dildos were omitted, and the definition of urolagnia for the purposes of judging potential obscenity gave support to draft BBFC policy. In this case the policy had been redrafted in 2009 after consultation with the CPS and kept on hold until the CPS's Guidance was formalized.

When the revised CPS Guidance was formalized the BBFC took several examples of urination and urolagnia to the Abusive and Extreme Images Unit (formerly the Obscene Publications Unit) of the Metropolitan Police Service. The Abusive and Extreme Images Unit investigates the distribution, making and possession of indecent, extreme and obscene images with a London-wide remit, but with the nature of investigations meaning that work is also undertaken outside London. Material under investigation can be found in hard copy format or on storage media having been downloaded from the Internet. While the Unit has evolved over the years, including changing its name, obscenity has been policed since the introduction of the OPA in 1959. While looking at examples of material previously submitted to the BBFC, consideration was given, among other examples, to urination during masturbation; smearing of urine caught in a cupped hand onto an individual's own breasts; dipping fingers into a bowl of urine; and urinating into a large water-filled bath in which individuals stay and engage in sexual activity. With consideration given to various such examples, and taking guidance from the police on what was likely to be subject to prosecution, with their experience of material also likely to be subject to conviction, the BBFC's revised internal guidance was put into practice with confidence that it was consistent with current interpretation of the OPA.

Further recent developments in the interpretation of obscenity

Whilst consideration of amendments to the BBFC's urolagnia policies were given the most attention following the revision of the Crown Prosecution Service Guidance, there were also significant changes to the way large dildos and wax dripping were treated. What constituted a large dildo was never well defined and there was certainly no clear guidance on dimensions. In the course of a decade, perhaps as a consequence of the lack of definition, only a handful of examples were ever cut. In each case, where cuts were required, scenes within the video work showcased penetration with dildos of exceptional size in comparison with adult video norms. In none of the submitted examples was it clearly evident that physical harm was resulting from the penetration. Under the 2010 CPS Guidance, the potential for large dildos to be considered obscene shifted from a question of size to a question of apparent or potential harm.

In 2007 a video work entitled *Butt Sluts 1* was cut by the BBFC on grounds of potential obscenity to remove an extended sequence of a man being anally penetrated with a large inflatable dildo. As the scene progressed and the dildo was further inflated it was clear that the size that was achieved far exceeded that normally depicted in sex works submitted to the BBFC for UK distribution. A determination was made that if this example did not constitute a 'large dildo' it would be difficult to determine what might. However, it was also apparent that the dildo was soft and pliable, being filled with air, that a substantial amount of lubrication was being used, and that penetration was slow and undertaken with a reasonable degree of care. Nevertheless more than 2 minutes 30 seconds was removed from the video work. Under the revised 2010 CPS Guidance it was unlikely this cut would be made. In this case the mitigating considerations, specifically the care with which the penetration is performed and the characteristics of the dildo, largely negated concerns about the potential for physical harm.

Under the 2010 CPS Guidance, concern about wax dripping also shifted from the nature of the act itself to contextual and harm-based considerations. In the preceding years several video works had been cut by the BBFC to remove sight of wax dripped onto the genitals or anus. Until 2010 examples of wax dripped on the genitals or anus, or less commonly wax being dripped within the context of a torture scenario, were considered likely to be prosecuted for obscenity. Several titles were cut, including *Doctor Sadistic*, *Freaky Extreme*, *Tranny Transformation* and *Reins of Discipline*. In 2010 wax dripping was subsumed into concerns related to sadomasochistic sex and, like oversized dildos, activities where physical harm was inflicted and where that harm might go beyond 'trifling' and 'transient'. Since this change was introduced, there have been no cases where cuts have been made for either wax dripping or penetration with large dildos.

Considerations of harm and consent

In December 1990, following the Operation Spanner police investigation, 16 men were convicted of assault occasioning actual bodily harm having been engaging in consensual sadomasochistic activity. Videotape that had been made of the activities was used in evidence. Despite appeals to the High Court, the House of Lords and the European Court of Human Rights, the convictions were upheld. At the heart of the judgement was the determination that a person cannot legally consent to an act that will cause actual bodily harm. In *R v Brown* (1993, 2 All ER 75) the Appellate Committee of the House of Lords, considering the 1990 convictions, made reference to *R v Donovan* that provides a definition of bodily harm as:

> 'bodily harm' has its ordinary meaning and includes any hurt or injury calculated to interfere with the health or comfort of the prosecutor. Such hurt or injury

need not be permanent, but must, no doubt, be more than merely transient and trifling.

(R v Brown, *1993, 2 All ER 75*)

Also found in *R v Donovan* is reference to the legal position on consent in these matters:

it is an unlawful act to beat another person with such a degree of violence that the infliction of bodily harm is a probable consequence, and when such an act is proved, consent is immaterial.

(R v Brown, *1993, 2 All ER 75*)

What constitutes injury that exceeds 'trifling' and 'transient' is undefined. But it has been accepted that this may include bruises or cuts, even where the injury heals completely in a short period of time (Spanner Trust 2011). The CPS's 2010 Guidance on the OPA underlines the definition in including 'sadomasochistic material which goes beyond trifling and transient infliction of injury' among the categories of material most commonly prosecuted. Prior to the 2010 Guidance, the BBFC had judged sadomasochistic works by applying the 'trifling and transient' test as a means of determining whether or not intervention is required. In addition to citing the OPA where cuts may have been required, the BBFC would also commonly cite the VRA.

In practice the application of the 'trifling and transient' test has led the BBFC to remove scenes in sadomasochistic and spanking fetish works where reddening of the skin gives way to clear bruising, weals being raised on the skin, or where skin may be broken. In November 2000, *A Caning for Miss Granger* became the first sex work to be rejected under the revised R18 Guidelines published in 2000. It essentially contains one extended role-play scenario in which a young woman is punished for being late for work. Although there were also serious concerns about consent, the injuries inflicted went beyond what would be considered 'trifling' and 'transient'. In its letter of rejection, the BBFC noted:

weals are visible on her buttocks and from an early stage there is considerable redness, bruising and swelling. The video focuses on the damage caused and goes some way beyond what might be regarded as 'mild consensual activity'.

(BBFC 2000c)

In 2005 the BBFC refused certification to *Severe Punishment*, a 37-minute sadomasochistic feature in which two restrained women are beaten and whipped by a third woman. In rejecting *Severe Punishment* the BBFC's reject letter was much more explicit in citing the 'trifling and transient' test:

The acts shown in *Severe Punishment* depict the infliction of real pain and injury and therefore go some way beyond the 'mild' activity that may be acceptable at 'R18'. The sole purpose of the work seems to be to invite sexual arousal at the sight of women being beaten, abused and caused real pain and injuries.

The position of UK law on sadomasochistic activities was established clearly in *R v Brown* (aka the 'Spanner Case') … The activities shown in this video, leading as they do to weals being raised on the skin, are considerably more than 'trifling and transient' and would therefore be likely to fall foul of UK law if carried out in the UK. Our understanding from the CPS and other enforcement agencies is that visual depictions of strong sadomasochistic behaviour are also liable to be found obscene under current interpretation of the Obscene Publications Act 1959.

(BBFC 2005)

In addition to spanking, caning and beatings, the 'trifling and transient' test has also been applied to acts of torture against the genitals. Cuts have included the yanking of penises, as opposed to the careful application of weights; trampling of penises against hard surfaces; the insertion of urethral sounds without apparent care; and damage to anuses by the misuse of vacuum pumps. Activities where it is apparent that care has been taken and where there is no evident risk of actual bodily harm have included the hanging of weights off genitals; penetration of the urethra, including with urethral sounds and multiple cotton buds; and play with low voltage electricity. These activities have been permitted at 'R18'.

Unlike certain acts where concerns about physical harm determine the likelihood of prosecution, 'fisting' remains an activity considered obscene under current interpretation of the OPA. In the case of *R v Slingsby* (1995, Crim LR 570) it is made clear that 'fisting', the insertion of the whole hand into the vagina or anus, does not constitute an act which in itself risks actual bodily harm. In this case the defendant was charged with manslaughter after his sexual partner died of septicemia as a result of cuts caused by the defendant's signet ring, which was worn during 'fisting' penetration of the woman's vagina and anus. It was accepted by the prosecution that 'the act of inserting fingers or hand into the vagina or rectum for the purposes of sexual stimulation would not, if consensual, amount to an assault or any other crime'.[1] It was determined:

that the sexual activity to which both the deceased and the defendant agreed did not involve deliberate infliction of injury or harm and but for the coincidental fact that the defendant happened to be wearing a signet ring, no injury at all would have been caused or could have been contemplated. The question of consent to injury did not, in fact, arise because neither anticipated or considered it.[2]

As an activity represented in sex works, 'fisting' nevertheless remains subject to prosecution under the OPA. As an activity listed in the CPS Guidance, the BBFC continues to define 'fisting' as penetration with all five digits beyond the last knuckle.

Conclusion

With new legislation on 'extreme pornography' introduced within the Criminal Justice and Immigration Act 2008, and 'prohibited images of children' within the Coroners and Justice Act 2009, the BBFC's intervention in sex works continues, in significant part, to be influenced and guided by the criminal law. With the precise nature of what may constitute 'extreme pornography' still being tested by the courts, there remains limited practical guidance on some aspects of the legislation including how realistic, if not actually real, need be an image of necrophilia; an act which threatens a person's life; or an act which results, or is likely to result, in serious injury to a person's anus, breasts or genitals. Most convictions for 'extreme pornography' have thus far been for relatively more straightforward images of bestiality. In practice little that might be considered 'extreme pornography' is submitted to the BBFC for classification and limited intervention has been required citing these grounds. Images of child characters featuring in animated sex works have occasionally been submitted and cut prior to classification. But these too are rare since the introduction of the Coroners and Justice Act 2009. It remains necessary for the BBFC to continue to understand the nature and type of material which is subject to prosecution. In this context the BBFC continues its current working relationship with the police and other enforcement agencies to ensure that up-to-date interpretation of the OPA, and other relevant legislation, is correctly and appropriately applied.

Despite new media developments having rapidly changed the way many people access sexually explicit material, the generally consistent nature of the material means legal concerns about obscenity, harm, indecency and extreme acts are set to continue – quite likely with further regulation of the online environment. The recent introduction of new legislation dealing with sexual content – extreme pornography and prohibited images of children – and the concerns the legislation reflects, underlines this expectation.

Notes

1 http://www.swarb.co.uk/lisc/Crime19951995.php (accessed 3 September 2011).
2 Ibid.

Bibliography

BBFC (2000a) *BBFC Annual Report*, London: BBFC.
——(2000b) *Record of the Enforcement Sub Group Meeting*, June, London: BBFC.
——(2000c) 'A Caning for Miss Granger: Letter of rejection', London: BBFC.
——(2005) 'Severe Punishment: Letter of rejection', London: BBFC.
——(2007) *BBFC Annual Report*, London: BBFC.
——(2009a) *BBFC Guidelines*, London: BBFC.
——(2009b) *Women Love Porn*, London: BBFC.
CPS (2010) *Obscene Publications: Legal guidance: The Crown Prosecution Service*. Online. Available at http://www.cps.gov.uk/legal/l_to_o/obscene_publications/index.html (accessed 3 September 2011).
Hanley, P. (2000) *Sense and Sensibilities: Public opinion and the BBFC guidelines*. Online. Available at http://www.bbfc.co.uk/download/guidelines/2000%20Guidelines%20Research%20-%20Sense%20and%20Sensibilities.pdf (accessed 28 May 2011).
Moalem, S. (2009) 'Everything You Always Wanted to Know about Female Ejaculation', *New Scientist*, Vol. 202 (Issue 2710): 31–3.
Spanner Trust (2011) 'The Spanner Trust'. Online. Available at http://www.spannertrust.org/documents/spannerhistory.asp (accessed 3 September 2011).
Wingrove, N. (1998) 'The Distributors Tale', *Sight & Sound*, 8(5): 16–17.

7

POLICING OBSCENITY

Dave McDonald

Introduction

Image, art, scandal: history abounds with occasions in which art, historical artefact and advertising have been the subject of intense controversy owing to their 'legitimacy'.[1] In such collisions, police often find themselves at a critical juncture. In May 2008, this was sensationally borne out when the internationally esteemed Australian artist Bill Henson was to have opened his latest exhibition at Sydney's Roslyn Oxley9 Gallery. On the afternoon before the exhibition's opening, New South Wales (NSW) police officers inspected the displayed works and ordered the temporary suspension of the exhibition. The following morning, a search warrant was obtained, the exhibition was formally shut down and a total of 32 images seized. The actions of police occurred alongside a nationwide debate that was both fierce and widespread. The then Prime Minister condemned the images as 'absolutely revolting' (*Today Show* 2008). The high-profile child advocate Hetty Johnston, who lodged the complaint initiating the intervention of police, declared that Henson's work 'is child pornography, child exploitation and it is a crime' (cited in Marr 2008: 15). In contrast, many came forward to defend both Henson as an artist and the principle of artistic freedom. Art critics located his work within a long historical tradition involving the representation of the nude child within art, while others condemned the intrusion of police into the sphere of the art gallery.

This chapter critically examines the scandal attending Henson's exhibition in order to explore the relationship between policing and the 'obscene' more broadly.[2] I use the term 'obscenity' within quotation marks to emphasize that policing of obscenity does not involve the policing of a straightforwardly discrete 'thing' that is easily defined as 'obscene'. I am indebted here to the work of Walter Kendrick (1996) and Lynda Nead (1999), whose contributions to obscenity and pornography reject the assumption that there are discrete attributes that designate a thing as obscene. Similarly, Leonard (2006: 202) usefully describes the nature of obscenity as a 'compelling *question'* (my emphasis). Whilst legal doctrine historically dictated that certain 'things' are, or are not, obscene, Kendrick (1996: xiii) observes that at the same time law 'fails to provide any guidance as to what this elusive thing really is'. Similarly, Adler (2001) argues that, in spite of the expansion of child pornography law since the 1980s, the very definition of child pornography itself is increasingly elusive (see also Chapter 8). Just as 'obscenity' is a concept marked by ambiguity, so too is the border that 'distinguishes' art from the obscene. This attests to the fact that art and obscenity are not absolute or exclusive categories. Instead, what tend to be taken as categories may instead more usefully be conceived as *processes* and, as such, 'rest upon acts of judgment performed by those who have particular knowledge and power' (Nead 1999: 205). The implication is that policing obscenity is complex, owing in large part to the act of judgement that it necessarily entails.

While the police investigation of Henson's exhibition has been documented elsewhere (Marr 2008; Meagher 2009), these accounts have tended to conceive of 'policing' in a formal sense. If, following Foucault (1980: 156), power is something not in one's possession, but instead 'a machinery that no one owns', the power to police obscenity cannot be reduced to state institutions or their actors, nor is it synonymous with 'the Police'. This chapter thus conceives of policing more expansively, locating formal policing practices alongside the national debate accompanying the images. This debate is as instructive of the manner in which 'obscenity' is policed as any formal police intervention that accompanies it. As Bhabha (1994: 24) attests, 'there is no knowledge – political or otherwise – outside representation'. It follows that knowledge of the 'obscene' is irrevocably intertwined with representation and discourse; debates about the extent to which an artwork constitutes obscenity are themselves occasions in which 'the obscene' is policed, in a regulatory sense. As the chapter demonstrates, the Henson scandal elicited a fierce discursive contestation, evoking ideas about childhood, of art and legitimacy, and of paedophilic desire. Discourse for Foucault (1978) is productive, which means that any desire for 'the Police' to exercise repressive control over obscene images is misplaced. My reading of this event draws on this conception of discourse and power, and as such constitutes a key point of departure from the way that others have conceived of the policing of Henson's images. For example, while Meagher (2009) uses the case of the Henson scandal to identify recommended changes to police investigations in order to more accurately reflect the present legislative regime, I read formal policing practices alongside the discursive controversy that the scandal itself elicits.

The chapter proceeds to explore how this discursive debate functions to produce and police both objects (the 'obscene') and subjects (childhood, viewers and illicit gazes) of art. The following section contextualizes the Henson scandal by reference to a broader relationship between art and obscenity, and by reference to an increasing concern about the nature of childhood sexualization in Australia in particular. I argue that this context renders the representation of an unclothed child as 'obscene', necessitating the intervention of police. The result is a contestation surrounding the permissible manner in which childhood may be represented and the policing of permissibility itself. The following section engages with the notion that *obscene gazes*

encounter the images, accounting both for the manner in which paedophilic subjectivity is evoked throughout the scandal and is itself subjected to discursive regulation.
In the conclusion, I consider the result of this particular policing effort, specifically
the apparent *failure* of a formal outcome arising from the police investigation of
Henson's images. In its entirety, the chapter seeks to provide an account of the
complex dynamics and implications that arise in the collision between artistic image
and obscene scandal.

Image and/as obscenity

On 22 May 2008, the day that Bill Henson's exhibition was scheduled to open, a column
was published in the *Sydney Morning Herald* by Miranda Devine. Devine (2008: 13)
argued that 'images presenting children in sexual contexts are so commonplace these days
they seem almost to have lost the capacity to shock'. Her critique of the continuing
sexualization of children centred specifically upon the invitation to Henson's exhibition.
This image, and the full exhibition that Devine had not yet seen, for her signified 'the
effort, over many decades by various groups – artists, perverts, academics, librarians, the
media and advertising industries, respectful corporations and the porn industry – to smash
taboos of previous generations and define down community standards' (2008: 13).
Specifically, she regards the sexualization of childhood as having been precipitated by
an amalgam of diverse interests – from 'respectful corporations' who market to children in
an increasingly sexualized manner, through to the pornography industry, even 'perverts'
themselves – and through which acceptable social mores are increasingly whittled
away. This effort, she argued, 'has successfully eroded the special protection once
afforded childhood' (2008: 13). The so-called sexualization of children has been of
increasing concern in Australia. Over the past decade, alongside an emerging anxiety
with 'raunch culture' (Levy 2005; Tankard Reist 2009), increasing concern has been
paid to the way this supposed culture envelops or objectifies girls in particular (Rush
and La Nauze 2006a, 2006b; SSCECA 2008). In short, Devine's column functioned
to distil through one of Henson's images a much broader context in which children
are sexualized and dispossessed of their innocence.

On the day of Divine's column controversy intensified, becoming the centrepiece
of afternoon radio and news programming. The exhibition's artworks had been
uploaded onto the gallery's website on the morning of the opening. During the
course of the afternoon, a prominent Sydney radio host, describing the images as 'disgusting', 'pornographic' and 'woeful', instructed listeners to access this website to see the
images themselves (Marr 2008: 10). With a throng of media positioned outside the gallery prior to the formal opening and a succession of threatening phone calls having been
received by the gallery, its owners and the artist called police for advice on how to
proceed. Two police officers, followed shortly afterwards by their commanding officer, arrived at the gallery for the purposes of crowd control. However, concern about
the potential for damage to the artworks quickly transpired into concern about the
nature of the images themselves. As a result, Superintendent Sicard requested the
exhibition's suspension in order to inquire into the images' legality (Marr 2008: 21).

The following morning, some twenty police officers, including Superintendent Sicard and members of the Child Protection and Sex Crimes Squad, returned to the gallery with a court-granted warrant (Marr 2008: 52). In total 32 images were seized. Addressing the media, following the raid, Sicard stated that several items has been seized 'depicting a child under 16 years of age in a sexual context. Police are investigating this matter and it is likely that we will proceed to prosecution on the offence of publishing an indecent article under the Crimes Act' (cited in Marr 2008: 52). In the weeks that followed, police investigated the seized images and progressively inspected numerous galleries around the country that were in posession of Henson's artworks, including the collection of the Australian Federal Parliament.

However, it is misplaced to suggest that the role of arbitrating the 'legitimacy' of Henson's images was one left to police. As the police investigation proceeded, so too did the impulse within the nation's media for Henson's detractors to establish his 'artwork' – if this was a point even conceded – as obscene and illegitimate. Young (2005: 20) writes that, 'since one of the common stories about art relates it to beauty, edification of the human spirit and the sublime, nomination of an artwork as disgusting seeks to exclude it from the very realm of art'. This observation was borne out on the morning of the police raid, where the story was covered exclusively on the *Daily Telegraph*'s front page. A photo occupying most of the page represented two uniformed police officers beside the sign 'Bill Henson' on the gallery's wall. It was accompanied by the large, bold headline 'Child Porn "Art" Raid' and a smaller reproduction of the invitation's image featuring the model's face (Masters and Vallejo 2008a: 1). Placing the term 'art' in inverted commas functions to critically undermine the artistic legitimacy of the images, designating them instead to the domain of child pornography. The subsequent by-line announced a 'Victory for decency as police close gallery' (Masters and Vallejo 2008a: 1).

On the same morning, the then Australian Prime Minister Kevin Rudd was interviewed on the breakfast television programme, the *Today Show*. The host evoked the brewing Henson scandal, saying: 'one critic says that he is an artist of ferocious integrity who depicts androgynous girls and boys adrift in the nocturnal turmoil of adolescence. What we say is, that is crossing the line' (*Today Show* 2008). Viewers were shown five images from the exhibition of the adolescent featured on the exhibition's invitation. Significantly, the network used black bars to 'censor' where the models' genitals would have 'appeared'. Holquist (1994: 14) writes that a paradoxical irony arises out of the censored text because it creates 'sophisticated audiences': 'the reader of a text known to be censored cannot be naïve, if only because the fact of interdiction renders a text parabolic ... readers must fill in with their interpretations' what was excluded. That the genitals themselves were not observable due to Henson's use of darkness and shade is a point which is abrogated: presumably, the black censoring bars signify that what is obscured is obscene and warrants obscuring.

On being shown these censored images, Kevin Rudd was asked 'how do they make you *feel*?' (*Today Show* 2008; my emphasis). The response was unequivocal: 'I find them absolutely revolting ... Whatever the artistic view of the merits of that sort of stuff – frankly, I don't think there are any – just allow kids to be kids, you know' (ibid.). What the exchange conveys is the *affective* dimension of the images, their powerful, at times forceful address to the spectator. Further, the statements constitute a moment in which the affective address of the spectator is transported into the language of disgust. In a parallel manner, in her complaint to the gallery, Hetty Johnston wrote the following:

> We would like to place it on record that we are disgusted and surprised at your gallery's decision to allow this display. Pictures portraying sexualized imagery of young girls can *never* be called art. It is child pornography, child exploitation and it is a crime.
>
> *(Cited in Marr 2008: 15; original emphasis)*

For Johnston, the fact that the images are of naked children invalidates their categorization as art: they can only ever be child exploitation. The threshold or boundary which differentiates the 'artistic' from the 'obscene' is rendered absolute, definable and containable. The images are pornographic, illicitly passing under the banner of art. As Johnston elsewhere states, 'you can call it anything you want, but at the end of the day, these are images of naked adolescents' (cited in Jinman and Tovey 2008: 7). In statements such as these, the photographic images become traces of a crime – one of child pornography, which through their production and subsequent display within the exhibition breaches childhood innocence.

On the afternoon that the exhibition was scheduled to open, the Sydney broadcaster Chris Smith stated on his programme that 'I don't think I've seen anything more disgusting'. He argued, it 'is disgraceful. It is disgusting. It is pornographic. It is woeful' (Smith 2008). The statement reveals something of the affective force of disgust. As Halsey and Young (2006: 276–7) observe, affect has to do with *intensity* and exceeds emotion in its physicality, its visceral or corporeal encounter with bodies. The affective experience of disgust for detractors such as Smith is revealed through his language, but also at the same time through his *struggle* to translate affect into language. Henson's images are 'disgraceful', they are 'disgusting', they are 'pornographic', they are 'woeful'. The words themselves and the manner in which they are enunciated underscore the *outrage* that is elicited by disgust's affective charge.

Photographs of course arise from a real encounter between actual people and, as such, in contrast to other representational mediums, have been the subject of more rigorous concern where children are involved (Higonnet 1998: 106). In the case of Henson's images, they are received as disgusting in particular because of the fact that they depict an actual child. Via her participation within Henson's artistic process, and the concomitant result that her naked body will forever be inscribed within the public domain through the display of Henson's art, the claim is that this particular child's innocence and modesty are therein diminished. By participating in the production of images of her unclothed body, it is held that the adolescent's right to innocence and modesty are denied.

Of particular relevance to this conception of the rights of the child is the manner in which the naked (child) body is conceived. The rhetoric of 'innocence' and 'modesty' are deployed in relation to the child with reference to sexuality, or sexual relations. Within the Henson controversy a threat to innocence and modesty is tied to the *naked* body. Accordingly, Henson's detractors demonstrate an implicit collapse or conflation between the non-sexual naked body and the sexual body. As Johnston (2008) states, 'given the photos focus on their nakedness (regardless of the "artistic" lighting, shadows, etc.) and that the artists [sic] stated intention is to focus on their transition from child to adult, that [sic] the images are clearly taken in a "sexual context"'. Here, the non-sexual naked body, a tradition within art that has long been legitimated, is decontextualized or delegitimated in the Henson controversy. The consequence is that the child's participation within Henson's artistic process is problematized on the basis of the *sexual* nakedness that participation entails.

Related to this is the issue of consent. Henson's detractors argue that the child lacks the capacity to meaningfully consent to their participation in his artistic process by virtue of being a child. For example, in an opinion piece in the *Sunday Telegraph*, federal Senator Mark Arbib asks:

> [H]ow can a young teenager, going through this complex developmental stage, have the maturity to properly consider the consequences of posing naked? And how can they grasp that any photos taken of them now will be forever available through the internet?
>
> *(Arbib 2008: 84)*

Similarly, Clive Hamilton, director of The Australian Institute, states the following: 'I argue that she, the girl, the model, could not possibly understand the implications of being presented naked to the world, even though the presentation is very aestheticized and that therefore she could not give informed consent' (*PM* 2008). In this way, the law's stipulation that the child cannot consent to sexual relations is transposed in such a manner to require that the child similarly lacks the capacity to consent to being photographed naked. On one level, this appears straightforward. However, that the law holds that a minor lacks the capacity to consent to sex does not also mean that the child *does* in fact also lack the capacity to consent to their own participation in an artistic process that involves their naked display for an artist. My point is not that the child *can* meaningfully consent to this per se so much as to problematize the a priori assumption that consenting to be photographed naked is akin to consenting to sexual relations (see Chapter 8 for discussion of this issue). Related to this, Higonnet (1998: 169) problematizes the way that the concept of consent is employed in debates about representations of children in art, stating: 'Consent, however, is not an infallible or conclusive test. Arguably, no person less powerful in any way than their photographer can give genuine consent: no person poorer, less mentally stable, racially discriminated against, socially marginal, etc.' This reliance upon the concept of consent – a concept the law uses in relation to sexual relations – reveals the manner in which it is assumed to apply equally to the act of modelling naked, in spite of the inherent complexity the concept of consent entails.

This is related to the subsequent claim that parents are negligent in their responsibility to their children by consenting on their behalf. Indeed, it is the case that a large proportion of those opposed to Henson's images directed their criticism not just to the artist but also to the child models' parents – criticisms that were, at times, vehement. Mark Arbib (2008: 84), for example, states that 'while the young girl in the portrait certainly didn't have the maturity to make the decision, her parents didn't have the right to give away her modesty either'. The then Premier of New South Wales similarly stated that 'as a father of four I find it offensive and disgusting. I don't understand why parents would agree to allow their kids to be photographed like this' (cited in Masters and Vallejo 2008b: 4). These statements insinuate that the children's parents are failing to attend to their duties as parents. It is not simply their decision to allow their children to model for Henson that is held as questionable but, rather, that they are in result complicit in their children's loss of innocence.

What these utterances about a child's inability to consent reveal, I contend, is a sense of loss and dispossession: the act of modelling naked for an artist 'sexualizes' the child, resulting in a loss of the child's innocence. The act of modelling for the camera naked is conceived here in a way that parallels the manner in which Susan Sontag has conceived of photography. Photography for Sontag is akin to a 'soft murder':

> To photograph people is to violate them, by seeing them as they never see themselves, by having knowledge of them that they can never have; it turns people into objects that can be symbolically possessed. Just as a camera is a sublimation of the gun, to photograph someone is a subliminal murder – a soft murder, appropriate to a sad, frightened time.
>
> *(Sontag 1978: 14–15)*

Following Sontag, what appears is a scenario through which Henson's photographing of the child is a moment of violation, of soft murder. In the commentary critical of Henson's photographing of naked child models, this conceptualization of the work of the camera, of photography, rings true: these are children whose innocence is lost through their naked encounter before the camera. The camera dispossesses them of their innocence.

However, this assumption fails to accord with what Henson's child models have articulated about their experience of modelling for him. Henson has for much of his 30-year career produced images of the naked child. At the same time there is to date no model who has publicly spoken negatively of the experience of modelling for him, or appearing naked in his images. SBS Television's programme *Insight* devoted an episode to the topic of the naked child in art in the weeks following the Henson controversy and included a number of commentators who had featured heavily in the debate. While child models of Henson's did not participate in the programme, former child models who had posed naked for other artists did speak of their experience. One woman named Marina, aged 25, who had previously modelled unclothed for the photographer Sandy Edwards, was asked how she feels now when she looks at her images, responding that 'I enjoy them just as much as I did when they were first taken' (*Insight* 2008). Elsewhere, another previous model, Zahava Elenberg, states of her experience of modelling for Henson as a 12-year-old some 20 years before:

'It [the location] was quite dark but I never felt uncomfortable. Bill made you feel incredibly safe and calm.' Contradicting the assumption that Henson's models inhabit a position of powerlessness before him and his camera, she states 'I was involved in the artistic process and I never felt that I wasn't in control' (cited in Bibby 2008: 1). Similarly, Joelle Baudet, who posed naked for Henson, states that 'the experience was enlightening. It never crossed my mind that what I was doing was pornographic' (cited in Bibby 2008: 1).

What such experiential accounts reveal is a disjuncture between those critical of Henson's work on the basis that the experience of modelling naked is harmful and the accounts provided by those who have modelled. To return again to Sontag's claim about the camera – 'a sublimation of the gun', 'a soft murder' – the disjuncture reveals the impossibility of conferring upon the camera (and, by extension, the photographer) an absolute, sovereign power over the camera's subject. These models' statements reveal that power lies not in an object or only at the disposal of one person over another. My claim is not that modelling naked for Henson *is* an empowering experience – but that it *may* be. Power is diverse in its possibilities, as is the camera: it may be 'negative', perhaps repressive, but it may also be productive, it may contain conditions for resistance, for agency, for self-realization. Power and powerlessness are unstable categories that refuse straightforward opposition based upon the dichotomy of adult/child. Whilst these critics accuse Henson of dispossessing his child models (of childhood innocence, of their rights as children), it might instead be said that these models are dispossessed, silenced or robbed in a different sense – of the capacity to articulate an experience of performative engagement with the camera that refutes the straightforward claims of Henson's critics.

Policing obscene gazes

Art critic John McDonald describes the experience of viewing Henson's images as an unnerving one: 'What may be most unnerving', he says, 'is that Henson turns every single viewer into a voyeur looking into the dark' (cited in Marr 2008: 35). The unnerving experience of looking at Henson's images of unclothed children is underscored by the *proximity* between the person who looks and the child who is looked at. These bodies are entwined through their proximity, but at the same time the child remains oblivious to this. The notion of looking is not a reciprocal one. It is in this way that the act of looking is figured as voyeurism. For McDonald, 'there must be many who find themselves transfixed by these pictures, while trying to summon up a stern resistance. Whether it be his landscape or the body, there is never a lure in Henson's work without some underlying threat' (cited in Marr 2008: 35). What remains to be considered in further detail is the notion of voyeurism that McDonald identifies and the potential for obscene gazes that are produced within, and policed by, the Henson scandal.

Marr (2008: 67) writes that 'of all the familiar figures present in this tumultuous debate, the most familiar yet mysterious was the figure of The Paedophile. His importance can't be exaggerated.' The broadcaster Derryn Hinch, for example, describes the images as being 'drooled over by paedophiles' (cited in Marr 2008: 69). Similarly, for Johnston, 'you have to understand that there are people who really enjoy looking at that, and would get a really sick little victorious giggle that they could have one of those images hanging up in their lounge room – and it's legal' (cited in Marr 2008: 64). These statements reveal an anxiety concerning the potential for improper acts of looking, for the voyeuristic gaze. However, to the extent that Henson's images produce a lure, coupled with a lingering sense of threat, there is an implicit contradiction within the criticism his images receive: the images are condemned as disgusting and simultaneously as sexual. These statements uphold the fact that the images are sexual in nature, but, in upholding this, they also simultaneously place it outside – upholding it, while also *disowning* it.[3] However, those voices or bodies for whom these images are *exciting*, or sexually affective, are repudiated. That is, while criticism of Henson is premised on the notion that the images are sexual in nature, it is only ever mysterious *others* who might engage with the images in such a manner. Through being disowned, this possibility is disavowed, placed elsewhere. The capacity to view the images sexually is thus simultaneously upheld (indeed, it is the very premise underpinning criticisms directed at Henson), but the subjects who specifically engage with them in this manner are always already located elsewhere – outlawed, mysterious, absent. In this regard, what may be observed is both a contradiction (the images are excitable, but only ever to mysterious, indiscernible *others*) and simultaneously a repudiation or disavowal of the potential for paedophilic desire.

McDonald's identification of a lure coupled with a threat in Henson's images is mirrored by Hamilton (2008), who declares the images 'imaginative, haunting and beautiful', but too dangerous to publish: 'That paedophiles not only find stimulation in media images of eroticised children but take them as a justification for their own predatory urges inescapably casts a darkness over the Henson photographs.' The danger is twofold: it lies in the potential for mysterious, unidentifiable others to look illicitly at the images, but subsequently also to legitimate this illicit look. That is, that the images are 'artistic' is conceived as conferring 'legitimacy' on the illicit look. Johnston exemplifies this anxiety, stating that where an image is designated as 'artistic', it is especially dangerous: 'because it's legitimate, it has credibility. It normalises this even more, says that it's quite normal and okay to portray children in a sexual context, naked kids, and throw them out there on the internet' (cited in Marr 2008: 69). Their 'artistic' status is seen as conferring legitimacy upon paedophilic desire, exemplifying their dangerousness.

To this end, in many respects the invocation of paedophilic desire throughout the Henson scandal functions to outlaw the potential to read images of children as sexual, at the same time that it simultaneously *produces* this possibility. Mohr (2004: 20) writes that 'paedophilic' images in which youthfulness is sexualized 'are surprisingly common in society – surprising given that society careers from hysteria to hysteria over the possible sexiness of children'. At the same time that particular images incite hysteria (e.g. Henson's images), a raft of other 'problematic' or 'sexualized' images are not conceived as sexual, or liable to charges of obscenity. However, where hysteria arises out of particular images then, as Mohr argues, this hysteria is productive.

'Society needs the paedophile: his existence allows everyone else to view sexy children innocently. But his conceptualisation by society must not be allowed to be rich enough to be interesting, to constitute a life' (2004: 20). Following Mohr, the Henson debate reveals a persistent contradiction in that his detractors *uphold* the sexual potential of the image. Mohr's claim is that hysteria about paedophilia 'springs mainly from adults' fear of themselves, but this fear issues from their half recognition that to admit it explicitly, as pornography does, that children are sexy would mean that virtually everyone is a paedophile' (2004: 28–9). Thus, the implicit acknowledgement of the threat constituted by adults is kept at bay by reference to the category of the illicit paedophile, therein quarantining 'us' from 'them'.

To the extent that these paedophilic others are invoked within the Henson debate, their shadowy, mysterious nature is informed through the Internet and technology. That the images are available *outside* the walls of the gallery that exhibits them is a source of anxiety that cannot be under-emphasized. As Johnston (2008) states, 'we know that art is no longer confined to the walls of the gallery, exclusively accessible by only its visitors. Today's technology means art is shared or "disseminated" globally within minutes.' Hamilton echoes this concern, stating that 'when they are placed on the internet, you know they're flashed around the world within hours and … can be used for all sorts of unpleasant purposes' (*PM* 2008). The advent of the Internet and digital photography for these commentators constitutes a moment in which art becomes accessible to improper audiences, exemplified by 'the paedophile' ('grubby old men' who sinisterly access, distribute or trade such images, sullying artistic intention illicitly). This is reinforced by the fact that the invitation was sent to approximately 3,500 guests. As Marr (2008: 5) writes, 'hanging on a gallery wall or tucked inside a catalogue, that image would not have provoked the same response'. In the context of an exhibition – an exhibition which features a number of images of naked children, but which importantly also features Henson's trademark images of clouds, of former grand buildings now lying derelict in ruins – the image itself is palatable for Marr. In isolation, on its own and sent outside the gallery in the form of an invite, it crosses the line, it exceeds the barriers that legitimate it. Thus, to the extent that the closeted realm of the art world is ruptured or disintegrated (one might say, democratized), then improper people may come into contact with the images. As Hamilton states:

> I think it's [the Internet] changed it [art] completely. I mean if we imagine going back 30 years and this sort of exhibition being put on in a gallery and it was seen by its intended audience, that is those who have presumably a sophisticated appreciation of photography as art, then I don't think, I certainly wouldn't have a problem with it. But when the same pictures become consumed, if I can use that commodified term, by a range of people for quite different and unintended reasons, which will have impacts on the child models in question, through the internet, then I think there are serious worries about that.
>
> (PM *2008*)

Underpinning this is an anxiety stemming from a perceived disintegration between the private and the public and, attached to this, an anxiety about readership and interpretation. It is not simply that these images can be shared, transported easily and become fluid in their origins and locales, but that we do not know, nor may we control, how they are gazed at.

In her influential work, Nead (1999) emphasizes the central role played by the 'connoisseur' in the history of obscenity. It is the 'connoisseur', she demonstrates, whose artistic taste and fluency is central to the designation of obscenity. Nead establishes her argument by reference to Naples' Museo Borbonico and its treatment of artefacts that were systematically excavated in the eighteenth century from the ruins of Pompeii. During the excavation, 'a problem immediately arose: what was to be done with the sexually explicit objects, which were turning up with increasing frequency as the excavations proceeded?' (Nead 1999: 203–4). Following the lead of other museums, artefacts deemed as obscene were designated to another space within the museum – *the secret museum*. By excising the 'obscene' in such a way, the intent is not to restrict encounters with such artefacts per se, so much as to regulate who is conferred with the legitimacy to encounter the obscene. 'Obscenity is judged and annexed' in the secret museum, writes Nead, 'and access to its pleasures and dangers is restricted to the same group that first classified the works' (Nead: 204–5). Determined less by any intrinsic quality of the work, the line differentiating art from the obscene is one determined by acts of judgement. However, the act of judgement is not a democratic one, a possibility proffered widely. Instead, it is conferred upon the body of the 'connoisseur'. Specifically, 'in any such judgment ... the judge must be beyond incrimination. The arbiter may only distinguish art and obscenity from a position that is outside of the attractions and impulses of sexual representation' (Nead: 205). The arbiter must be one for whom the sexual impulses arising from the obscene work are disavowed. As the connoisseur entrusted with the authority to catalogue the archaeological finds from Pompeii writes in his compilation, 'it has been our intention to remain calm and serious throughout. In the exercise of this holy office, the man of science must neither blush nor smile. We have looked upon our statues as an anatomist contemplates his cadavers' (Barré cited in Nead 1999: 207). It is thus an exclusive 'privilege' conferred upon the connoisseur, defined as 'he' that can resist the affective address of the work or artefact.

To return again to the Henson scandal, the fact that the images were not 'confined' to the private space of the gallery, but were instead reproduced on the gallery's website and in the form of the invitation, constitutes a moment in which the privilege conferred upon the connoisseur is ruptured. Historically, the connoisseur – sophisticated, knowledgeable in the traditions of photographic art – may legitimately encounter the image. To the extent that the image exceeds the private confines of the gallery, it may be encountered by mysterious, sinister paedophiles whose look exceeds regulation. As Higonnet (1998: 142) writes, 'exposure becomes frightening when it is to strangers' eyes'. It is to these strangers that the potential for an illicit look is deferred within the Henson debate.

Conclusion: en/countering the obscene

After almost three weeks of inquiries, inspections of galleries around the country and statements to the contrary, the police investigation of Bill Henson ultimately led to 'nothing'. Australia's Classification Board judged the central image in question, *Untitled* (#30), mild and justified by context; the NSW Director of Public Prosecutions ruled that the prospect of a conviction against the artist was negligible; and NSW Police (in contrast to their earlier statements) ruled out prosecution.[4] The seized images were duly returned and the exhibition subsequently proceeded. As Johnston laments of the NSW Crimes Act, 'it's toilet paper' (cited in Marr 2008: 131). In the face of the law's failure to police filthy or dirty images, she evokes an abject metaphor itself in order to deride the legislative regime. If there was to be any consensus between those who decried Henson's images as obscene and those who defended the artist, his work and the principle of artist freedom, it may well have been the question: what went *wrong* (albeit entailing very different responses)?

That the Henson scandal did not lead to formal charges against the artist or the gallery lends itself, on one level, to the observation that policing of the 'obscene' here constitutes a failure and that such investigations are futile. Hetty Johnston describes the outcome 'disgusting … a major victory for paedophiles and paedophile suppor-ters', one which comes 'at the expense of children' (Drummond 2008). Similarly, Meagher (2009: 297, 300) describes the police investigation as a 'costly and unnecessary mistake' owing to the 'futility of criminal prosecution'. Meagher's claim about the futility of criminal prosecution is an argument he establishes based upon the law's recognition of 'artist value' as a legitimate defence within obscenity prosecutions. The recognition of this defence, he writes, is to 'tip the balance firmly in favour of artistic discretion' (ibid.: 300). While I agree with aspects of Meagher's analysis, I reject the idea that the Henson scandal, and the policing of the obscene more generally, is usefully conceived as futile. To do so is to overlook the very tangible consequences flowing from the scandal itself. The preceding discussion has offered an account of the manner in which the 'obscene' is policed as a site of discursive contestation. However, tangible effects extend beyond this: for example, in response to the outcry, the Australia Council revised protocols regulating artists who receive federal funding for work involving the depiction of children, paralleling changes to National Endowment for the Arts funding that occurred in response to similar crises concerning 'obscene' or 'disgusting' artwork in the United States (Australia Council for the Arts 2008).[5]

That NSW police did not pursue the prosecution of Henson is in certain respects, I contend, immaterial. I have argued that Henson's images were framed as emblematic of a broader cultural anxiety about the sexualization of children. To this end, in spite of the absence of formal criminal charges, in many respects the 'charge' directed at Henson and charted implicitly throughout this chapter within the national debate, 'sticks'. As a result, Henson is not known as an artist of international standing, one whose work has represented Australia at the Venice Biennale, whose works are held in some of the most respected collections internationally. Instead, he is framed as the 'artist' who photographs naked children, as *artist provocateur*. He becomes the *cause*, and the epitome, of this context, the agent that brought this crisis in the ideal of childhood to bear. Further, Henson *continues* to be policed: in October 2008, upon the revelation that he had previously been escorted around a school to select children to photograph, he was the subject of another intense episode of controversy and criticism (Cazzulino 2008: 1; *Herald Sun* 2008: 18). Similarly, his subsequent exhibitions have been 'policed' for the extent to which he continues to photograph children (see Hardy 2010a, 2010b).

Further to this, the view that this episode signals a failure in policing obscenity implicitly assumes that the law indeed may have (but in this instance lacks) the power to *govern* images. Instead, I see within scandals such as this a more complex relation between law and the image. While the story of legal governance is one in which law takes precedence over images and maintains the capacity to control such images, Young (2005: 10) usefully conceives of the relation between law and image as 'one of *co-implication*, in which law and the image are enfolded within each other, their contours and their substances passing through and around each other' (original emphasis).[6] The dichotomy of law–image functions to assume 'that the realm of the cultural is subject to legal processes and is the object of law's subjective governance' (Young 2005: 8). In contrast, the complex interplay, charted in this chapter, that arises between policing and the 'obscene' is demonstrative of the fantasy of law's capacity to unilaterally 'govern' images. Following Foucault (1980: 158), power is not reducible to law, or to state apparatuses such as 'the Police'. Similarly, Butler (1998: 256) writes that if 'power is instanced as the act of censorship, figured as an efficacious action that one subject performs upon another', then 'power is reduced to that which is externally imposed upon a subject'. While I observe within this particular case study an episode in which 'obscenity' *is* policed, policing itself can never constitute simply a sovereign agency to censor troublesome images (Müller 2004: 5). Further, that for Foucault power produces the capacity for resistance is itself evident throughout the Henson controversy. This may be witnessed via Henson's child models who speak positively of their experience of modelling naked before the camera. Similarly, it can be witnessed in the decision of the National Gallery of Victoria to retrieve Henson's images from storage at the height of the scandal and place them on display alongside a curator's didactic panel placing Henson's images within an artistic tradition of the nude child (see Marr 2008: 93).

However, if there is a failure to be observed in policing of the obscene, it is the failure of censorial desire itself. Holquist (1994: 17) writes that 'censors never succeed (or at least never succeed for long) in totally instrumenting their desire to purge'. This observation gives way to an implicit paradox that underpins the manner in which Henson's 'obscene' images were policed: rather than counter, repress or excise from view the troublesome image, the opposite occurs. These images are *incited into discourse* and, through this, the image for which law and police desire to be suppressed, contained or hidden, ruptures these confines, is *ungovernable*. Writing of the attempt over centuries to hunt down, confiscate and burn pornography, Kendrick (1996: 238) writes that 'the dismaying consequence was that ... its nature [was] made so public that the effort to stifle it became a corrupting influence. The real problem – though no one recognized this – was publicity itself, the permeation of the culture by images'. In the move to police the obscene, to annex it from view, the result in the Henson scandal is that few now no longer know who Henson is; images which would have gone largely unremarked have been endlessly reproduced and poured over. Aided and abetted by the technology of the Internet and mass media, the ostensibly obscene image is rendered easy to encounter. In seeking to repress the obscene, to counter the spectatorial relation between image and publics, this encounter itself is *invited*.

Notes

1 Internationally, artists such as Sally Mann, Robert Mapplethorpe, Jock Sturges, Nicholas Nixon, Tierney Gearon, Judith Black and Dick Blau have all been the subject of at times vehement criticism for the manner in which children have featured in their work. For a detailed account of the controversy surrounding many of these artists, see Higonnet (1998). On scandals surrounding the use of children in art see also Crimp (2002); Edge and Baylis (2004); Kidd (2003); Kleinhans (2004); Mohr (2004); and Smith (2004). On broader debates about controversial or 'obscene' art see Butler (1990, 1997, 1998); Sigman (2003); and Young (2005).
2 For an analysis of legal frameworks regarding obscenity in the United Kingdom, the United States and elsewhere, see Adler (1990); Gurstein (1996); Manchester (1999); Shek (2002); and Thomas (2007).
3 In a parallel manner, Adler convincingly argues that child pornography law itself para-doxically functions to invite scrutiny of pictures of children in the manner that paedo-philes do. As she states, 'child pornography has changed the way we look at children. I mean this literally. The law requires us to study pictures of children to uncover their sexual meanings, and in doing so, it explicitly exhorts us to take on the perspective of the paedophile' (Adler 2001: 256).
4 For a more thorough chronological account of the interactions between Australia's Classification Board, the Director of Public Prosecutions and NSW Police in relation to the Henson scandal, see Marr (2008: 113–27) and Meagher (2009).
5 On changes arising from scandal in relation to the National Endowment for the Arts see Young (2005).
6 See also Douzinas and Nead (1999) for a thoughtful problematization of the manner in which law posits itself as a discourse about all other practices and discourses, and the relation between law and image.

Bibliography

Australia Council for the Arts (2008) *Protocols for Working with Children in Art*, Sydney: Australia Council for the Arts.
Adler, A. (1990) 'Post-modern Art and the Death of Obscenity Law', *The Yale Law Journal*, 99: 1359–78.
——(2001) 'The Perverse Law of Child Pornography', *Columbia Law Review*, 101: 209–73.
Arbib, M. (2008) 'A Child's Innocence is at Stake here', *Sunday Telegraph*, 15 June: 84.
Bhabha, H. (1994) *The Location of Culture*, London: Routledge.
Bibby, P. (2008) 'This is not Porn, say Henson's Models', *Sydney Morning Herald*, 26 May: 1.
Butler, J. (1990) 'The Force of Fantasy: Feminism, Mapplethorpe, and discursive excess', *Differences: A journal of feminist and cultural studies*, 2: 105–25.
——(1997) *Excitable Speech: A politics of the performative*, New York: Routledge.
——(1998) 'Ruled Out: Vocabularies of the censor', in R.C. Post (ed.) *Censorship and Silencing: Practices of cultural regulation*, Los Angeles: Getty Research Institute.

Cazzulino, M. (2008) 'Henson Stalked School for Model', *Daily Telegraph*, 4 October: 1.

Crimp, D. (2002) *Melancholia and Moralism: Essays on AIDS and queer politics*, Cambridge, MA: MIT Press.

Devine, M. (2008) 'Saturated with Sex: The campaign to save young minds', *Sydney Morning Herald*, 22 May: 13.

Douzinas, C. and Nead, L. (1999) 'Introduction', in C. Douzinas and L. Nead (eds) *Law and the Image: The authority of art and the aesthetics of law*, Chicago, IL: University of Chicago Press.

Drummond, A. (2008) 'No Charge over Henson's Naked Kid Photos', *Ninemsn*, 7 June. Online. Available at http://news.ninemsn.com.au/entertainment/575939/no-charge-over-hensons-naked-kid-photos (accessed 26 July 2011).

Edge, S. and Baylis, G. (2004) 'Photographing Children: The works of Tierney Gearon and Sally Mann', *Visual Culture in Britain*, 5: 75–89.

Foucault, M. (1978) *The History of Sexuality: Volume 1, an introduction*, London: Penguin.

——(1980) *Power/Knowledge: Selected interviews and other writings 1972–1977*, New York: Pantheon Press.

Gurstein, R. (1996) *The Repeal of Reticence: A history of America's cultural and legal struggles over freedom of speech, obscenity, sexual liberation and modern art*, New York: Hill & Wang.

Halsey, M. and Young, A. (2006) 'Our Desires are Ungovernable', *Theoretical Criminology*, 10: 275–306.

Hamilton, C. (2008) 'Henson Fracas: Art the victim of child sexualisation', *Crikey*, 23 May. Online. Available at http://www.clivehamilton.net.au/cms/media/documents/articles/henson_fracas__art_the_victim_of_child_sexualisation.pdf (accessed 26 July 2011).

Hardy, M. (2010a) 'Artists Be Warned: Big brother is watching', *The Drum*, 3 May. Online. Available at http://www.abc.net.au/news/stories/2010/05/03/2888521.htm?site=the-drum (accessed 26 July 2011).

——(2010b) 'Henson's Exceptional Talent Cowed?', *ABC Arts*, 7 May. Online. Available at http://www.abc.net.au/arts/stories/s2893550.htm (accessed 26 July 2011).

Herald Sun (2008) 'Tawdry Tour: Editorial', *Herald Sun*, 6 October: 18.

Higonnet, A. (1998) *Pictures of Innocence: The history and crisis of ideal childhood*, New York: Thames and Hudson.

Holquist, M. (1994) 'Corrupt Originals: The paradox of censorship', *PMLA*, 109: 14–25.

Insight (2008) 'The Naked Eye', 24 June, Television programme, Sydney: SBS Television.

Jinman, R. and Tovey, J. (2008) 'Career Framed by Controversy', *Sydney Morning Herald*, 24 May: 7.

Johnston, H. (2008) 'Hetty Johnston: Henson debate a healthy sign', *Crikey*, 2 June 2008. Online. Available at http://www.crikey.com.au/2008/06/02/hetty-johnston-henson-debate-a-healthy-sign (accessed 26 July 2011).

Kendrick, W. (1996) *The Secret Museum: Pornography in modern culture*, Berkeley, CA: University of California Press.

Kidd, D. (2003) 'Mapplethorpe and the New Obscenity', *Afterimage*, 30: 6–7.

Kleinhans, C. (2004) 'Virtual Child Porn: The law and the semiotics of the image', *Journal of Visual Culture*, 3: 17–34.

Leonard, S. (2006) 'Pornography and Obscenity', in H.G. Cocks and M. Houlbrook (eds) *The Modern History of Sexuality*, New York: Palgrave Macmillan.

Levy, A. (2005) *Female Chauvinist Pigs: Women and the rise of raunch culture*, Melbourne: Schwartz Publishing.

Manchester, C. (1999) 'Obscenity, Pornography and Art', *Media and Arts Law Review*, 4: 65–87.

Marr, D. (2008) *The Henson Case*, Melbourne: Text Publishing.

Masters, C. and Vallejo, J. (2008a) 'Child Porn "Art" Raid', *Daily Telegraph*, 23 May: 1.

——(2008b) 'Who Would Call this Art? As a father I find it offensive and disgusting – Morris Iemma', *Daily Telegraph*, 23 May: 4.

Meagher, D. (2009) 'Investigating "Indecent, Obscene or Pornographic" Art: Lessons from the Bill Henson controversy', *Media and Arts Law Review*, 14: 292–307.

Mohr, R. (2004) 'The Paedophilia of Everyday Life', in S. Bruhm and N. Hurley (eds) *Curiouser: On the queerness of children*, Minneapolis, MN: University of Minnesota Press.

Müller, B. (2004) 'Censorship and Cultural Representation: Mapping the territory', in B. Müller (ed.) *Censorship and Cultural Regulation in the Moral Age*, Amsterdam: Rodopi.

Nead, L. (1999) 'Bodies of Judgment: Art, obscenity, and the connoisseur', in C. Douzinas and L. Nead (eds) *Law and the Image: The authority of art and the aesthetics of law*, Chicago, IL: University of Chicago Press.

PM (2008) Radio programme, 23 May, Melbourne, ABC Radio.

Rush, E. and La Nauze, A. (2006a) *Corporate Paedophilia: The sexualisation of children in Australia*, Canberra: The Australia Institute.

——(2006b) *Letting Children be Children: Stopping the sexualisation of children in Australia*, Canberra: The Australia Institute.

Shek, T.R. (2002) 'Obscenity Laws and Art Exhibitions', *Art and Antiquity Law*, 7: 349–69.

Sigman, J. (2003) 'Self-mutilation, Interpretation, and Controversial Art', *Midwest Studies in Philosophy*, 27: 88–114.

Smith, Chris (2008) *The Chris Smith Afternoon Show*, Radio programme, 22 May, Sydney: 2GB.

Smith, L. (2004) 'Lewis Carroll: Stammering, photography and the voice of infancy', *Journal of Visual Culture*, 3: 95–105.

Sontag, S. (1978) *On Photography*, Harmondsworth: Penguin Books.

SSCECA (2008) *Sexualisation of Children in the Contemporary Media*, Canberra: Senate Standing Committee on Environment, Communications and the Arts.

Tankard Reist, M. (ed.) (2009) *Getting Real: Challenging the sexualisation of girls*, Melbourne: Spinifex Press.

The Today Show (2008) Television programme, 23 May, Sydney: Channel Nine.

Thomas, D. (2007) 'The Relationship between Obscenity Law and Contemporary Art in the United Kingdom, the United States and Other Jurisdictions', *Art Antiquity and Law*, 8: 337–60.

Young, A. (2005) *Judging the Image: Art, value, law*, London: Routledge.

8

SEXTING, INTIMACY AND CRIMINAL ACTS: TRANSLATING TEENAGE SEXUALITIES

Jo Moran-Ellis

This chapter examines the legal regulation of young people under the age of 18 with respect to the practice that has come to be called 'teenage sexting'. Sexting is a term now used mainly to describe the texting of nude or semi-nude pictures, although it can also be used to denote the sending of erotic texts. Media reports and legal responses in the past few years have been highly concerned with sexting by 'teenagers'. Despite this media focus on what has been called a 'sexting craze' (Pilkington 2009) and the use of labels such as 'Generation sexting' (Marshall 2009) there is a lack of clarity about the scope or the boundaries of the phenomenon. Furthermore, whilst the term 'teenagers' might seem to indicate fairly clearly who is the focus of attention in naming 'teenage sexting' as a specific activity, it denotes an ambiguous subject position both socially and legally. In social terms the category technically means someone between the ages of 13 and 19 years, but is more often used to indicate the middle section of that range or the lower half. It carries connotations of change and transition (to adulthood) embedded within particular stereotypes of behaviour, and in effect is imprecise in its implication of delineating a homogeneous group, structurally or socially. In relation to legal regulation, 'teenager' has no meaning since age-related matters such as culpability, capacity to consent to sexual activity and the age of majority are tied to speci-fied (albeit differing) ages. Nonetheless, social and legal complexities notwithstanding, media reports and social commentaries flag 'teenage sexting' as a unitary phenomenon.

A second area where clarity is lacking is in relation to the term 'sexting' itself. In popular reporting it is applied to a range of practices which are united in that they all involve digital erotic images and phones but diverge in terms of the production of the 'sext' and the audiences for it. For example, sexting has been used to describe the act of sending of erotic images to a lover, the act of circulating a sext to a wider audience without permission of the subject of the sext, the posting of self-made erotic images on social networking sites, the circulation of mobile phone video-recordings of sexual assaults by teenagers and the circulation of voyeuristically obtained sexual images. The use of one term to describe this range of practices has obscured differentiations between them including the differentiation of harms. This is potentially problematic for legal regulation since the various forms of sexting could carry different legal implications in relation to what kind of crime is being (or could be) committed and by whom, and what kind of judicial response is or is not warranted.

Using studies, case material and newspaper reports from the USA, Canada and the UK, and drawing on some ideas from actor–network theory (Latour 1987) I look at how teenage sexting has been regulated legally and informally. I argue that where legal governance is deployed, both sexting and teenagers are shaped in particular ways to make them available for a judicial response through processes of 'translation' (Brown and Capdevila 1999). These processes of translation are the product of, and also depend on, networks of actors – human and non-human – which produce and assemble the social category of 'sexting teenagers'[1] and hence as a particular category of actor for scrutiny, classification and control in specific contexts. In different contexts, networks and translation processes produce different kinds of 'sexting teenagers' – the criminal, the misguided, the immoral or the romantic. These different kinds of sexting teenagers are produced out of the part the law plays in the regulation of this erotic practice (including when it plays little part at all) but their production is simultaneously also part of the mechanism by which the law is or is not deployed as a source of control.

The phenomenon of sexting

Whilst it is difficult to trace a starting point for sexting as a practice generally, and for teenage sexting in particular, its emergence in UK press reports as a problem in need of intervention seems to start in 2002, with newspaper stories about teenagers who were victims of adult exploitation via mobile phones. The *Daily Mail*, for example, reported the prosecution of a police officer who 'bombarded a teenager with 800 messages with requests for sex' (Powell 2002) and in the same year the *Daily Express* ran a headline that proclaimed 'perverts use phone text to lure children' (Lambie 2002). This latter news story focused on 'paedophiles' posing as teenagers and texting children in order to establish a sexual relationship with them. By 2009 in the UK, sexual texting between teenagers had become the dominant focus of media coverage. In that year the plethora of newspaper reports in various UK newspapers primarily focused on two topics: first, that teenagers (and that group specifically) were routinely sending sexualized pictures of themselves to each other (e.g. see Marshall 2009 and Barbieri 2009); and, second, that in the USA young people had been prosecuted for sending and receiving sexts under the laws that make child pornography illegal (Henderson 2009). These articles portrayed teenage sexting as a highly problematic activity both in terms of dangers attendant on sexting (including the risk of criminal prosecution), and in terms of the vulnerability of teenagers to sexual predation by adults. In the UK, the media are still reporting on sexting, with some continued focus on prosecutions in the USA (*Daily Star* 2011; *Mail Online* 2011; Collins 2011).

Alongside an increased focus on teenage sexting as a problem, the range of activities labelled as sexting by the press has grown and what counts as sexting has became more complex and contextual. By the end of 2009 it was possible to identify at least four types of digital action being called sexting. The first type involves a person taking a photograph of themselves (naked, semi-naked or in a sexualized pose) and sending it to a particular person who may be someone they wish to start dating, with whom they are flirting or is an intimate/romantic partner (e.g. see reports by Barbieri 2009, Marshall 2009 and Loveys 2011). Alternatively two people together might take a picture of themselves or of each other in some kind of intimate act and share the picture between them. So, this first type of sexting is between two people, is mutual, is freely agreed to by both and sharing of the images is confined to them. In this sense, this form of sexting is both consensual and bounded.

The second type of practice that features in newspaper reports as sexting involves the posting of sexual pictures of oneself on social networking sites, such as Facebook (e.g. Ahmed 2009). This is a less 'bounded' form of sexting since the images are not made for a specific person but, rather, are designed for a bigger, albeit invited, audience – in effect their availability for viewing is still authorized by the subject of the photograph even though the audience is bigger than in consensual bounded sexting.

Reports of this type of sexting – consensual but in effect semi-bounded – position it as an unequivocally dangerous activity because of the risk that the images will escape out of the author's control. The capacity of the person who posted the picture to actually control who sees it, and/or downloads it, may be compromised by the technological limitations to the security the site claims to offer (Livingstone 2008) or usurped by people who gain access to 'private' images through duplicity (e.g. adults posing as teenagers to become an individual's 'Facebook friend' in order to download images for their own purposes). Some newspaper reports also frame the danger of such postings in terms of the images having an enduring life on the Internet and hence having the capacity to cause embarrassment to the author in the distant future. Whether or not this is a realistic concern, here we see a familiar emphasis on futurity when it comes to young people (Moran-Ellis and Cooper 2000), an emphasis which couples together their imagined future with their present-day actions and positions them in terms of what they will become with an emphasis on the significance of the here and now for this future. In effect, this is a concern that young people, through their naiveté or recklessness, fail to invest properly in their own futures through such sexting practices.

The third set of practices that have generated media interest and moral concerns overlaps with that outlined above but concerns those situations in which a sext is circulated without the author's consent to a wide audience of recipients who (usually) know the subject of the image(s). This practice is generally associated with malicious intent. Whilst this has also been labelled sexting in media reports, it involves no element of consensuality with respect to distribution and is unbounded. Such sexting may occur as an act of boasting by the original recipient of the text, or as an act of revenge following the breakdown of the relationship. In other circumstances a sexted image may be obtained by a third party peer and distributed as a form of humiliation or taunting. The wider distribution of these pictures is usually around peer networks but it can be broader than that, in some cases including family members of the victim of the malicious act (Ellis 2009).

There is a final set of practices that have been labelled sexting and these involve the sharing of images which do not include any initial consent to the making of the picture (or video-recording). Legally, these images can fall into the category of voyeurism (e.g. see sections 67 and 68 of the Sexual Offences Act 2003 in England and Wales) and examples involve: the filming of an act of sex without the knowledge of at least one person party to the sexual encounter; the use of mobile phone cameras to take uninvited pictures of people who believe themselves to be in a private space, such as in bathrooms or shop changing-rooms; photographing up women's skirts without their consent (so-called upskirting); and the filming or photographing of sexual assaults and the circulation of those pictures to others. In Australia and the USA specific offences of 'Upskirting' have been created (e.g. Summary Offences Amendment (Upskirting) Act 2007, Vic.). In Australia, Anastasia Powell (2010) has argued that the filming of sexual assault and the distribution of that film should both be legally recognized as violations of sexual autonomy and prosecuted as such. Under the legislation for England and Wales, this type of recording is legally recognized via the imposition of harsher sentences in cases where sexual assault is accompanied by a recording of the incident and the distribution of that recording (see Sentencing Guidelines Council 2007).

Although all these practices have been subsumed under the single label of 'sexting' in media reports and other places, they can be differentiated from each other in terms of consent, non-consent and imputed dissent. From sexting between two individuals for mutual pleasure, to posting an image on a social networking site, to mobile phones being used to record a sexual assault, there is an increasing gradient of non-consent and one might impute an increasing likelihood that the subject of the images would dissent from participating in these practices.

However, this distinction notwithstanding, sexting of all kinds arouses considerable moral outrage and even the most consensual bounded form is seen as a problematic teenage activity. In the USA consensual teenage sexting has been subject to criminal prosecution under child pornography laws in several States (Humbach 2010; NCSL 2011) and in other countries it has been the subject of professional intervention by schools and the police, and a topic of extensive social commentary. However, in general, finding a judicial space in which to locate these acts so they can be policed is not straightforward. It seems that to inject criminality into any of the events described as sexting requires them to be repositioned as an event which has already been rendered illegal: child pornography. This necessitates the 'translation' of both the image and the parties involved in sexting into the kinds of image and kinds of subject that child pornography laws regulate. The rest of this chapter is concerned primarily with the role of translation in the regulation of consensual teenage sexting, the version of sexting that seems on the surface to be the least likely practice to involve questions of criminality.

The prevalence of sexting

Empirical evidence suggests that sexting is a practice many teenagers are aware of (Phippen 2009). However, other empirical research suggests that the actual practice of teenage sexting may not be as common as some commentators would suggest. In the USA, Mitchell et al. (2007) conducted a random sample survey of 10- to 17-year-olds and concluded that most requests for sexts came from adults to young people rather than from members of their own peer group, and that such requests were received by around 4 per cent of their respondents in one 12-month period. A large-scale survey by Livingstone et al. (2010) of 11- to 16-year-olds in the UK established that 12 per cent had received sexts from peers and 4 per cent had sent them, a level of engagement similar to that found by Lenhart (2009) in the USA amongst 12- to 17-year-olds. So, although the work by Phippen (2009), for example, found a high percentage of 11- to 18-year-olds in their survey indicated they knew about sexting and knew of incidences of people sexting, the actual level of engagement in the practice by individuals may be quite low.

Whether or not sexting is a common practice or more a common idea, as Bond (2010a, 2010b) notes, in her work on the role of mobile phones in the sexual lives of young people, young people use texting as spaces and sites for 'doing' being sexual, performing their sexual identities, and formulating and realizing sexual aspirations, desires and longings. She likens this to the idea of teenage sexual encounters 'behind the bike shed'. Her work suggests that young people themselves see sexting as a generally unremarkable part of the everyday sexual lives of their age group, and that they were unconcerned about consensual sexting of erotic images. However, they expressed strong disapproval of unauthorized circulation of sexts. So, the moral limits set by young people are organized around consent and dissent rather than content of the sexts. Other work also suggests that young people are not particularly exercised by pictorial displays of sexuality, situating them as acceptable acts of intimacy or simply as acts of bravado in more public displays of sexual self-images (Bond 2010a; Lenhart 2009; Phippen 2009). This suggests a peer group normalization of the idea of sexting independent of how common it is in practice. This normalization is reflected in some suggestions that consensual sexting is a digital version of 'normal' teenage sexual life practices of sending (explicit) love letters (Day 2010: 1; Wood 2010: 1), or that it is a practice intrinsically bound up with intimacy and should be understood as such (Slane 2010). These normalizations stand in contrast to media and expert portrayals of consensual sexting as warranting concern, anxiety and intervention.

Regulating teenage sexting

Despite empirical research suggesting relatively low levels of teenage sexting, it has been the subject of considerable official response. The use of the law to police teenage sexting where it is consensual is not an obvious move. The use of child pornography laws in the USA to control teenage sexting, including consensual sexting, has resulted in young people being prosecuted for the making, distributing and/or viewing, or possession of child pornography. For example, in Florida in 2009 (cited in Jolicoeur and Zedlewski 2010: 7) the state prosecuted a 16-year-old girl and her 17-year-old boyfriend for the production, direction and promotion of child pornography following the discovery on their phones of sexts they had only shared between the two of them.

To address the question of how it is possible for consensual sexting to be regulated as child pornography I will focus on a case in Tunkhannock, Pennsylvania, USA, drawing on the Court accounts of this case (*Miller v Pennsylvania*, Injunction 2010;[2] *Miller v Pennsylvania*, Opinion 2010[3]).

In 2008 a teacher in a school in Tunkhannock confiscated some students' mobile phones and discovered on them pictures of female students from the same school in which they were nude, semi-nude or 'scantily clad'. Following this discovery the school passed the pictures to the District Attorney (DA), who then threatened the students identified in the pictures and those who had them on their mobile phones with charges for the possession and distribution of child pornography unless they attended probation and completed a programme of 're-education'. Three of the girls and their parents refused this and challenged the circumstances in which they were threatened with a felony offence. The girls argued that their pictures were not pornographic – they consisted of two girls in their underwear, one making the 'peace' sign and the other talking on her mobile phone, and a second picture of a girl, with a towel around her waist (and hence topless), who had just come out of the shower. This counter-interpretation of the images allowed the girls to portray the taking of the pictures and the pictures themselves as a form of the self-expression which is protected under the First Amendment. The parents' arguments were made against the re-education programme on the basis that this compromised their rights as parents under the Fourteenth Amendment to 'direct their children's upbringing' (*Miller v Pennsylvania*, 2010 Injunction: 10). The girls also challenged the re-education programme requirements on the basis that it required 'compelled speech', against which they were protected by the First Amendment, which provides that 'Government action that requires stating a particular message favored by the government violates the First Amendment right to refrain from speaking' (*Miller v Pennsylvania*, 2010 Opinion: 25-6). These arguments were upheld and a permanent injunction was issued restraining the DA office from pursuing the prosecution of the three girls.

This example contains several important points concerning the legal regulation of consensual teenage sexting. First, it is an example of how positioning images as child pornography produces the images and all associated actions (production, possession, dissemination) as criminal acts. In actor-network theory terms, the images are translated into the kind of event that the law deals with: one that involves harm or disgust. This translation, however, requires a number of elements: the images have to register as pornography, the subject of the images has to register as a child, and the production, distribution and/or viewing of the images have to be of the same mode as found in child pornography. It is, however, also an example of a failure of that translation.

In the USA the law that criminalizes child pornography comes out of a series of legal cases (*New York v Ferber*, 1982, 458 U.S. 747; *Roth v United States*, 1957, 354 U.S. 476; *Osborne v Ohio*, 1990, 495 U.S. 103; *United States v Williams*, 2008, 553 U.S. 285) and, as Humbach (2010) shows, these established that sexual images of children are not images which have the protection of the First Amendment[4] under any circumstance. Unlike adult pornography, which can enjoy First Amendment protections providing it is not legally deemed obscene (as established under *Roth v United States*, 1957, 354 U.S. 476 and *Miller v California*, 1973, 413 U.S. 15), an image of a child (under 18 years of age) in a sexual situation or pose is always exempt from the protection of the First Amendment and so is prosecuted without reference to questions of obscenity (Humbach 2010: 446). Further, a ruling in *New York v Ferber* in 1982 (458 U.S. 747) provided that the production of child pornography by definition involves a child (or children) being harmed and this outweighs whether or not the image would meet the test of obscenity set down in relation to adult pornography. This means that US law considers that a sexualized image of a child is always a depiction of some form of child sexual abuse or sexual exploitation. In 1990 following *Osborne v Ohio* (1990, 495 U.S. 103) the courts ruled that the possession and viewing of child pornography creates a further harm since it is not only a continuation of the original abuse of the child in the image, but it also creates a commercial market for its production, creating further future victims (Humbach 2010: 452). Thus the range of offences that can be prosecuted cover the production of the image, its distribution and its viewing. All of these offences are serious felonies and carry the possibility of sex offender registration.

However, such absolutes still leave open the question of what constitutes a sexualized image of a child in the first place, and the definition of child pornography does vary from state to state (Jolicoeur and Zedlewski 2010), although all have in common the centrality of the person depicted being under the age of 18.

This construction of child pornography as a crime on the basis of the age of the person depicted in a sexual pose is what enabled the DA in the Tunkhannock case to pursue charges against the young people for their sexting acts, even though no crime was recorded by the images. This positioning of the consensual sexts within the reach of the laws which prohibit child pornography involved three key translations: translating the images into pornographic images of children; translating the girls' agency into incompetence; and translating the boys and girls into perpetrators of a crime.

In respect of the first translation, the images were of minors so the key translation required the images to be recognized as sexualized images remained.[5] If this is accomplished the girls' claims to freedom of expression (and hence protection of this under the First Amendment) is negated since if the images meet the definition of child pornography there can be no protection of expression. This then affords the second translation: the girls' agency into incompetence. The establishment of the images as child pornography reshapes the girls' decision to take the pictures into a decision to engage in self-harm by choosing to be victims of a crime. The legitimacy of the girls choosing to portray themselves in a particular way is thus negated.

If the girls are the subjects of child pornography images, however, determining who to prosecute is a problem since the girls are then in the role of victims and yet they created the images, i.e. they are perpetrators of the child pornography offence. Here a third translation occurs which divorces the authors of the sexts from the subjects of the sexts (even though they are one and the same) and locates these authors (the girls) in the network of legal action as perpetrators for producing the images and distributing them, and the boys as perpetrators as viewers and/or further distributors of the images. The status of victim is removed.

These translations are central to the operation of law in this case since, without them, consensual sexting does not warrant criminalization – there is no harm to the participants, there is no entry into a market of exploitation, and no illegal sex act has been committed or is portrayed as having been committed. Without this translation into child pornography and the repositioning of the girls and boys as perpetrators, consensual sexting is not available for this kind of formal regulation.

When the DA offered an exit from this network of legal regulation via probation and attendance on a re-education programme, the refusal of this created a resistance to the translations the legal regulation required and as such they opened up the possibility of the sexting act being outside the reach of current law. The assertion of the right of parents to determine the upbringing of their children draws the child away from the grasp of the state. The claim for rights to uncompelled speech insists on the state's own protection of the citizen from undue interference being accorded to children. The contestation of what does and does not constitute erotic or sexually provocative poses challenges the authority of the state's determination of what is or is not sexually arousing in this case. This is an alternative translation of sexting and in this move the legal regulation of sexual acts is ousted from being at the centre of a network of official actors, and in its place are the rights of the citizen to freedom of expression and protection from undue interference.

There are further alternative translations which can be effected, or for which arguments have been made. These alternatives rely on yet other positionings of the act of sexting within juridical networks or the relocation of sexting into an alternative network of informal regulation. The US law positioning relies on the age of the subjects of the images as the key point of departure for reframing sexting as child pornography. The alternatives rely on enrolling privacy rights into the legal network (in the case of an argument made from Canada), or enrolling the concepts of risk and futures into a network of educationalists and parents with the police as associated actors (as in the UK), leaving the law on the margins of the network as an actor-in-waiting.

Making sexting look like privacy violation?

In contrast to the USA, no cases in Canada to date have prompted legal response on the scale of the main cases reported in the USA. However, Canada is of interest because its operation of privacy legislation affords an alternative approach to the legal regulation of consensual teenage sexting. In Canada the translation of sexting for regulation via child pornography legislation does not necessarily require the production of the subject of the images as either a victim or a perpetrator in the first instance, nor the production of the recipient of the images as a perpetrator for viewing the images. Canada still uses child pornography legislation to regulate sexting but, as Slane (2010) shows, primarily where the consent of the subject of the images has been breached through unauthorized distribution of them by the initial recipient. I draw heavily here on Slane's paper to illustrate how alternative translations could be/are accomplished in differently configured networks.

Slane argues that in Canada there is scope for a dignity-based approach to sexting which combines protections against harms with rights to bodily integrity. She makes her case in relation to sexting via two positionings of sexting teenagers, and differentiations between sexting practices. With respect to teenagers, one position is as citizens who enjoy privacy rights under Human Rights legislation and the other as persons whose sexuality is expressed through romantic and intimate acts. Jolicoeur and Zedlewski (2010) and Day (2010) have also positioned sexting as being rooted in romance and intimacy, and this is echoed by Slane in her argument. This positioning of teenagers in networks of romantic love grants them sexual autonomy and rights to intimacy. This means that arguments for privacy rights can be applied where sexts are located in acts of romance and intimacy. The findings of the survey by Jolicoeur and Zedlewski (2010) supports this romantic ontology to consensual teenage sexting: 69 per cent of sexts are sent to boy/girlfriends, 39 per cent to someone the sexter has dated and 30 per cent to someone the sexter would like to date. Slane argues that, under Canadian law, this opens up a space for the protection of consensual teenage sexting through the legal principles which provide for the protection of reputation (Slane 2010: 50). This protection means that a right to moral and physical integrity is not lost when images are made public without consent. She contrasts this to the USA position on privacy which allows for the right not to be subject to public exposure in the first place, but which offers no protection once public exposure has occurred.

So, under Canadian Law, according to Slane, it is possible that only the circulation of a sext beyond the intended recipient is a matter for the law in respect of the maintenance of the original subject's right to privacy. In contrast, under US law, the production and sending of the consensual sext is a crime in the first place, and further unauthorized circulation of it is not protected under privacy laws. For example, in the Florida case cited earlier, an appeal by the girl defendant to the Florida Supreme Court which argued that the state had no right to violate the privacy of the two consenting sexting defendants was rejected on the basis that the couple had no 'expectation of privacy when it comes to nude photographs' (A.H. v Florida 2007 cited in Jolicoeur and Zedlewski 2010: 8). This ruling was based on the view that taking pictures of sexual activity involved the creation of a record which could potentially be shared with others and this potential mobility of the photographs excised the context of privacy in which they were made. Day (2010) also reinforces this point. Put simply in US law, once a photograph is taken one cannot imagine it is possible to always keep it private hence it cannot be protected by privacy legislation. Slane argues that the Canadian position is different.

This alternative legal approach is possible in Canada because the network in which the law performs includes privacy and intimacy as 'non-human actors' (Lee and Stenning 1999) by which I mean that concepts of privacy and intimacy form part of the legal network. Brown and Capdevila (1999: 40) argue that the agency of objects can be conceptualized where 'an artefact disrupts the space in which it is placed'. Non-human agency does not involve intentionality, only the capacity for an artefact to change what occurs in a network, sometimes expressed as the capacity to create 'folds' in the network which bring different parts of it into proximal relation, be that in time or space. Actor-network analyses require a symmetrical consideration of human and non-human actors. So ideas of, and claims to, privacy and intimacy and the performance of privacy and intimacy can be understood as actors in the Canadian regulatory network but not in the US networks. Where privacy is part of the network which produces teenage sexting for legal governance it locates consensual sexting as a private, intimate act which can therefore be outside the reach of the law. At the same time this creates a legal space for the subject of the images to be considered a victim of a crime if a sext is distributed to a wider audience without consent. In addition, if the sext is shared with others outside the intimate setting without authorization, then the person who breached the sharing consent becomes a perpetrator of a crime, albeit a crime of child pornography not a crime of privacy violation. So, who and what is/is not within the reach of the law changes depending on whether the sext remains in the intimate domain or is distributed beyond that without the agreement of the original author.

The few prosecutions of teenage sexting in Canada have been primarily brought in respect of a consensual sext being distributed maliciously by the recipient to a wider audience without the author's consent. These prosecutions tend to have been brought in situations where the malicious distributor has been an adult who was in an intimate relationship at some point with the author. In *R v Walsh* (2006, cited in Slane 2010: 54), for example, Walsh was a 23-year-old male who circulated sexts he had been sent by his 15-year-old girlfriend following the break-up of their relationship. He sent the photographs on to at least one friend, who then further distributed them to others, including the family of the girl and her school peer group. The judge determined that Walsh was guilty of child pornography offences on the basis that his intention in distributing the pictures was to gratify his own desires, even if they were desires for revenge at the girl ending the relationship rather than sexual desires, and the result was an offence against the girl's 'dignity-based privacy interests by treating her as a degraded sexual object rather than respecting her as a person' (quoted in Slane 2010: 56). So, as in the cases in the USA, child pornography laws were used to bring a prosecution, but here the charge was concerned with the non-consensual distribution of the sext, not the original production and sharing/viewing. This translation into a child pornography crime was accomplished via legal protection of the dignity of the subject. The unauthorized distribution of the images violated the dignity that the author of the sexts could reasonably expect to be preserved at the time of making and sending the sext to her boyfriend. In effect, the unauthorized distribution recontextualized the images such that they now constituted child pornography, given that they were images of a minor and were circulated for reasons of gratification by another. In the context in which they were originally produced, an intimate relationship, they could not be framed as child pornography as they were private and consensual. As Slane (2010: 56) notes: 'Cases of malicious distribution fit most easily within the existing conception of harm set out in the child pornography jurisprudence.' However, she also notes that police discretion is extensive with regard to whether or not prosecutions for this are taken forward, and that many cases of malicious distribution by younger people are dealt with by diversion into the juvenile welfare system.

In this approach, concepts of privacy and intimacy effect legal protection of consensual sexting and militate against breaches of consent. The translation of a sexted image into a child pornography image occurs when the image leaves the intimate shared space without consent. The distributor is then translated into the perpetrator subject position, and the subject of the image gains the protections afforded to the victim of the crime. This alternative translation is accomplished by privacy and dignity operating as actors in the legal networks, in contrast to the US cases where they are kept outside that particular network.

Making sexting look like risk?

Child pornography laws in the UK also allow for consensual teenage sexting prosecutions,[6] as in the USA. However, such prosecutions have not been pursued in the UK to date. Instead, the main response has been orientated to non-legal mechanisms of control, and organized around ideas of risks and the future well-being of the young person as opposed to criminality. Media reports are a key element in this informal social control, acting as both a source of 'information' on sexting as a current phenomenon and as a key actor in producing it as a problem. For example, in 2009, the *Daily Mail* carried a report of an 'investigation' carried out by Penny Marshall, 'mother of three', into the prevalence of sexting amongst teenagers at a 'prestigious school'. Her report focused on what she considered the nonchalant acceptance of sexting as a normal practice amongst the teenagers and she raised concerns about their lack of awareness of the implications and risks of what they are doing. She also raised the spectre of ignorant parents who lack Internet skills, concerns about the acceptance of pornification by the current young generation, and in wider society more generally, and the loss of innocence of childhood – the latter a theme which is not uncommon when adults are considering questions of sexuality and young people or children (see Kitzinger 1988).

Other reports have focused on the prevalence of sexting, although often reporting quite differing rates, with headlines such as 'Sexting Boom' (*Daily Star* 2011), 'One in Four Pupils Swap Porn Images of Themselves' (Loveys 2011), 'Sexting Youths Dial up a Storm' (*Sunday Times* 2009). A more lengthy piece in the *Guardian* summarized the general media position: 'You don't know what sexting is?: texting explicit photographs has become a common part of courtship among teenagers. But the consequences can be tragic' (Barbieri 2009). This latter article covered the campaign by the Beatbullying charity and focused on an account of the distress sexts can cause to recipients who don't want to receive them and to the subjects of sexts which are circulated without consent. It also reported teenagers' own views that sexting was normal and not a problem, and that it offered a safer way of engaging sexually with someone than physical contact.

Other reports also focus on bullying and danger. The *Daily Mirror* in 2009 (Ellis 2009) drew on a report by the campaign charity – Beatbullying – which focused on the coerced production of sexts within peer relations where the boy is cited in that report alongside warnings from police experts in the form of a report produced by the Child Exploitation and Online Protection Centre (CEOP) on the dangers of sexting as well. The views of Beatbullying and CEOP are repeated in other newspaper reports and, in addition, the *Daily Mirror* carried an article written by Lakeman (2009) – an Internet safety expert – about how paedophiles make use of consensual sexted images posted on social network sites.

Media reports of the dangers of sexting also focus on the dangers of consensual semi-bounded sexting – posting of images on social network sites. The fear that is flagged up is that pictures can be accessed and downloaded by sexual offenders who are interested in grooming young people for illegal sex. This fear of predation was widely reported on the 5 August 2009 in UK newspapers: *The Times* headlined an article on sexting: 'Sexting Teenagers Drawn into Online Lair' with a sub-heading of 'Paedophiles trawl social networking sites' (Ahmed 2009: 15) whilst Ellis (2009: 31), in the *Daily Mirror*, reported a similar message from the police on the same day. *The Times* also cited a warning from an authoritative source, the police Child Exploitation and Online Protection Centre (CEOP), that ' … as well as blackmailing children with the pictures, paedophiles have also pretended that they are the person in the picture to snare another victim' (Ahmed 2009: 15). Regulation of this type of sexting practice is presented as falling within the domain of the police in respect of the images being used for the actual commission of a crime such as grooming (prohibited in England and Wales under sections 14 and 15 of the Sexual Offences Act 2003, and in Scotland under The Protection of Children and Prevention of Sexual Offences (Scotland) Act 2005), and within the domain of the police and 'Internet experts' as agents who have knowledge of how images circulate and are deployed on the Internet.

Whilst these warnings and concerns act together to create a climate of moral anxiety about sexting, the capacities of parents as moral managers of teenagers are portrayed as limited by their lack of knowledge about Internet matters. This perceived limitation is addressed directly in newspaper articles detailing advice to parents on how to govern their children's use of the Internet (e.g. Marshall 2009), whilst schools are pressed to develop better IT safety education programmes for their pupils (ibid.).

The school as a site for education on Internet safety and self-protection features extensively in many newspaper reports, and in addition school teachers themselves take on a role of warning of the dangers. For example, in 2010 the *Daily Mail* (2010) ran a headline announcing 'The Dangers of Sexting Added to Curriculum', and in 2011, the *Daily Telegraph* (Collins 2011: 13) headlined a report with 'Teachers Warn of Rise in Sexting' followed by a report that a teacher, head of Spanish, 'told MPs and school leaders at a Westminster Education Forum meeting that she was aware of a "gradual desensitization" among young people to sexual images being transferred between peers'.

An additional actor in this network of informal control is the unconcerned, risk-taking teenager. Barbieri (2009) makes reference to this formulation of the sexting teenager, as does the article by Marshall (2009) described earlier. Such views are in line with those reported by Bond (2010a, 2010b) and Phippen (2009) in their research, but young people holding these attitudes tend to be portrayed as naive or misguided rather than agentic, competent social actors.

Here, then, a third form of regulatory network is assembled which involves: the police, but in the context of their concerns about the activities of paedophiles rather than in their judicial regulation of young people; schools, in the context of their concerns about bullying, safety issues with respect to Internet 'predators', the moral domain of sexualization and 'pornification'; and parents, who are simultaneously positioned as concerned and as naive. Within this network time and anxieties about risks circulate to produce concerns about immediate dangers of harm, and risks to the future selves of the teenagers. Thus, consensual sexting is not performed in this network as a romantic or intimate act, nor as an expression of sexual identity, but as a product of a wider cultural degradation of society in relation to sexuality, or as acts of naiveté with respect to risk and danger, reflecting the incapacity of teenagers to make wise decisions for the future. In the UK consensual sexting has not to date been translated into questions of child pornography which need to be prosecuted, nor to questions of privacy rights and violations. Teenagers are positioned as pedagogical subjects who are slipping out from under the pedagogical relationships with schools and parents in which they should be located until they are able to act independently. This network of informal regulation is firmly located in the moral domain with legal actors providing expertise about the crimes linked to sexting, but not sexting itself as a crime.

Conclusion

The actor–network approach allows us to raise several questions about the processes by which the act of sexting enters into the legal realm and into other networks of governance. This approach invites us to consider how actors and networks produce consensual teenage sexting as a crime and/or an object of regulation, and the process by which regulation of a consensual act is accomplished. I have argued that in the US context pre-existing laws are complexly articulated with the age of the subject to sustain a translation of sexting as child pornography and hence make it available for criminal prosecution. However, this relies not only on law enforcement agents but also on the enrolment into the legal network of: teachers or other adults who confiscate/examine mobile phones without recourse to legal warrant (Wood 2010); moral views of what constitutes a sexual image of a young person; parents who comply with the legal view (as opposed to those who resist); and young people placed in subject positions which put them outside constitutional protections (a move which sometimes fails). Here the subjecthood of agentic teenage actors is evicted from the network and replaced by the deviant criminal subject(s) with no scope to consent to produce or share images of themselves in a sexual context. Under these conditions, sexting of any sort has scope to be a crime if the subjects of the image are under the age of 18 years.

The translation of consensual teenage sexting into child pornography is not, however, stable. Moves have been made in the USA in favour of translating teenage sexting into a crime that carries a less serious penalty than the current felony status accorded to producing, distributing and/or possessing child pornography (NCSL 2009, 2010, 2011; Weins and Hiestand 2009) which affords the possibility of imprisonment and registration on the sex offenders' register. In 2009, a bill was put forward that proposed to class sexting as a misdemeanour (U.S., H.B. 132, 128th Gen. Assem, Reg. Sess., Ohio, 2009 cited in Slane 2010: 58) and other examples have followed (although they still do not remove consensual teenage sexting from being a criminal offence, so the USA remains a jurisdiction which prosecutes consensual teenage sexting).

In Canada, consenting teenagers can be accorded a degree of sexual autonomy and agency in as much as they are free to share images of themselves with each other in the context of intimacy and romance. However, once the image leaves that intimate circle the actor who breached the consent is produced as a criminal and the subject of the image is then the victim of a crime. This legal approach is possible where privacy is an actor in the network of regulation. Consensual teenage sexting is thus not a crime, but breach of that privacy is. Age is rendered relevant for the victimhood status of the subject of the image if privacy is breached. Authorship and image remain integrated, unlike in the USA where they are divorced from each other to accomplish the translation of the subject of the image into a perpetrator.

A third alternative network is highly visible in the UK wherein educators, Internet safety experts, the police and parents produce sexting as a risky enterprise for future moments in the lives of young people. Risk is articulated with the age of the sexter and also with time in terms of imagined future consequences for the subject of the sext. Anxieties about this risk, and other more immediate risks such as being bullied or sexually preyed on through the image becoming publicly available, articulate with the perception that it is almost inevitable that a sexted image will escape the original bounds of consent and control. In this respect, the network produces and sustains anxiety and moral responses in place of criminality.

All three networks have at their centre the mobile phone with digital photographic capacity, the Internet, teenagers, sexual activity and sexual identity. And, yet, these actors are routinely decentred by adults and child pornography. At the same time, in the different networks and the different translations which those networks enact and sustain, consensual teenage sexting emerges consistently as a potentially troubling practice albeit troubling in different ways. Actor-network theory insists that divisions and differences are outcomes of the network, not features on which the network relies, and that the network itself limits the possible relations and characters of those things that are the outcome (Law 1999: 7). In other words, what a thing is 'can only be discerned by following the way it moves through encounters, relations and networks' (Brown and Capdevila 1999: 41). By approaching the regulation of sexting via some of the ideas from actor-network theory it is possible to see that the law, as an instrument of regulation, produces and is produced by a network that brings together institutional actors, technologies, 'aged' subjects and particular translations of a consensual act into criminal acts, but that differing actors in the network may lead to differences in how the legal regulation is effected. In contrast, other non-legal networks and actors generate translations of consensual teenage sexting which reproduce current anxieties about risks and the futures of young people, and decentre the law as a means of regulation in favour of moral regulation. Here teenagers emerge not as criminals but as innocents whose own naiveté makes them gullible, unruly, vulnerable and in need of pedagogical rescue.

Acknowledgement

My thanks to Geoff Cooper for suggesting the term 'sextualities' that is used in the title of this chapter.

Notes

1 For the sake of simplicity I retain the use of the term teenagers, but throughout this it refers to young people who are at least 13 years old but are below the age of majority.
2 *Miller v Pennsylvania*: Injunction, 2010 – United States District Court for the Middle District of Pennsylvania. No. 3:09cv540. Online. Available at http://www.jlc.org/files/ Order-for-Permanent-Injunction.pdf (accessed 17 August 2011).
3 *Miller v Pennsylvania*: Opinion, 2010 – United States Court of Appeals for the Third Circuit. No 09-2144. Online. Available at http://www.jlc.org/files/briefs/miller_opinion. pdf (accessed 17 August 2011).
4 The First Amendment includes a prohibition on any law being made which 'abridges' the freedom of speech. This is in effect a protection against government limitation of freedom of expression.
5 Given these self-authored images of the girls did not depict any sexual activity this translation was a challenge. The DA declined to explain his interpretation to the parents and the court did not concern itself with this question since they addressed the complaint that the DA acted with a retaliatory prosecution against the girls and parents for exercising their constitutional rights in refusing to agree to the probation and the re-education pro-gramme (*Miller v Pennsylvania*, Opinion: 31).
6 For England and Wales, see section 1 of the Protection of Children Act 1978, which regulates taking, distribution, possession and/or publishing of any indecent photograph or pseudo-photograph of a child under the age of 16; section 160 of the Criminal Justice Act 1988 which regulates possession of an indecent photograph of a child or pseudo-photograph; section 45 of the Sexual Offences Act 2003 which amends the Protection of Children Act 1978 to include children aged 17 and 18. For Scotland see section 52(a) M1 Civic Government (Scotland) Act 1982, which regulates the possession of indecent photographs of children.

Bibliography

Ahmed, A. (2009) 'Sexting' Teenagers Drawn Into Online Lair: Paedophiles trawl social networking websites', *The Times*, 5 August: 15.
Barbieri, A. (2009) 'You Don't Know What Sexting Is?', *Guardian*, 7 August: 18.
Bond, E. (2010a) 'The Mobile Phone = Bike Shed? Children, sex and mobile phones', *New Media & Society*, 13(4): 587–604.
——(2010b) 'Managing Mobile Relationships: Children's perceptions of the impact of the mobile phone on relationships in their everyday lives', *Childhood*, 17(4): 514–29.
Brown, S.D. and Capdevila, R. (1999) 'Perpetuum Mobile: Substances, force and the sociology of translation', in J. Law and J. Hassard (eds) *Actor Network Theory and After*, Oxford: Blackwell Publishing/Sociological Review.
Collins, N. (2011) 'Teachers Warn of Rise in Sexting', *Daily Telegraph*, 18 March: 13.
Daily Mail (2010) 'The Dangers of Sexting Added to Curriculum', *Daily Mail*, 9 March.

Daily Star (2011) 'Sexting Boom', *Daily Star*, 19 March: 16.

Day, T.R. (2010) 'The New Digital Dating Behavior – Sexting: Teens' explicit love letters: criminal justice or civil liability', *Hastings Communications & Entertainment Law Journal* 33(1), 69–95. Online. Available at http://Works.Bepress.Com/Terri_Day/6 (accessed 31 May 2011).

Ellis, M. (2009) 'Teen Sex Texts Found on Pervert Websites: Paedos pouncing on intimate snaps', *Daily Mirror*, 5 August: 31.

Henderson, P. (2009) 'Teens charged for nude texting', *Daily Telegraph*, 9 February: 13.

Humbach, J.A. (2010) '"Sexting" and the First Amendment', *Hastings Constitutional Law Quarterly*, 37(3): 433–85. Online. Available at http://ssrn.com/abstract=1470819 (accessed 31 May 2011).

Jolicoeur, M. and Zedlewski, E. (2010) 'Much Ado About Sexting', Document Number 230795, National Institute of Justice Report Discussion Paper, Online. Available at http://www.ncjrs.gov/pdffiles1/nij/230795.pdf (accessed 31 May 2011).

Kitzinger, J. (1988) 'Defending Innocence: Ideologies of childhood', *Feminist Review (Special Issue on Family Secrets: Child Sexual Abuse)*, 28: 77–87.

Lakeman, G. (2009) 'Generation Sext: Paedo warning to teenagers texting intimate pics to pals', *Daily Mirror*, 1 December: 33.

Lambie, D. (2002) 'Perverts use Phone Text to Lure Children', *Daily Express*, 8 September: 17.

Latour, B. (1987) *Science in Action: How to follow scientists and engineers through society*, Milton Keynes: Open University Press.

Law, J. (1999) 'After ANT: Complexity, naming and topology', in J. Law and J. Hassard (eds) *Actor Network Theory and After*, Oxford: Blackwell Publishing/Sociological Review.

Lee, N. and Stenning, P. (1999) 'Who Pays? Can we pay them back?', in J. Law and J. Hassard (eds) *Actor Network Theory and After*, Oxford: Blackwell Publishing/Sociological Review.

Lenhart, A. (2009) 'Teens and Sexting: How and why minor teens are sending sexually suggestive nude or nearly nude images via text messaging', Pew Internet and American Life Project. Online. Available at http://www.Pewinternet.Org/~/Media//Files/Reports/2009/PIP_Teens_And_Sexting.Pdf (accessed 31 May 2011).

Livingstone, S. (2008) 'Taking Risky Opportunities in Youthful Content Creation: Teenagers use of social networking sites for intimacy, privacy and self-expression', *New Media and Society*, 10(3): 393–411.

Livingstone, S., Haddon, L., Gorzig, A. and Olafsson, K. (2010) 'Risks and Safety for Children on the Internet', The UK Report, LSE London. Online. Available at http://www.eukidsonline.Net (accessed 31 May 2011).

Loveys, K. (2011) 'One in Four Pupils Swap Porn Images of Themselves', *Daily Mail*, 18 March 2011.

Mail Online (2011) 'Boy of 14 Accused of Child Pornography after Convincing Girl His Age to Send Him Sex Text', 6 March. Online. Available at http://www.dailymail.co.uk/news/article-1363445/Sexting-case-asks-14-year-old-child-pornogragher.html (accessed 10 August 2011).

Marshall, P. (2009) 'Generation Sexting', *Daily Mail*, 18 March.

Mitchell, K.J., Finkelhor, D. and Wolak, J. (2007) 'Online Requests for Sexual Pictures from Youth: Risk factors and incident characteristics', *Journal of Adolescent Health*, 41: 196–203.

Moran-Ellis, J. and Cooper, G. (2000) 'Making Connections: Children, technology, and the national grid for learning', *Sociological Research*, 5(3). Online. Available at http://www.socresonline.org.uk/5/3/moran-ellis.html (accessed 20 July 2011).

NCSL (2009) 'Year-end Summary of 2009 Sexting Legislation', National Conference of State Legislatures. Online. Available at http://www.ncsl.org/?tabid=17756 (accessed 9 June 2011).

——(2010) '2010 Legislation Related to "Sexting"', National Conference of State Legislatures. Online. Available at http://www.ncsl.org/?tabid=19696 (accessed 8 July 2011).

——(2011) '2011 Legislation Related to "Sexting"', National Conference of State Legislatures. Online. Available at http://www.ncsl.org/default.aspx?tabid=22127 (accessed 10 July 2011).

Phippen, A. (2009) 'Sharing Personal Images and Videos Among Young People', South West Grid for Learning. Online. Available at http://media.education.gov.uk/assets/files/pdf/r/10%20%20%20sharing%20personal%20images%20and%20videos%20among%20young%20people.pdf (accessed 11 May 2011).

Pilkington, E. (2009) 'Sexting Craze Leads to Child Pornography Charges', *Guardian*. Online. Available at http://www.guardian.co.uk/world/2009/jan/14/child-pornography-sexting (accessed 11 May 2010).

Powell, A. (2002) 'PC Bombarded Schoolgirl with Lewd Texts to her Mobile, Court Told', *Daily Mail*, 3 September: 31.

——(2010) 'Configuring Consent: Emerging technologies, unauthorised sexual images and sexual assault', *The Australian and New Zealand Journal of Criminology*, 43 (1): 76–90.

Sentencing Guidelines Council (2007) *Sexual Offences Act, 2003: Definitive guideline*, Sentencing Guidelines Council. Online. Available at http://sentencingcouncil.judiciary.gov.uk/docs/web_SexualOffencesAct_2003.pdf (accessed 8 January 2011).

Slane, A. (2010) 'From Scanning to Sexting: The scope of protection of dignity-based privacy in Canadian child pornography law', *Osgoode Hall Law Journal*, 48: 3. Online. Available at http://Ssrn.Com/Abstract=1800047 (accessed 5 May 2011).

Sunday Times (2009) 'Sexting Youths Dial Up a Storm', *Sunday Times*, 22 March: 12.

Weins, W.J. and Hiestand, T.C. (2009) 'Sexting, Statutes, and Saved by the Bell: Introducing a lesser juvenile charge with an "aggravating factors" framework', *Tennessee Law Review*, 77: 1–56.

Wood, R.H. (2010). 'The First Amendment Implications of Sexting at Public Schools: A quandary for administrators who intercept visual love notes', *Journal of Law and Policy*, 18: 701–37.

Part 4
Policing and the 'sex industry'

9

POLICING COMMERCIAL 'SEX WORK' IN ENGLAND AND WALES

Teela Sanders

Introduction

This chapter is intended to be a reflection on the 'busy' policy and legislative reforms that have taken place in England and Wales to govern, control and police the commercial sex industry. Here, I am dealing specifically with adult prostitution that takes place in the street sex work market, as well as indoor markets such as brothels. However, the focus of government has been largely on the street, and also on those men who buy commercial sex. This chapter will track the recent development (from 2000) of a criminalization agenda and examine the reforms (and the ideologies that underpin them) that have created a system of 'policing' with the objective of eradicating prostitution. Reflecting back on the historical legacies that have informed the current context, this chapter looks particularly at key policy and legislative activities, as well as providing a critical analysis of the consequences of a criminalizing approach on a vulnerable group of women in society. Finally, the consequences of this approach will be assessed within the wider context of 'responsibilization', 'risk' and 'forced welfarism'.

What is meant by policing?

As this book demonstrates, 'policing' is a fluid concept and set of practices. In this chapter, the term is used in two ways. First, I use it to denote the formal role of state police actions that are governed by the law and official guidance. Different tactics in policing will also be referred to, as these can sometimes be inconsistent and haphazard across England and Wales as individual police forces reflect different approaches and regimes in their attempt to manage prostitution. Elsewhere in this chapter, I use 'policing' to refer to other groups who are charged with the task of 'helping' vulnerable sex workers (often through criminal justice initiatives), but are in fact welfare agencies policing through interventions and assistance.

The importance of history: prostitution policy in context

Looking through an historical lens it is clear that we have not arrived at the state by which prostitution is managed in England and Wales without some influence from perspectives and laws that have gone before. Ostensibly, the 'common prostitute' has always been policed by the state through dominant pieces of legislation such as the Vagrancy Act 1824 and, later, a set of three Contagious Diseases Acts (1864, 1866 and 1869) that gave the police various powers to contain and lock up women they expected to be spreaders of diseases (see Self 2003 for an extensive account of the historical context). Whilst women involved in prostitution have historically been tarnished as vectors of disease and as 'deviants' (see Caslin 2010), there was a period of repeal as a more tolerant approach to sexuality appeared in the mid-twentieth century.

In some ways the relatively liberal treatment of the issue in the 1950s seems an out of reach era compared to contemporary approaches. Whilst there was the offence of living off the immoral earnings of prostitution under the Sexual Offences Act 1956, the benchmark for the prevailing decades regarding prostitution law was the Wolfenden Report (Home Office 1957) that also set out the reform to decriminalize homosexuality. The Wolfenden Committee made sharp distinctions between the public and private faces of prostitution, noting that 'public nuisance' was the business of the state as that constituted crimes of public decency. The concern with public nuisance led to the outlawing of street prostitution in the Street Offences Act 1959, for which heavy penalties were introduced for soliciting and loitering. But, as Day (2008: 51) discusses, upholding the difference between the street and the private realms of sexual activities between two consenting adults was an important distinction in law. Indeed, this distinction shaped the state of the sex industries and how they were policed (or not in the case of indoor sex markets) throughout the remaining twentieth century and up to very recent times.

The Wolfenden perspective was that private acts (of any form of sexual activities) were tolerated in law, leading to a demarcation that visible prostitution was not acceptable, but invisible commercial sex was not really the business of the state unless other crimes occurred. Day (2008: 53) neatly reflects how this law enabled women in the 1960s and beyond to find 'spaces of freedom' where they could carry on their sex work discreetly, as long as they were out of the public eye. What this did was to encourage the state to abdicate any responsibility for addressing prostitution as an income-generating activity or economic enterprise and to turn a blind eye as commercial sex went mostly underground. Indoor prostitution was pushed away to the sidelines of the informal economies, severed from any infrastructures or accountability by the state. This latter point, that 'sex as work' is not acknowledged by the state, is one of the few tenets that are currently visible in the management of prostitution in the current decade.

Recent history: leading up to the current blueprint

Whilst there was little state intervention and formal policing of the sex industry during much of the 1980s and 1990s, with vice squads being disbanded in the 1990s, the change of government to New Labour in 1998 heralded a new wave of state attention to 'the problem of prostitution'. Supported by two pieces of government-funded research into the relationship between drug markets and street prostitution (Hunter and May 2004) and reducing prostitution by getting women to leave it (Hester and Westmarland 2004), the first government consultation on prostitution, *Paying the Price*, was launched in 2004 (Home Office 2004).[1] As I have stated elsewhere (Soothill and Sanders 2004), the picture of prostitution and the direction of the reform outlined in *Paying the Price* did not engage any reflection on the historical legacy of prostitution; rather, it presented scattered misinformation about the nature and extent of the industry that created the great danger that the whole issue would be mismanaged. What started as a welcome opportunity to take stock of antiquated law, *Paying the Price* painted only the very harsh negative aspects of street prostitution, perpetuating myths that those involved in street work are always coerced, abused and at the hands of criminals and violent punters. The exercise was focused on 'doing something about prostitution' rather than reviewing the realities, complexities and options for the management of commercial sex in the UK. The intentions were about preventing prostitution, enabling women to leave and sanctioning those who stayed involved or fuelled 'demand'.

Official policing support is crucial when government tries to implement one-dimensional approaches to a 'problem'. The then Labour government received overt support from the Association of Chief Police Officers (ACPO) who, in 2004, made their first statement on prostitution policy in many years and declared that their focus would be to address the severe criminal activities that can be associated with prostitution – such as trafficking, corruption and extortion that lead to the physical and emotional harm of (mainly) women. ACPO (2004: 4) stated that, in focusing its attention in this area, it was making 'difficult operational choices necessary in a world of competing priorities'. Yet what was experienced, particularly at a grassroots level, was not policing practices focused on these highly criminal activities. Rather, individual women who worked on the street were targeted by Anti-Social Behaviour Orders (often issued under inequitable circumstances) and, when they breached these Orders because of the unrealistic and unobtainable conditions they set, they found themselves serving a custodial sentence for a non-imprisonable offence (see Sagar 2007). Located firmly within the newly established 'Crime and Disorder Partnerships', ACPO afforded visible street prostitution the status of an unwanted blight on society that should be tackled through criminal procedures. This standpoint is confirmed by the outright rejection by ACPO of other alternatives to manage street sex work, for instance through managed zones. Despite there being strong evidence that some partnerships between police, health authorities, residents and sex worker communities could work together to provide safer working conditions through managed zones, such solutions were not considered appropriate but instead law-breaking (Bellis et al. 2007).

Unlike in other European countries where the 'sex as work' discourse has been evident amongst debates in parliament (Hubbard et al. 2008; Kantola and Squires 2004), the UK parliamentary discussions have been burdened by an over-emphasis on drugs, public nuisance and disorder, and the horrors of those who buy sex. Little attention, in the formal discussions regarding prostitution, was given to why women enter into the trade, the link between poverty and social exclusion, or the realities of violence for many sex workers. Instead, the 'problem' was framed as one that could be linked to deviant and non-conformist women.

The *Coordinated Prostitution Strategy*

After accumulating over 800 responses to the *Paying the Price* consultation, in January 2006, what is now the blueprint for managing prostitution in the UK was published. The *Coordinated Prostitution Strategy* (hereafter, 'the Strategy'), set out the overall aim: 'to disrupt markets' through a three-pronged approach of deterring punters, accelerated routes out of prostitution, and preventing entry (Home Office 2006: 13). The multi-agency partnerships which were called upon to work towards eradication were given five areas of priority:

- *Prevention*: The first concern was that there was a considerable effort made from a range of cross-cutting agencies to prevent vulnerable people becoming involved in prostitution. Rightly, young people and children were flagged as particularly vulnerable to prostitution and early stage interventions were welcomed.
- *Tackling off-street prostitution*: Largely ignored in the consultation document, the Strategy states that there is also an official intention to reduce the activities of indoor sex work in order to 'disrupt the sex markets' overall (see Sanders 2007b). The welcomed aspects of this focus were the concentration on young and underage people who were sexually exploited in the sex industries (see Pearce 2006). Second, reinstating the need to police indoor markets appeared to be presented as driven by the need to address sex trafficking. As a result of this, two large-scale policing operations were conducted on the indoor markets, aimed at finding trafficked people. The outcomes of these were that very few people who were arrested defined themselves as trafficked, when they were indeed voluntarily involved.[2]

  Again, any forward-thinking solutions to managing indoor sex work in a safer way, such as making it legal for two women to work together in the interest of safety (originally proposed in the consultation document), were rejected for fear this would cause an explosion of brothels in suburbia. Instead, there was a focus on reinforcing the existing laws against brothels which threatened the status quo that had developed between policing agencies and sex work businesses, which rested on the police having a working understanding of, and often productive relationships with, sex workers in order to aid the investigation of serious criminal activities.
- *Developing routes out*: Whilst it was appreciated that sex workers needed more services and holistic long-term support to make changes, the emphasis here was that the criminal justice system would also be used to enable women to leave prostitution. Enforcement was seen to be a bedfellow with providing services, particularly for the women who were highly excluded from other services. Whilst recognition was given to the different health, welfare, housing, benefit and social support needed by women who have often experienced long-term disenfranchisement, no resources or funding was given to the agencies that were expected to work with this group.

- *Ensuring justice*: It was acknowledged that this group of women is amongst the most vulnerable in society, often experiencing violence and abuse on the streets. Three core objectives were set: enhancing personal safety; encouraging reporting and improving the response from the criminal justice system to victims of violent and sexual crimes; and a new guide to the law on effective investigating and witness support.
- *Tackling demand*: Negative experiences from communities were prioritized as the justification for enforcing the existing kerb-crawling legislation and a new approach was issued to enforce soliciting and loitering laws. There was renewed emphasis on stamping out kerb-crawling using the following tactics: informal warnings; court diversion (the widely criticized 'John's Schools');[3] and prosecution. For street workers, a more detailed arrest and prosecution process was to be used, ensuring that they were drawn closer into the criminal justice system. For the first time in recent history a new rehabilitation approach was taken to address loitering, which was later to appear in the statutes in 2010 as Engage and Support Orders (see below).

These five key priority areas set out the new wave of the formal policing of sex workers, both on and off the street, as well as those involved in purchasing sex (mainly 'kerb-crawlers'). Little new legislation was drafted as a result of the blueprint, with an emphasis put on intensifying existing powers that had previously been regarded as a low priority in policing.

The absence of male sex work

One theme in this chapter is the contradiction between the apparent gender neutrality of the laws and policy recently created to address prostitution, with the reality that in practice they are heavily biased to different genders at different times. Whowell and Gaffney (2009) explore how the *Coordinated Prostitution Strategy* ignores the presence and differences in relation to male sex work, demonstrating that the motivation to 'do something about prostitution' is entirely about female street prostitution that is seen as problematic. The historical legacy that has essentially focused on the deviant woman remains today, and the absence of the male sex worker in formal policy is incredible given both the presence of male sex work in cities and on the Internet (and contrasts sharply with the preoccupation of law enforcement officials with male homosexual sex in public places detailed in Chapters 1, 2 and 5). Whowell (2010) summarizes the ways in which men who sell sex are absent from the key documents and the impacts of the measures to regulate prostitution per se are not considered in relation to the male sex worker population. The male identity as a sex worker is ignored in policy and therefore any consideration for resources, interventions and even 'routes out' are framed towards female street sex workers. As a result of this absence in policy, the policing of male sex work, if at all, takes place through different guises and more often by assessing young men on the street as anti-social youths rather than as persons involved in nefarious commercial sex. This means that their vulnerability and potential safety issues are not recognized. Understanding this invisibility can only be done by examining further the construction of the male sex worker in popular culture, which is far removed from the deviant female 'whore' on which medical and legal discourses have been created.

Tackling demand: criminalizing the purchase

Earlier, under the Sexual Offences Act 2003, it was stated that henceforth law should be 'gender neutral', finally recognizing that law could not be designed 'for women' only. Whilst this did make important changes, such as finally removing the term 'common prostitute' from law (in the Policing and Crime Act 2010), it also paved the way for men who buy sex to be targeted as part of the broader efforts to eradicate prostitution. Prior to the New Labour relaunch of how prostitution is managed, Brooks Gordon and Gelthorpe (2003) documented the increasing police powers to arrest and prosecute men for kerb-crawling during the 1980s. The *Paying the Price* consultation document set out the parameter for which men who buy sex were to be treated and understood: 'every effort must be made to deter men from this activity, sending a clear message that it is seriously anti-social, that it fuels exploitation and problematic drug use, and that going to prostitutes contributes to the spread of HIV/Aids and STIs' (Home Office 2004: 97). The 'anti' message in terms of the 'demand' for prostitution was an easy target against a group of men that had little overt support in society or collective identity (see Brooks Gordon 2006; Sanders and Campbell 2007).

In 2008, the government ratcheted up the focus on 'demand', funding another six-month review: *Tackling Demand for Prostitution: A review* (Home Office 2008). This 'review' included a (cursory) summary of academic literature and visits from ministers to Sweden and the Netherlands to examine alternative systems. Kingston (2010: 26) describes the recommendations from this review as a mixture of public awareness of sex trafficking, anti-kerb-crawling messages, and a removal of the requirement of kerb-crawling to be 'persistent' before charged (hence reducing this to a first-time offence). This review was significant as it recommended that a new strict liability offence should be created which made it a crime to pay for sex with anyone 'controlled for another person's gain'. In reality this meant that anyone assisting consensual commercial sex would be committing a crime: so receptionists, drivers, partners and landlords would all fall under the 'control' definition even where activities were consensual.

There was much opposition to the blank introduction of a law which blatantly tried to outlaw paying for sex in a similar vein to the Swedish system. The outcry was heard, and a reworded version of the recommendation appeared in the Policing and Crime Bill 2009. It stated that it would be a crime to pay for sex from anyone who has been subject to 'force, deception, coercion or threats'. This is still a strict liability offence which essentially means that ignorance (i.e. not knowing that someone was forced) is no means of defence (see Kingston 2010 for a more detailed critique of this). The underlining principle that it is wrong to pay for sex, and something to be discouraged in a civil society, still remains at the core of the prostitution policy.

Anti-trafficking campaigns

The backdrop to domestic policing of prostitution are wider 'concerns' relating to sex trafficking. As in other countries, the idea of the 'forced prostitute' has become written into domestic policy as trafficking is translated into anti-prostitution policies and practices (see Weitzer 2010 referring to the USA). Equally, as there is confusion over the term and status of voluntary migrant sex workers (see Agustin 2006), all migrants who are in the UK to work in the sex industry are clumped together under the umbrella of trafficked victims. The lack of nuance in understanding those who voluntarily pay smugglers to enter the UK, or are consenting to their movement into the sex trade, means that operations to find victims of sex trafficking become raids that seek out migrant sex workers. For instance, Ward and Wylie (2010) describe how lap-dancing venues in Ireland were raided with the intention of seeking out trafficked women who were being forced to work there, yet the police could not find anyone that admitted to being forced, despite several different nationalities arrested. What we know from the most comprehensive research into migrant workers in the sex industry by Mai (2009) is that very few are actually forced and trafficked. This research acknowledges that there may be elements of exploitation and a lack of alternative choices to work in other industries because of limited citizenship and work rights, but this did not constitute trafficking.

Direct policing resources have been funnelled into policing prostitution borne out of real concerns that people are forced into prostitution. In 2006, the UK Centre for Human Trafficking was opened with the intention of making the UK a hostile environment for this form of organized crime. Set up as both a prevention agency and one to work in partnership with all other policing agencies, the emphasis was on investigating cases of prostitution where there were concerns about coercion. As the evidence shows (see Note 2), Operation Pentameter 1 and 2 found low levels of trafficking in the UK in comparison to what was expected. However, as such operations and investigations have resulted in small numbers of victims, it is argued that the laws to manage prostitution can be interpreted as laws to police migrant sex workers under the guise of international concerns with the problem of sex trafficking (see Andrijasevic 2010).

Policing through welfare

The upshot of the legislative and policy changes, coupled with a strong abolitionist message from government over the past decade, is that prostitution has been redefined as a 'social disorder'. What is more notable is that the raft of new anti-social behaviour mechanisms which have been used to control and constrain sex workers (see Sanders 2009a) demonstrates that the application of the new agenda has a specific gendered dimension. Most obvious are the Engage and Support Orders, (discussed below) which are the latest anti-social behaviour mechanism. These Orders are, in practice, only used to control women who are considered in need of forced treatment to desist from prostitution. As I have argued elsewhere (Sanders 2009a), these orders constitute 'forced welfarism' as they essentially act as a criminal sanction that orders women to make changes to their personal and private lives, and in particular their sexual behaviour. Whilst not unlike penal welfarism, which offers offenders the right to make changes and take up opportunities in prison, forced welfarism acts as a means of introducing coercive change in a community setting and for non-criminal activities. Forced welfarism ties coercion to behavioural change which is deemed by the courts to be in the welfare interests of the individual and for the benefit of the community. By insisting that women engage in an exit process, to rid themselves of a lifestyle of vice and decay, 'forced welfarism' is presented as a gentle persuasive measure to insist that women change for their own good (and that of their children) and to be rehabilitated back into the community (Sanders 2009a: 9).

The *Coordinated Prostitution Strategy* (Home Office 2006: 14) stated that 'this [namely the problem of prostitution] is a partnership issue' and lists the following agencies who should be involved in policing prostitution: community safety teams; local strategic partnerships; local safeguarding children boards; social services; health agencies; housing agencies; drug action teams; enforcement agencies; domestic violence organizations and job training agencies. This vast range of welfare agencies, many of which are either directly from the criminal justice system or increasingly funded through community safety partnership initiatives, is increasingly where the focus of intervention comes from. The widening out of policing to multi-agency partnerships has been heralded as a successful departure from previous approaches which involved a revolving door of arrests and fines (see Matthews 2005). However, this simplistic view of the impact of multi-agency policing of prostitution masks the realities of who is policed and how. Widening out the policing of vulnerable women to other agencies (some of which present as not part of the criminal justice system) only increases the number of agencies involved in the surveillance of sex workers and equally devolves social control mechanisms to non-statutory agencies.

Ultimately the UK now promotes a system of policing (of mainly street sex workers), through multiple agencies, using different mechanisms of control and constraint to simply remove women from the streets and a 'life of vice'. The consequences of focusing on removing individual women are that the underlining reasons why women enter into the sex industry, particularly the harsh environment of street prostitution, are not addressed. Scoular and O'Neill comment that the:

> Absence of analysis of the structures and processes that create and sustain particular sets of social relations that underpin involvement in sex work leads to partial analysis and the positioning of a partial subject, cast as a victim, whose agency to exit can be supported by welfare backed up by enforcement to exit.
>
> *(Scoular and O'Neill 2007: 769)*

Whilst the Orders are in their infancy, it is unknown what happens when women breach them (i.e. don't exit); but, like breaches of Anti-Social Behaviour Orders, this can result in custodial sentences (see Sagar 2007).

Theorizing these mechanisms, Scoular and O'Neill (2007) articulate how the rhetoric to assist sex workers, posited as attempts to remove them from marginalized positions and reintegrate them through a model of social inclusion, is in fact a disguise for gendered social control practices. Reflecting the wider agenda of New Labour that set out to responsibilize those who were not active citizens, or indeed acted 'uncivil', the 'progressive governance' model moves away from state police but instead uses welfare agencies to provide 'help', which in reality is the checking, surveillance and constraining of women. Responsibilization, Scoular and O'Neill (2007) argue, is presented as protecting vulnerable victims from risk. Sex workers are constructed as 'risky subjects' undertaking risky sexual practices and decision-making about their lives. Women who work on the street are usually drug users and, as Malloch (2004) neatly documents, the concepts of responsibilization for drug users have been gendered around risky behaviour and offending. Scoular and O'Neill summarize the effects of the individualization of risk:

> Consequently, material realities and structural exclusions recede from official attention, which, instead, becomes focused upon individual needs and in protecting women from risk. Hence the very realities of violence and vulnerability are not the focus of policy but instead removing uncivil individuals from streets and communities is the priority.
>
> *(Scoular and O'Neill 2007: 770)*

Engage and support orders

These orders were introduced under the Policing and Crime Act 2010. They are compulsory orders which are given to those street sex workers who are arrested three times and hence considered 'persistent' offenders. There is no element of voluntary engagement or active participation in the programme, which essentially ignores the growing body of literature that highlights the long-term complexities of making changes to a lifestyle of prostitution (see Cusick and Hickman 2005; Sanders 2007a; Baker et al. 2010). The Order sets out three meetings that the individual is expected to attend with a suitable practitioner and demands that they must show progress in addressing their (now defined) 'criminal' behaviour. Whilst this may well be probation services, other third sector organizations who already work with sex workers may tender for this work. On the one hand this is positive as the surveillance will be carried out by those practitioners who are well aware of the deep-rooted nature of a lifestyle of prostitution and the entrenched issues that are associated with leaving it. However, the contradiction is that those organizations, which may well have sex worker rights and empowerment as their ethos, become servants of the criminal justice system, ultimately engaged in a process of checking, insisting on change and notifying courts if this has not taken place within the allocated time framework. While it is well established how the penal system is the ultimate means of surveying the body (Foucault 1977), it is the contemporary reinforcement of this focus and control of the undeserving docile body through criminal justice interventions that demonstrates the gendered dimensions to policy developed under the New Labour government.

Again, policing by third parties that are not directly the state is the modus operandi that seeks to control the practices of a small group of women. This is indeed intense policing, as the numbers of women who will receive Engage and Support Orders are most likely to be small and concentrated in specific city locations. This highly gendered policy that is part of the 'clean up the streets' agenda (Hubbard 2004) ignores key issues for sex workers such as safety and the realities of sex work which will most likely persist during the Order. Resources are criminal justice agency led, with little new resources allocated to other interventions outside the criminal justice system.

How can this form of policing through rehabilitation orders be understood? Whilst sex workers are not the only group of 'uncivils' who are subject to specific orders which target their individual behaviour, it is the Engage and Support Order that explicitly targets female sexual behaviour. Harrison and Sanders (2006) understand this form of social regulation by looking at the dynamic relationship between structure and agency. In this case, labelling behaviours 'anti-social' *and* 'vulnerable' at the same time justifies further exclusion, incarceration and inequalities of treatment. Welfare support is offered alongside disciplinary mechanisms as individuals are expected to be responsible for their lifestyle and actions which are often out of their control. Where there is no evidence that individuals are conforming or on a path to change, they are threatened with withdrawal of welfare or indeed incarceration as the final option. In what Dwyer (1998) terms the age of 'the conditionality of welfare', support is only offered with deterrence, containment and discipline. Indeed, in the case of prostitution, this gendered surveillance and control is in fact coercion to 'change' and 'exit' a lifestyle to become 'better' and move from being a 'bad' to a 'good' woman.

Conclusions: consequences of social control practices

Those scholars, practitioners and activists who have engaged in the responses to government, organized campaigns, spoken to ministers and lobbied MPs and the House of Lords over the past decade have been motivated by the damaging consequences of abolitionism and criminalization. Not always, but often located in a sex worker rights framework, drawing on human rights principles and a pragmatic approach to safety, scholars have highlighted the negative consequences of the framework of criminalization for sex workers (e.g. see Goodyear and Cusick 2007; O'Neill 2010; Phoenix 2008; Scoular et al. 2007). Key concerns are the effects of heavy policing on street prostitution as women move away from traditional areas and do not use trusted tactics to keep themselves safe as their priority lies with getting off the street to do business. Whilst it has been evidenced that in the UK the indoor markets are relatively safer than the street (Sanders and Campbell 2007), with the remit to 'disrupt the sex markets', coupled with immigration-based policing of the brothel industry, those working and managing indoor sex work are under threat and scrutiny. This is a departure from how the indoor sex industries have been discretely managed for the past fifty years, as brothels were often tolerated under certain compliant conditions and cooperation with the police (see Sanders 2005, chapter 5). Now, in all

areas of sex work, there is suspicion of the authorities because of the fear of criminalization, presenting particular issues in terms of engaging vulnerable women with
health and social care services. With no evidence of any change in approach under
the new UK Conservative–Liberal Democrat government since their arrival in 2010, the
existing remit of criminalization and using Engage and Support Orders to 'rehabilitate'
wayward women seems to have a foothold for the future.

What is certain and evident from this review of policy is that the New Labour
government set out to eradicate female prostitution by using several aspects of formal
and informal policing, surveillance and forced welfare. To justify and indeed
normalize this intense intervention of a relatively minor criminal activity, there has
been a process of redefining what prostitution is. By defining the activity as a 'social
disorder', and those involved as sellers, buyers or organizers as 'uncivil' and in need
of rehabilitation through mechanisms in the criminal justice system, intense policing
activities have gone relatively unchallenged. There was little emphasis on voluntary
engagement but instead forced change through orders and rehabilitation programmes.
There most certainly has been a revolution in the amount of legislation, guidance,
policies and initiatives targeted at this phenomenon but, as Day (2008: 57) states,
the 'revolution in prostitution control, however, is repressive and discriminatory
overall'.

The context of prostitution policy with its abolitionist tones and desires to achieve
eradication of commercial sex needs to be considered within the broader context of
the criminalization of sexual relationships and behaviours since the 1990s (see
Phoenix and Oerton 2005, for a review of different spheres where regulation has
been introduced). Over the past decade there has been a return to drawing sexual
relationships between consenting adults into the criminal justice system through laws,
policing policies and practices as well as welfare agencies taking on an increasing role
of the third arm of the state. Attempts to invert and control behaviours that are
considered 'anti-social' and therefore risky can be documented across different groups
and activities. For instance, Johnson (2007) discusses how under the Sexual Offences
Act 2003 the offence of 'sexual activity in a public lavatory' was reintroduced, specifically to target male homosexual cottaging activities. Regulating public sexual
behaviour is continually a concern of the police yet is not gender-neutral in the way
policing operates, but targets cruising and cottaging done by gay men (see Chapters 2,
3 and 5). Wider concerns about the 'pornographication of society' through Internet
availability of explicit sex and sexual images, led to calls for further legislation to ban
all pornographic images as 'extreme' images under the Criminal Justice and Immigration
Act 2008 (which has been referred to as the 'Dangerous Pictures Act') (Attwood
and Smith 2010). Furthermore, a Home Office commissioned report by Dr Linda
Papadopoulos on the sexualization of children spread hyper-concern about the ways
in which children are overexposed to sexual images, leading to severe consequences
regarding gendered expectations and male dominance. Debates around the report
called for legislation to be used to limit, curb and reduce imagery and viewing
for children, showing how the criminal justice system and legislative powers are
considered the first response for regulation.

Taking these examples, and that specifically of prostitution policy (with its emphasis on criminalization and the criminal justice system), the mechanisms employed to solve the 'problem' are part of a broader neo-liberal governmentality anxious about that which is not neatly part of the rhetoric of civility. This anxiety leads to social sorting practices which are both oppressive and counterproductive, as individual behaviour is the target rather than structural problems which contribute to the behaviour. However, social control practices of the most vulnerable become legitimated when they are masked as protection. Narratives of the 'anti-social' morph into that which characterize individuals as risky and a threat to society as concepts of vulnerability and risk are drawn together. It is under these conditions that state and other policy proliferates probably more so than ever in the history of prostitution management, whilst at the same time women involved in commercial sex remain marginalized, vulnerable and outcast.

Notes

1 Concurrently the Scottish government (2004) were also in consultation on the paper 'Being Outside: Constructing a Response to Street Prostitution'.
2 Operation Pentameter 1 in 2006 visited 515 premises and found 188 potential victims of trafficking; 88 were confirmed as trafficked persons, including 12 under the age of 18. Operation Pentameter 2 in 2008 searched 822 premises and found 167 confirmed trafficked persons, 13 aged 14–17; 528 arrests were made resulting in 88 charges relating to human trafficking (CPS 2006; Brain 2008).
3 'John's Schools' are the common name for kerb-crawler rehabilitation programmes. For detailed critiques see Campbell and Storr (2001) and Sanders (2009b).

Bibliography

ACPO (2004). *Policing Prostitution: ACPO's policing strategy and operational guidelines for dealing with experience and abuse through prostitution*. Association of Chief Police Officers. London: Home Office.

Agustin, L. (2006) 'Migrant Sex Work and Trafficking', in R. Campbell and M. O'Neill (eds) *Sex Work Now*, Cullumpton: Willan.

Andrijasevic, R. (2010) *Migration, Agency and Citizenship in Sex Trafficking*, Basingstoke: Palgrave.

Attwood, F. and Smith, C. (2010) 'Extreme Concern: Regulating "dangerous pictures" in the UK', *Journal of Law and Society*, 37(1): 171–88.

Baker, L., Dalla, R. and Williamson, C. (2010) 'Exiting Prostitution: An integrated model', *Violence Against Women*, 16(5): 579–600.

Bellis, M.A., Watson, F.L.D., Hughes, S., Cook, P.A., Downing, J., Clark, P. and Thomson, R. (2007) 'Comparative Views of the Public, Sex Workers, Businesses and Residents on Establishing Managed Zones for Prostitution: Analysis of a consultation in Liverpool', *Health & Place*, 13(3): 603–16.

Brain, T.J. (2008) 'Report of the Chief Constable'. Online. Available at http://www.bran deis.edu/investigate/pol/trafficking/docs/Report%20of%20Gloucestershire%20Con-stabulary%20about%20Operation%20Pentameter%202.pdf (accessed 28 May 2011).

Brooks Gordon, B. (2006) *The Price of Sex: Prostitution, policy and society*, Cullompton: Willan.

Brooks Gordon, B. and Gelsthorpe, L. (2003) 'Prostitutes' Clients, Ken Livingstone and a New Trojan Horse', *The Howard Journal*, 42(5): 437–51.

Campbell, R. and Storr, M. (2001) 'Challenging the Kerb Crawler Rehabilitation Programme', *Feminist Review*, 67 (Spring): 94–108.

Caslin, S. (2010) 'Flappers, Amateurs and Professionals: The spectrum of promiscuity in 1920s Britain', in K. Hardy, S. Kingston and T. Sanders (eds) *New Sociologies of Sex Work*, Farnham: Ashgate.

CPS (2006) 'Report of Operation Pentameter', July. Online. Available at http://www.cps. gov.uk/Publications/docs/pentameter_0706.pdf (accessed 16 January 2012).

Cusick, L. and Hickman, M. (2005) '"Trapping" in Drug Use and Sex Work', *Drugs: Education, prevention and policy*, 12(4): 369–79.

Day, S. (2008) 'Wolfenden 50: Revisiting state policy and the politics of sex work in the UK', in V. Munro and M. Della Giusta (eds) *Demanding Sex: Critical reflections on the regulation of prostitution*, Aldershot: Ashgate.

Dwyer, P. (1998) 'Conditional Citizens? Welfare rights and responsibilities in the late 1990s', *Critical Social Policy*, 18 (57): 493–517.

Foucault, M. (1977) *Discipline and Punish: The birth of the prison*, Paris: Gallimard.

Goodyear, M. and Cusick, L. (2007) 'Protection for Sex Workers', *British Medical Journal*, 334: 52–3.

Harrison, M. and Sanders, T. (2006) 'Vulnerable People and the Development of "Regulatory Therapy"', in T. Newburn, A. Dearling and P. Somerville (eds) *Supporting Safe Communities: Housing, crime and communities*, London: Chartered Institute of Housing.

Hester, M. and Westmarland, N. (2004) '*Tackling Street Prostitution: Towards a holistic approach*', London: Home Office.

Home Office (1957) *Report of the Committee on Homosexual Offences and Prostitution* (Cmnd 247), London: HMSO.

——(2004) *Paying the Price: A consultation paper on prostitution*, London: HMSO.

——(2006) *Coordinated Prostitution Strategy*, London: HMSO.

——(2008) *Tackling Demand for Prostitution: A review*, London: HMSO.

Hubbard, P. (2004) 'Cleansing the Metropolis: Sex work and the politics of zero tolerance', *Urban Studies*, 41(9): 1687–702.

Hubbard, P., Matthews, R. and Scoular, J. (2008) 'Regulating Sex Work in the EU: Prostitute women and the new spaces of exclusion', *Gender, Place and Culture*, 15(2): 137–52.

Hunter, G. and May, T. (2004) *Solutions and Strategies: Drug problems and street sex markets. Guidance for partnerships and providers*, London: Home Office.

Johnson, P. (2007) 'Ordinary Folk and Cottaging: Law morality and public sex', *Journal of Law and Society*, 34(4): 520–43.

Kantola, J. and Squires, J. (2004) 'Discourses Surrounding Prostitution Policies in the UK', *European Journal of Women's Studies*, 11(1): 77–101.

Kingston, S. (2010) 'Intent to Criminalize: Men who buy sex and prostitution policy in the UK', in K. Hardy, S. Kingston and T. Sanders (eds) *New Sociologies of Sex Work*, Basingstoke: Ashgate.

Mai, N. (2009) *Migrant Workers in the UK Sex Industry: ESRC findings*, Institute for the Study of European Transformations, London: Metropolitan University.

Malloch, M. (2004) '"Not Fragrant At All" Criminal Justice Responses to Risky Women', *Critical Social Policy*, 24(3) 385–405.

Matthews, R. (2005) 'Policing Prostitution: Ten years on', *British Journal of Criminology*, 45(6): 877–95.

O'Neill, M. (2010) 'Cultural Criminology and Sex Work: Resisting regulation through radical democracy and participatory action research (PAR)', *Journal of Law and Society*, 37(1): 210–32.

Papadopoulos, L. (2010) *The Sexualisation of Young People Review*. Online. Available at http://www.drlinda.co.uk/pdfs/sexualisation_review.pdf (accessed 17 April 2012).

Pearce, J. (2006) 'Finding the "I" in Sexual Exploitation: Young people's voices within policy and practice', in R. Campbell and M. O'Neill (eds) *Sex Work Now*, Cullompton: Willan.

Phoenix, J. (2008) 'ASBOs and Working Women: A new revolving door?', in P. Squires (ed.) *ASBO Nation: The criminalisation of nuisance*, Bristol: Policy Press.

Phoenix, J. and Oerton, S. (2005) *Illicit and Illegal: Sex, regulation and social control*, Cullompton: Willan.

Sagar, T. (2007) 'Tackling On-Street Sex Work: Anti-social behaviour orders, sex workers and inclusive inter-agency initiatives', *Criminology and Criminal Justice*, 7(2): 153–68.

Sanders, T. (2005) *Sex Work: A risky business*, Cullompton: Willan.

——(2007a) 'Becoming an Ex-Sex Worker: Making transitions out of a deviant career', *Feminist Criminology*, 2(1): 1–22.

——(2007b) 'No Room for a Regulated Market? The implications of the co-ordinated prostitution strategy for indoor sex industries', *Community Safety Journal*, 6(1): 34–44.

——(2009a) 'Controlling the "Anti Sexual" City: Sexual citizenship and the disciplining of female sex workers', *Criminology & Criminal Justice*, 9(4): 507–25.

——(2009b) 'Kerbcrawler Rehabilitation Programmes: Curing the "deviant" male and reinforcing the "respectable" moral order', *Critical Social Policy*, 29(1): 77–99.

Sanders, T. and Campbell, R. (2007) 'Designing Out Violence, Building in Respect: Violence, safety and sex work policy', *British Journal of Sociology*, 58(1): 1–18.

Scoular, J. and O'Neill, M. (2007) 'Regulating Prostitution: Social inclusion, responsibilization and the politics of prostitution reform', *British Journal of Criminology*, 47(3): 764–78.

Scoular, J., Pitcher, J., Campbell, R., Hubbard, P. and O'Neill, M. (2007) 'What's Anti-Social About Sex Work? The changing representation of prostitution's incivility', *Community Safety Journal*, 6(1): 11–17.

Self, H. (2003) *Prostitution, Women and Misuse of the Law: The fallen daughters of Eve*, London: Frank Cass.

Soothill, K. and Sanders, T. (2004) 'Calling the Tune? Some observations on "Paying the Price: A consultation paper on prostitution"', *Journal of Forensic Psychiatry and Psychology*, 15(4): 642–59.

Ward, E. and Wylie, G. (2010) 'Lap Dancing Clubs and Red Light Milieu: A context for sex-trafficking of women to Ireland?', in G. Wylie and P. McRedmond (eds) *Human Trafficking in Europe*, Basingstoke: Macmillan.

Weitzer, R. (2010) 'The Movement to Criminalize Sex Work in the United States', *Journal of Law and Society*, 37(1): 61–84.

Whowell, M. (2010) 'Male Sex Work: Exploring policy in England and Wales', *Journal of Law and Society*, 37(1): 125–44.

Whowell, M. and Gaffney, J. (2009) 'A Co-ordinated Prostitution Strategy and Response to Paying the Price: But what about the men?', in J. Phoenix (ed.) *Regulating Sex for Sale: Prostitution policy reform in the UK*, Bristol: Policy Press.

10

THE 'PROBLEM OF TABLETOP DANCING'

Antonia Quadara

Introduction

Prostitution businesses have been legal in the state of Victoria, Australia, since 1986. In 1994, new legislation was introduced that further treated prostitution like any other trade (though with a much higher degree of regulatory requirements). Police are involved in policing the industry to the extent that operators (i.e. managers and owners) run foul of, or are clearly operating beyond, the legislative framework. Such situations range from the plainly prohibited (i.e. street-based sex work; employing underage workers) to practices that contravene the legislation, such as operating a brothel without a licence, serving alcohol, not meeting certain occupational health and safety (OH&S) standards, or having an interest in more than one brothel. Relative to other Australian states, police powers for controlling sex workers and the industry are fairly restricted (Quadara 2008). Thus, the central mechanism that controls prostitution is the Prostitution Control Act (PCA) 1994. It defines: *what* a 'sexual service' is; the *type* of business that can provide it; *who* can be involved (as a worker or an operator); and *where* such businesses can be located. This chapter is not about prostitution; it is about tabletop dancing. It reflects on the emergence of tabletop dancing in Melbourne and how it was seen as undermining the capacity of the PCA to be that central control mechanism.

The effectiveness of the legislation depends on recognizing which activities are sexual services and so subject to the provisions of the Act, and those activities, which, although sexual in nature, comprise some other aspect of the sex industry (i.e. adult entertainment, which is controlled through planning permits and liquor licensing conditions). In 1999, the definition of 'sexual service' was expanded in order to ensure that illegal prostitution was not occurring through tabletop dancing venues. Any club where it was determined that sexual services were provided would lose its liquor licence.

However, the problem that tabletop dancing presented was not simply about the ways in which it was a conduit for illegal (i.e. unlicensed) prostitution. At the heart of the media and policy debates was the capacity of tabletop dancing to blur the central distinction between *looking* (the strip club) and *touching* (the brothel). As one man said of the effects of having attended a tabletop dancing club: 'My first reaction upon leaving the venue was one of wanting to reach out touch and be touched.'[1] It is this blurring and the anxiety it occasioned that is the focus of this chapter. Specifically, it is how this blurring revealed the male desiring body at the heart of commercial sex – and the extent to which controlling it is really about concealing this body – that is my interest. Now, it may seem obvious that men and their desires are at the heart of commercial sex. Yet, it has not been their bodies that have been policed (see Chapter 9). Frameworks for controlling commercial sex – from pornography to stripclubs to prostitution – result in economies of desire in which men's access to and consumption of women's sexual (ized) services are concealed. Whether the model is prohibition, legalization or decrimi-nalization, what has typically resulted is a subterranean sexual economy in which men's bodies have remained unmarked, and almost invisible. In other words, such classification and policing is invested in the production of a gendered and bounded commercial sex economy. As has been amply demonstrated by the research literature, this economy has put the body of female sex workers under a harsh disciplinary gaze while the male desiring body (i.e. the client) remained invisible and unproblematic (Allen 1984; Godden 2001).

The collective anxiety over tabletop dancing stems precisely from the way men's bodies and desires became visible to this regulatory framework. The nature of tabletop dancing – its closeness, its explicitness – combined with alcohol, pulsing music, dim lights, mirrors and 'lots and lots of [the] young wiggling flesh'[2] of dancers circulating the club produces two things. On the one hand, a carefully crafted space of gendered relaxation (Frank 2003), which offers both more and less than climaxes. This is more ambiguous than sexual arousal by just watching naked women. Tabletop dancing venues are spaces of fantasy and 'counterfeit intimacy' (Wood 2000), in which dan-cers create an illusion for men: sexually available, welcoming, sexually interested in them, attentive, flirty – *and* they get naked. Hence, more than a strip, since it's also about stroking the male ego in a world that no longer caters exclusively for him, but less than a service because masturbation and orgasm are not meant to be provided. On the other hand, this space has the potential to produce an 'unruly' male body upon his exit to the city street – aroused, sensitized, inebriated. Indeed, one concern about tabletop dancing venues in city areas is their link to violence between groups of drunk men leaving clubs, as well as how these titillated men threatened the safety of women who are 'legitimately' going about their business (i.e. not dancers) because they cannot control the urge to reach out and touch. Underlying these public safety concerns – which ultimately becomes the remit of police – are assumptions about the nature of (hetero)sexual desire. Namely, that aroused men are uncontained men and that this is a natural consequence of seeing naked women. Thus, perhaps it is better to have 'gratified' male bodies (i.e. arousal/erection/ejaculation/closure) rather than titillated male bodies (i.e. arousal/deferred gratification/no closure). This points to broader cultural scripts about (hetero)sex, men's entitlement to it and women's role in rationing it. Such scripts inform law enforcement and criminal justice responses to men's sexual behaviour and sexual violence.

The first section of this chapter describes how 'the problem of tabletop dancing' was framed within sites of public discourse, namely print news media and parliamentary debate. The second section analyses the parliamentary debate over the amendment bill for an expanded definition of sexual service to see just how the law necessarily polices sex, bodies, gender and desire in controlling prostitution. The final section examines how the properties of tabletop dancing undermine the self-evidence of 'sexual service', and bring a desiring male body into the open.

The problem of tabletop dancing

In the early 1990s, a new type of adult entertainment arrived in Melbourne's Central Business District (CBD), which was viewed as doing something different than 'simple' stripping due to the explicitness of the dance and the proximity between dancer and customer. Dances are performed on tabletops, stages and within customers' immediate personal space, and can feature open-leg work and the removal of all clothing, including G-string. As a carefully crafted space of gendered relaxation (Frank 2003) tabletop dancing offered both *more* and *less* than sexual gratification. From the early 1990s to 1999, the 'both more and less' troubled city officials and state government. Tabletop dancing, they declared, was a problem. However, over the six years in which tabletop dancing was debated as a social issue – about which something needed to be done – the kind of problem it represented changed from one of civility and public order to one of law.

Tabletop dancing's combination of explicitness, proximity and alcohol at first generated concern about the state of Melbourne as a 'capital' city. Media coverage began in 1993, where tabletop dancing was described as 'the new American craze'.[3] News headlines proclaimed that the city must 'Keep the street life out of the gutters'[4] to ensure that it would not become a 'seedy city'.[5] Articles explained 'How sleaze entered the city's mainstream'[6] and heralded a 'city sex trade attack',[7] while others fretted: 'Is Melbourne the right place for a naked city?'[8] and 'Should this be banned in the CBD?'[9] These concerns were met at first with a number of 'public order' controls. For example, liquor licensing requirements were intensified, changing from the same requirements as any other hotel, to with an additional 14 requirements specified. Following this, several venues had their operating permits revoked and were required to go through the Victorian Civil and Administrative Tribunal to have them reinstated. This gave the city an opportunity to close some venues down altogether. The register at which these discursive practices operate involve notions such as the right of citizens to enjoy the amenity of the city, public order and civility. Whether such activity was permissible under law (its legality) was not yet at issue. Indeed, early parliamentary debates about the proliferation of tabletop dancing venues in King Street did not recognize the disruption necessarily as a juridical one.[10] An early editorial on the problem of King Street pointed to the proliferation of tabletop dancing venues, stating 'although there is no suggestion these new flesh clubs are doing anything illegal, their arrival will do nothing to ease the problems'.

By 1999, this had changed. The issue was now about the way tabletop dancing blurred the distinction between service and entertainment. Three somewhat contradictory problems were identified by the government. First, it was suggested that illegal prostitution was taking place via tabletop dancing venues. The argument presented by the Attorney-General at the introduction of the bill, was whether tabletop dancing venues 'can or do lead to acts of prostitution', that is, whether tabletop dancing venues were conduits for prostitution. The purpose of the new definition was, in part, 'to reduce the likelihood of such entertainment functioning as a channel into the prostitution industry'.[11] In other words, the redefinition would ensure the integrity of Victoria's business licensing system for sex work.

Second, tabletop dancing muddied the distinction between 'service' and entertainment. The PCA regulates what is arguably a narrow slice of commercial sex, for under the umbrella of 'sex-industry' falls a wide range of activities: bondage and discipline providers, production and distribution of pornographic films, magazines, books and sex toys, and sexually explicit entertainment – peep shows, stripping and tabletop dancing. The PCA defines the parameters and sets up the relations not only of what constitutes prostitution, but also creates a zone of approach in which the distance of other actions and behaviours are judged as being either closer to, or further from, 'sexual service'. What is not considered a sexual service, falls to other legislation, for example the Liquor Control (Reform) Act 1998, Summary Offences Act 1966 and the Planning and Environment Act 1987. Hence, it is essential to maintain the distinction between 'service' and 'entertainment', since other regulatory mechanisms depend on it.

Related to this, a third problem emerged: confusion over the nature of 'service' itself. The practice of tabletop dancing encouraged 'titillation' rather than 'gratification', thus it was seen to be increasing violence around the King St area and in the workplace because, it seemed, men *weren't* being sexually satisfied:

> As I said, customers go to brothels, pay their money and, to use a well-known phrase, take their choice. However, with sexually explicit entertainment, which is normally held in licensed venues, customers arrive expecting to be entertained … People drink copious quantities of alcohol. The entertainment at those venues is sexually explicit. One could argue that sexual gratification is provided by peep-shows but may not be provided by lap dancing. People leave the venues tanked up but not having had the sexual gratification they thought they would.[12]

Given that sex work in Victoria is so thoroughly regulated through legal statute, the definition of 'sexual service' is absolutely crucial. Law is fundamentally a system of classification. Thus the anxiety over tabletop dancing's blurring of the lines. Prior to the problematization of tabletop dancing it was a relatively simply exercise – at least technically – to tell the difference between forms of sexual exchange or, in the language of regulation, to distinguish which providers needed to obtain a licence under the Prostitution Control Act 1994 from those who were required only to conform to general venue licensing controls.

As noted, these problems were to be resolved through the PCA and specifically through an expanded definition of 'sexual service', which would, it was argued, capture the 'more and less' of tabletop dancing. A Foucauldian reading of this solution sees it as an exercise in codification. Law is characterized by its penchant for coding bodies (human and inhuman) and the relations between them according to a variety of classifications, for example as analogous (comparative relationships), dichotomous (binary relationships) or series (sequential relationships). This process is one of capture and containment, abstraction and concretization. A feminist reading would add that this is a codification which instantiates (hetero)sexual difference. The next section briefly expands on the significance of governmental regulation of commercial sex.

Governments and the regulation of prostitution

When introducing the amendment bill into parliament, the then Attorney-General reflected on the significance and consequences of regulating sex and the role of sexuality for the modern subject:

> The question one must ask is: why legislate to cover sexual activity at all? Sexuality is legislated all the time, but one must ask why? ... Sexuality affects absolutely everything we do. There is a constant dichotomy between ration-ality and instinct, objectivity and emotion, and mind and body. It is important to focus closely on sexuality because it has such a powerful impact on the way we dress, the way we talk, the action we take and so forth ... We as a society have decided that prostitution is an activity that should be licensed ... to bring it out in the open and let everyone see it and to make rules and regulations about it.[13]

However, more than a simple or passive exercise to control some natural force as this reflection seems to suggest, legislating sex actively produces the object of regulation itself. Foucault's analyses of government regulation of bodies, behaviours and their interactions as the modern form of power are familiar, and I will not rehearse them here. Suffice to say that it was through the control and containment of various 'improper' populations that modern *forms* of power were articulated to *objects* of that power – bodies, behaviours or biopower – and *rationalized politically* as the purpose of government and the mechanism by which individual and social health are achieved (biopolitics).[14] Sexuality in particular becomes an arrangement through which power operates: 'Through the themes of health, progeny, race, the future of the species, the vitality of the social body, power spoke of sexuality and to sexuality; the latter was not a mark or symbol, it was an object and a target' (Foucault 1990: 147). These insights describe how the body and its capacities – including its sexual and desiring capacities – are articulated to the philosophy and machinery of the modern state. For Foucault, this political rationality does not just control bodies, it actively produces bodies and makes more or less possible the type of connection it has with other bodies.

The remaining discussion in this chapter outlines the new definition of sexual service that was debated. The debates demonstrate an assumed naturalness and obviousness about what sex 'is'. My question here is what kind of sexed bodies are produced through and underwrite this self-evidence. Following this, I consider how tabletop dancing disrupts this self-evidence and how, going back to the idea of both more and less, tabletop dancing reveals the male desiring body the prostitution regulation has historically tried to conceal.

Solving the 'problem of tabletop dancing'

As indicated earlier, the nature of the problem that tabletop dancing presented for Melbourne changed, and it was only later in the public debate that the problem became one of what exactly – in terms of the paradigm reflected through the PCA – tabletop dancing was: a service or a form of entertainment? Parliament evidently decided that it fell somewhere between the two. The legislative solution was to expand the definition of 'sexual service' such that a range of more 'interactive' behaviours could constitute a service. Thus, the definition went from 'taking part in an act of sexual penetration within the meaning of Subdivisions (8A) to (8G) of Division 1 of Part 1 of the Crimes Act 1958; and masturbating another person' (Prostitution Control Act 1994 s.3), to include this:

c) permitting one or more other persons to view any of the following in their presence

   i. two or more persons taking part in an act of sexual penetration;

   ii. a person introducing (to any extent) an object or a part of their body into their own vagina or anus;

   iii. a person masturbating himself or herself or two or more persons masturbating themselves or each other or one or more of them in circumstances in which

   iv. there is any form of direct physical contact between any person viewing the occurrence any person taking part in the occurrence; or

   v. any person viewing the occurrence is permitted or encouraged to masturbate himself or herself while viewing and for the purposes of this definition, a person may be regarded as being masturbated whether or not the genital part of his or her body is clothed or the masturbation results in orgasm.[15]

In addition, the payment of admission fees to these clubs constitutes payment for the sexual service. This amendment, referred to as Clause 4 in the debates, was one of six others being debated at this time.

This definition is remarkable for its breadth. What it now includes within its purview are viewing acts of live sex between one or more people, masturbation and penetration (including self-penetration), where there is *any* physical contact between *any* person viewing this or where the viewer is allowed or encouraged to masturbate themselves while viewing (and note the scope of masturbation). However, the parliamentary debate did not necessarily regard this breadth as a problem. Ostensibly, the issue of tabletop dancing and the parliamentary debates generated was concerned with closing a 'loophole' through which 'many illegal brothels had opened via tabletop dancing'. Some noted that, although it appeared broad, underneath it all we know what sort of behaviours we mean. Others disagreed. My interest in the next section is to determine just how it is that, despite the expansion, it is self-evident what a sexual service is.

Defining 'sexual service'

Speaking of the philosophical debates around the moral defensibility in selling sex, Satz (1995: 65) makes the observation that there is a tendency to treat sex 'as if the term referred to something as obvious as "table"'. What we see in the parliamentary debates about Clause 4 however is, on the one hand, a tendency to treat commercial sexual exchange as though it were perfectly obvious what 'sex' is, and on the other, a concern about the breadth of the definition and anxiety that 'government was opening a can of worms'. The shadow Attorney-General said of the Clause:

> It is an extremely broad definition ... [Issues have been raised] whether ... widening of the definition will have a more extensive impact than first thought. The broadened definition of 'sexual services' will encompass some of the peepshows which – where someone pays money to watch a person strip, which encourages that person to masturbate – and which currently do not come under the umbrella of the prostitution control legislation. For example, gay saunas will come under the definition of premises that provide sexual services. Such premises will in future be required to conform with the stringent requirements of the regulations under the Prostitution Control Act. Activities such as peep-shows should not be included in the wider definition of 'sexual activity'.[16]

The Attorney-General responded:

> It is in fact not complicated ... the definition of sexual services is clear. If the audience participates in the sexual acts that are part of so-called peepshows or floor shows, the house is a brothel and should be licensed. It is important to remember that the government is not saying that activities of that kind cannot occur; rather, it is saying that the whole philosophy behind the bill is that prostitution and brothels need to be brought out into the open and licensed so that they can be controlled. If the activity is effectively prostitution, and everyone knows that it is prostitution despite the façade, it has to be licensed. Everything else flows from that – the health inspectors, the inspections relating to crime, and so on. It is a simple process.[17]

The 'obviousness' of sex was invoked as a counter-argument to these concerns and the Attorney-General put forward this formulation:

> If it is purely a strip, it is not covered by the bill, unless there is interaction between the stripper and the members of the audience. It could be that

members of the audience are encouraged to masturbate, or it could be that members of the audience are invited to come up and take part in a sexual activity.[18]

What we can infer from this is that live sex shows and shows such as vibrator strips are the proper targets of the legislation. The ability to identify these occurrences is, as Dean states, 'simple', based on clear understandings and principles. However, there is nothing in the legislation itself to suggest such limitation since its language suggests that any person participating in, or any person viewing, a wide array of genital-based sexual activities in venues where an admission fee has been paid, is effectively a brothel. Hulls's reference to gay saunas makes this plain. There is no logical reason, given the legislation, why an event such as SEXPO[19] cannot be considered a prostitution service provider. Yet the rejoinder to these concerns refuses any possible ambiguity inhering in the definition. It does this by drawing on the truth of sex. That is, while language may complicate matters, the 'meaning of things' underpinning words are clear. Further, this meaning – or rather the things themselves – is known by all; we all are able to recognize an activity as prostitution 'despite the façade'.

What is the 'meaning of things' referred to here, the truth of sex behind the facade of language and context that will ensure the expanded definition does not capture the wrong kind of bodies, desires and relations? Perhaps law itself could offer some clarity.

Adjudicating 'sexual service'

Although rare, the meaning of 'sexual service' for the purposes of regulation has not gone entirely without legal consideration. In *Rowell v City of Yarra* (1994, 14 A.A.T.R)[20] the breadth of 'sexual service' was discussed and, contrary to Dean's sentiments, the definition of 'sexual service' as it stood prior to the amendments described as a 'vague, difficult and doubtful concept'. In part, the tribunal members suggested that this was a result of the inferior drafting of the definition. It was also a result of the width and variety of services that can be considered sexual within everyday culture:

> In ordinary English, sexual services is a fairly wide concept extending far beyond intercourse and masturbation. A striptease show in front of an audience would, we would have thought, be a service, and, indeed, a sexual service. It is the undressing and subsequent nudity or near nudity of a striptease show that makes it interesting to an audience and this is an element of a sexual nature, whether or not the performance has any other merit of an artistic kind. We would distinguish a striptease show from a performance in legitimate ballet, opera or drama where nudity or undressing may be justified as part of a genuine artistic performance. Even a much more minor thing might be regarded as a sexual service. Would the lending of a pornographic magazine not be a sexual service? Indeed, if done for money, would it not fall within this definition?[21]

These reflections serve to further obscure what might fall into the definition of 'sexual service', since it is being suggested that the realm of the sexual extends far beyond what is intended by the definition, or indeed what could possibly be included within the codes of law. It also make two contradictory statements, insofar as it suggests on the one hand, that what is sexual – what makes it interesting to an audience – resides in the act of getting naked itself, regardless of whatever else is intended. Yet it simultaneously asserts the classic separation between artistic (legitimate and genuine) forms of nudity, which would not fall into sexual service, and nudity for the sake of sexual interest, raising the question of just where 'the sexual' resides (see Chapter 7). The members seem to be saying that it is at once a property of nakedness, yet this is somehow counteracted by the context of artistic performance. As it is with Clause 4, the 'meaning of things' is less than clear, and the question thus becomes 'if everything that can be fairly described as "sexual services" is too wide for the purposes of this definition, how then is the concept of "sexual services" in this context to be read down?'

In having regard to a range of common law cases, the members ask whether physical contact is a valid criterion in establishing 'sexual service'. A criterion such as this would mean that viewing sexual acts where there is a partition separating patron and performer would not be defined as a sexual service (so what is envisaged here are venues and clubs where performers might engage in forms of sexual penetration or masturbation, and patrons are invited to view this from a private and partitioned room offering the opportunity to masturbate to climax). Similarly, it would potentially include situations such as 'a kissing booth at a church fair' at least, as the tribunal qualifies, when that kissing is on the lips, belly dancing and 'other erotic dancers' who sometimes touch or invite touching by the audience. As far as the tribunal goes, neither example 'would amount to prostitution in any ordinary sense of the term, and we do not really think that either of them would be intended to be included within the Planning Scheme definition of prostitution'.[22] In *Rowell*, the provision of privacy, plastic buckets and tissues are significant insofar as the patron 'is provided with an opportunity and an invitation (implicit or explicit) to achieve sexual gratification and sexual climax'. It is this criterion that is used as the test for establishing 'sexual service' and is treated within the case as settling as much as possible what sexual service might entail:

> The alternative test then is that 'sexual services' in the definition should be read down to services which provide an opportunity and invitation to attain sexual gratification and sexual climax … On this basis penetration and masturbation by one person of another would be included, but so would other situations which might not necessarily requiring [sic] physical touching.[23]

The 'meaning of things' thus becomes – it is hoped – clear: it is in the words of Catharine MacKinnon (1989: 325), 'whatever it takes to make a penis harden and shudder'. In other words, we know it's a sexual service because there is an erection and ejaculation. Thus 'sexual service' refers to a closed circuit of desire/arousal/erection/ejaculation/departure. This closed circuit which acts to conceal male desiring bodies within the commercial sex industry is elaborated on in the next section.

Concealing male corporeality and desire

The self-evidence of sexual service is self-evident to the extent that it expresses a hydraulic masculine desire. Following the logic of *Rowell* it is the circuit of male orgasm – arousal, stimulation, climax – this signifies a 'sexual service'. In contrast to the constant seepage of women that must be policed – breast milk, menstruation, pregnancy – and sex workers as vectors of disease, there is no acknowledgement of a masculine corporeality which is also fluid; it is as though men had no blood, urine, semen coursing through their bodies.[24] Although *Rowell* seems to make semen a central part of recognizing when a sexual service has taken place, and which venues were in this regard brothels, it is not semen, however, but ejaculation which is the key term here. Ejaculation is an *action* of the penis, a completion of arousal, and confirmation not only of masculine potency, but willed arousal. Seminal fluid on the other hand resides within the male body, incomplete, virtual, its actualization not always expected.[25]

Semen has thus largely been absent from discourses of sexuality, and is instead 'understood primarily as what it makes, what it achieves, a causal agent, and thus a thing, a solid' (Grosz 1994: 199). Within such a seminal economy, 'purely a strip' is somehow empirically different from a tabletop dance, and this from a sexual service. What is being instituted is a model of masculine sexuality that is classically hydraulic. That is, it is 'getting hard and getting off' that designates that something has been exchanged, that a service has taken place (at least up until the amendment). This reflects not only a masculinist order of desire, but a social imaginary of embodiment per se:

> Part of the process of phallicizing the male body, of subordinating the rest of the body to the valorised functioning of the penis, with the culmination of sexual activities occurring, ideally at least, in sexual penetration and male orgasm, involves the constitution of the sealed-up, impermeable body.
>
> *(Grosz 1994: 200–201)*

A sealed-up impermeable body is essential to the understanding of sexual service as a form of contractual exchange. The service contract that is the model for prostitution turns the *completed* circuit of male orgasm into a legal concept. This has informed the state's response in that sex workers are defined by their function, i.e. having sex with men.[26] What is most visible in the current terrain of commodified sex then is not men's desire for it and their purchasing of it, but woman as the cause, receptacle and locus of male desire. That is, the sex worker has stood in for both parts of the exchange and has been surveilled accordingly.

'Closing the loophole' or opening a 'can of worms'?

To return, then, to the question of what the loophole is that Clause 4 attempts to close. The previous section demonstrated that 'sexual service' is a territorialization of sexed spaces, marked by thresholds of value. The feminine body, and particularly parts of it (e.g. genitals, breasts), becomes complicit, discursively, with the tumescence and unity of penis. The Prostitution Control Act 1994 as a regulatory exercise attempted to keep the circuit of the consumption of the feminine complete and discrete (i.e. gratification/climax), for it is this discretion that permits distinctions between sexual economies, allowing private reproductive romantic sex to be normalized as the true and the good (and the free of charge), but allows the commercial non-reproduction sex to remain concealed, and within which the desiring masculine subject remains invisible. The problem of tabletop dancing when it arrived was that that circuit of pleasure is not closed, but deferred:

> Under the current Prostitution Control Act a brothel has no liquor licence and no alcohol is provided on the premises. One assumes that customers arrive at brothels in relatively sober frames of mind, pay sums of money, and one would argue obtain sexual gratification. They get what they pay for and walk away … However, with sexually explicit entertainment, which is normally held in licensed venues, customers arrive expecting to be entertained … People drink copious quantities of alcohol. The entertainment at those venues is sexually explicit. One could argue that sexual gratification is provided by peepshows but may not be provided by lap dancing. People leave the venues tanked up but not having had the sexual gratification they thought they would. That has happened in some tabletop dancing venues. They are indirectly providing a sexual service and are therefore illegal.[27]

The concern presented here is rather different from the argument presented by the Attorney-General at the introduction of the Bill, where the language used suggested that the issue was whether tabletop dancing venues 'can or do lead to acts of prostitution' – that is, whether tabletop dancing venues were conduits for prostitution. The above diagnoses a different problem: there is something in the performance itself that functions like a service. Indeed the presentation of the problem is intriguing. On the one hand, the problem with tabletop dancing is that customers are *not* gratified; on the other, the problem is that customers get *more* than what the performance itself provides. The more relates both to the libidinal excesses of explicitness, liveness and proximity and to the very gendered 'leisure space' such venues provide. Describing the relationship between the activities within tabletop dancing venues and their effects as indirect, yet also as a type of gratification, suggests a proximal, impersonal zone between clients and dancers that is more than their own participation, something the legislators were aware of in naming admission fees 'payment' for sexual services. Somehow, whatever is exchanged within tabletop venues, it cannot be contained between the direct parties. In other words, libidinal, liminal excesses are generated by the performance, signalling the limitation of understanding the commercial sexual exchange as the satiation of sexual desire. The following discussion draws out several key ways tabletop dancing 'blurs the line between entertainment and service', a line which, as the previous discussion demonstrates, is a political organization of sexed bodies. Primarily, 'blurring the lines' relates to what could be called the 'sensorial milieu' of tabletop dancing, where the experience of exchange and the parties involved enter into zones of indetermination, thus disturbing the self-evidence of sexual service.

Tabletop dancing's sensorial milieu: vision and/as touch

Tabletop dancing presented a confusion between 'looking' and 'touching' that disrupted the classificatory system by which prostitution and non-prostitution activities have traditionally been regulated. It did more than this, however. In the tabletop dancing space, vision and touch enter into each other's system of bodily organization, thereby scrambling their impacts on the body. The result is 'one of wanting to reach out touch and be touched'. The following section examines how the vision–touch confusion created 'more than a strip'; the subsequent section examines the lack of gratification – the failure to close the circuit of male desire.

One crucial way tabletop dancing disrupts the distinction between the 'pure strip' and 'service' is through the capacity and sense of vision. The libidinal excess of tabletop dancing was most readily expressed in the parliamentary debates as a consequence of the performance's explicitness (i.e. open leg work). Thus, it was declared, tabletop dancing is like live pornography.[28] As an object of research, pornography has been attributed causal properties, both physiological and psychological.[29] Thus naming tabletop dancing 'live pornography' makes explicit the connection between the explicit image, titillation and (re)action.

However, it is not only the explicitness of what is seen that makes tabletop dancing excessive; there is the additional complication of proximity and liveness. As a sense and as an epistemological tool, sight is understood as distal, able to unify objects or events in a field simultaneously, providing a distance or separateness between seer and seen and in this way, organizes the other senses below it (Grosz 1994: 97).[30] Touch as a contact sense provides successive information based on differentials between surfaces, and in comparison across surfaces.[31] 'Purely a strip' conforms with this distal element of sight, removing the body from the field of vision: it is entertainment. In the case of tabletop dancing, where private dances are given, where the dancer is less than one foot away, swaying, grinding, undulating in a river of skin and perfume, the seeing subject is also the assailed by his sense of smell, his ears respond to conversation, his hands might fleetingly sweep a thigh when he places money in a garter. Sight, instead of organizing the sensing body hierarchically, in line with the supremacy of vision, is now amongst a sensorial overload, and a kind of synaesthesia[32] is produced. This has less to do with tabletop dancing itself, than it does with the sensorium of the body.

In the context of tabletop dancing the eye and the hand communicate with and amplify each other (Merleau-Ponty in Grosz 1994: 99) resulting in men wanting to reach out and touch and be touched by any woman in the street following a voyeuristic interlude at a tabletop venue. This is a communication lubricated with alcohol.[33] In short, the nature of looking in the tabletop dancing venue is in itself a mode of consumption which threatens, rather than ensures, the autonomous spectator-subject. Vision takes place, in other words, in a haptic space in which the function of vision as a distance sense is corroded. Rather, it becomes consumptive, proliferative, multiple. This 'visual gastronomy', (Falk 1994: 54) collapses the distance between self and other, subject and object. Tabletop dancing locates vision within a network of hearing, smell and the potential fantasized touch. In this way, sight, as the simultaneous, coordinated and thereby extensive, is disrupted by this sensory jumble of inter-connectedness and irreducibility. This has an effect not only on the corporeal cartography of masculine desire, but also on the surveilling gaze of regulation. One limitation on the definition was that 'only venues which provide entertainment involving actual sexual intercourse between performers, lap dancing and other prostitution-type ser-vices are regulated under the act. Performances that involve 'simulated sexual activities will not be affected'.[34] However, this caveat, rather than clarifying things, produced more questions:

> The bill will apparently use fair trading inspectors, who look after motorcar sales agents, travel agents, credit providers and estate agents, to monitor prostitute ser-vices, escort agencies, tabletop dancing and peep shows. They will be charged with deciding when a performance moves into a sexual act – and presumably whether someone is faking it. What qualifications will those inspectors have, Mr. Deputy President? It would surely be advisable that the inspectors were women and trained to [be] attuned to the women, and indeed to the men concerned.[35]

The redefinition of sexual service involves now a series of other acts that must be *determined* to be sexual. Thus the legislation, through attempting to make the grey area black or white, in fact institutes a perpetual uncertainty about what is being seen and confers a policing role onto fair trading inspectors who will be responsible for making discernments about real masturbation, simulated masturbation, real climax and simulated climax.

Conclusion: a can of worms?

Tabletop dancing generates a zone of proximity between service and entertainment, touching and looking, where the availability of the sexualized feminine form (in looking, in conversation, in the purchasing of a dance) is an act of consumption itself. Thus, against the bounded economy that 'sexual service' is meant to operate within, what is being offered in tabletop dancing is something else, not gratification, but titillation. In terms of the new amendment to sexual service, it is not the invitation and encourage-ment to masturbate to climax that is the defining feature of the broadened definition, as would be suggested by *Rowell*, where private booths, plastic baskets and tissues are evidence of such encouragement, but the potential to be 'turned on' – to be titillated – that is the key issue. This is signalled by the stipulation that masturbation may be said to occur 'whether or not the genital part of his or her body is clothed or the masturbation results in orgasm' (section 3c PCA). Vision, touch and liveness are 'knots of complication' in the discursive and disciplinary ordering of the commercial sexual exchange, knots of intensity which are antithetical to the closed, civil(ized), gendered, system of the regulatory economy.

The expanded definition of 'sexual service' as a solution to the problem of tabletop does indeed open a can of worms. On the one hand, Clause 4 attempts to respond to the deterritorializing elements of tabletop dancing, which consisted of the perceived collapse of a distinction between service and entertainment, based on the interaction between looking, touching and liveness, and the kind of pleasure (i.e. the kind of exchange) permitted in each of these activities. On the other, the definitional amendment becomes fundamentally contradictory insofar as it seeks to atomize and contain this corporeal *interactivity*. This expanded definition does not institute a closing of the loophole, but rather produces an indefinite multiplication of that which it seeks to contain. The entire object of section C is to set limits on the interaction of what can be viewed, bodily presence, touch and the invitation to touch; and to set limits on how these intensities circulate across the assemblage that is the dancer, the dance and the customer. This ultimately is futile because it is precisely these intensities skittering across the categories of 'dancer' and 'customer' that link them together in a state of inter-subjectivity, and in which the dance is produced *between* dancer and customer:

> [A young cowboy was at the club. He] politely put a tip onstage while I danced, placing it rather than throwing it. I watched him watch me with his chin on his hand ... When he was ready [for a private dance], I led him over to the platforms and chose the most private corner, farthest from the bar and the rest of the club. I told him it was twenty-five dollars a dance and climbed the narrow stairway to the platform so that I stood above him. He leaned back and tilted up the brim of his hat. I took hold of the pole and swung, coiling my body into S-shapes and spirals. I removed my bra and miniskirt and just before the song ended I pulled my thong to one side and let it snap back into place. He looked flushed. Without a word he held up his left hand and circled his index finger. "You want me to keep going?" I asked and he nodded. As the next song began I took off my thong and lowered myself to the floor so that my body was level with his face. I rolled arched, licked my lips – at this he shook his head slowly – did the splits, stood up and twirled. As the second song ended he circled his finger in the air, languidly. I was surprised. Easy money, I thought – no hustling on the floor, just continuous dancing. I reminded myself to move slowly. He was quiet and intent, and I tried to match his mood, to keep him in this state ... He raised his finger one more time for a fourth dance. Now I was the one lulled into a trance, hypnotized by my own movements, locked in his gaze. I lost my sense of time. At the end I wished he would ask for more. He didn't. I picked up my clothes, put them on, and descended the stairs. He handed me a hundred. 'Worth every penny', he said. I thanked him and told him to have a nice night.
>
> *(Eaves 2002: 286–7)*

Clearly what the young cowboy is after and what he gets are qualitatively different from the phallocentric 'closed circuit' discussed earlier. I see the problem of tabletop dancing as a productive problem we need to pursue because it raises fundamental questions about commercial sex, heterosexuality and men as desiring bodies. Tabletop dancing defers men's sexual gratification and, it seems to me, exposes the way in which the control of prostitution – whether legalized or prohibited – requires men and their desires to be concealed and contained. Such concealment is not only about the 'unsavoury' aspects of selling sex, but is fundamentally about ensuring the naturalness of the phallogocentric order of sexual difference and sexual desire, of what is sex, what is 'sexy', and maintain the cultural distinction between what is 'paid for' and what is 'free'. The element of performance points to the fact that in the clubs, finally, a price is put on a *masculine* sexual imaginary. What erotic dancing does, as a performance and through the 'less and more' it generates, is commodify men's need not of having access to women's sexual body, but to the fiction of feminine reciprocity and mirroring their own desires back to them. This is not unique to tabletop dancing. It is simply that tabletop dancing made this fact stand out in relief and highlighted the inadequacy of current ways of thinking about and controlling commercial sex.

This 'closed circuit' assumption about sexual service means that sex industry workers' status is subordinated to that function: to generate erections and sexual gratification in men. Several consequences arise from this. First, it increases the range of control brothels, escort agencies, tabletop dancing venues can have over a worker's body, types of service provided and appearance because her job is limited to gratification rather than the creation of a sexualized fantasy and interaction. Second, there remains an inability to recognize violence against sex workers as both a workplace issue and a criminal issue, with a view 'that just because you work in the industry that you'll do anything … because that's what we do … we do anything … at any time … we have no morals or boundaries … we're on men's beck-and-call all the time … even when we're not working' (Steph in Lantz 2003: 298) shaping the behaviour of clients and indeed the reactions of police to incidents of violence. Research has noted that male client violence seems to occur as a result of conflicting notions about the exchange (Whittaker and Hart 1996). Some clients believe that payment entitles them to control over the sex worker's body – to services they have not paid for, that a worker will not do as a matter of course, or to be as rough as they want (Monto 2004; O'Neill 2001; RhED 2002). The expanded definition of 'sexual service' is unstable, contradictory and extremely broad. But what the debates really point us to is the necessity of developing a definition of 'sexual service' based on what sex industry workers do (including tabletop dancers) from *their* perspective.

Notes

1 *The Age*, 12 March 1995: 16. *The Age* is a broadsheet newspaper that covers events in the City of Melbourne in the State of Victoria.
2 Ibid., 16 January 1994: 3.
3 Ibid., 16 January, 1993: 10. The opening of Crown Casino in November 1993 in Southbank (which abuts King Street, the central location for tabletop dancing venues in Melbourne) amplified the anxiety over tabletop dancing.
4 Ibid., 1 November 1993: 16.
5 Ibid., 26 April 1997: 6.
6 Ibid., 10 March 1997: 11.

7 Ibid., 5 April 1998: 1.
8 Ibid., 16 January 1994: 10.
9 Ibid., 16 January 1994: 3.
10 Ibid., 1 November 1993: 16.
11 Prostitution Control (Amendment) Bill, Assembly, 6 May 1999: 811.
12 Prostitution Control (Amendment) Bill, Assembly, 25 May 1999: 1206.
13 Ibid.: 1199.
14 I am deliberately spanning the breadth of Foucault's concern with government, power and bodies in this one sentence.
15 Part 1 Definitions section 3 Prostitution Control Act 1994.
16 Prostitution Control (Amendment) Bill, Assembly, 25 May 1999: 1197.
17 Ibid.: 1200.
18 Ibid.: 1210.
19 The 'Sexuality, Health and Wellbeing' Exhibition is popular with many segments of the population and is an attempt to destigmatize the adult sex industry. SEXPO makes a successful play at female consumers of sex. A crèche is provided and opening day is ladies day.
20 This case involved determining whether an inner-city venue was providing prostitution services or live adult entertainment as defined by the Richmond Planning Scheme. The venue had provided a showroom in which a striptease act followed by an act of inter-course (between the stripper and the owner of the venue) could be viewed by clients from within a private cubicle.
21 *Rowell v City of Yarra* 1994, 14 A.A.T.R: 61.
22 Ibid.
23 Ibid.: 63
24 Ibid.
25 See Lingis's discussion of the anthropological research done with the Sambia, a Mela-nesian culture organized through an economy of masculine fluids (Lingis 1994: 133–58).
26 I am thinking here of 'premature ejaculation', which suggests that men's climaxes and emission of semen ought to be willed and at an appropriate time. 'Wet dreams' attribute seminal seepage to the unconscious (although even this is antithetical to shared assumptions of men's sexual bodies – semen doesn't seep: it explodes, erupts, it makes the passage from inside to outside definitively).
27 Prostitution Control (Amendment) Bill, Assembly, 25 May 1999: 1207.
28 *The Age*, 26 February 1995: 12.
29 For example loosening sexual inhibitions (Zillman and Bryant 1989), encouraging sexist and misogynist attitudes towards women, or increasing feelings of aggression and violence (Donnerstein 1980; Malamuth 1984).
30 Sight is clearly much more than a sense. It is the organizing principle for Western, phallo-gocentric discourses as such. On the epistemological importance of vision see Levin (1997).
31 There are several dimensions to touch: contiguous access to an object; touch may produce (along with vision) the notion of shape or form, but (unlike vision, which gives shape its simultaneity or synchronicity) touch only yields successive or additive, diachronic notions of shape; touch grants the subject access to the texture of objects (which vision only intimates).
32 Synaesthesia is a condition in which one type of stimulation evokes the sensation of another, as when the hearing of a sound produces the visualization of a colour, or hearing a word such as 'sock' produces a taste. See Baron-Cohen and Harrison (1997).
33 Brothels do not have liquor licences. Strip clubs usually do. In relation to tabletop dancing the Liquor Licensing Commission and VCAT revoked and reviewed liquor licences and planning permits in the hope of halting the proliferation and concentration of venues.
34 Prostitution Control (Amendment) Bill, Assembly, 6 May 1999: 811.
35 Ibid.: 966.

Bibliography

Allen, J. (1984) 'The Making of a Prostitute Proletariat in Early Twentieth Century New South Wales', in K. Daniels (ed.) *So Much Hard Work: Women and prostitution in Australian history*, Sydney: Fontana/Collins.

Baron-Cohen, S. and Harrison, J. (eds) (1997) *Synaesthesia: Classic and contemporary readings*, Malden: Blackwell Publishing.

Donnerstein, E. (1980) 'Aggressive Erotica and Violence Against Women', *Journal of Personality and Social Psychology*, 39: 269–72.

Eaves, E. (2002) *Bare: On women, dancing, sex and power*, New York: Alfred Knopf.

Falk, P. (1994) *The Consuming Body*, London: Sage Publications.

Foucault, M. (1990) *The History of Sexuality: The will to knowledge*, London: Allen Lane.

Frank, K. (2003) '"Just Trying to Relax": Masculinity, masculinizing practices, and strip club regulars', *The Journal of Sex Research*, 40: 61–75.

Godden, L. (2001) 'The Bounding of Vice: Prostitution and planning law', *Griffith Law Review*, 10: 77–98.

Grosz, E. (1994) *Volatile Bodies: Toward a corporeal feminism*, St Leonards: Allen and Unwin.

Lantz, S. (2003). 'Sex Work and Study: Students, identities and work in the twenty-first century', unpublished doctoral dissertation, University of Melbourne.

Levin, M. (1997) *Sites of Vision: The discursive construction of sight in the history of philosophy*, Cambridge, MA: MIT Press.

Lingis, A. (1994) *Foreign Bodies*, New York: Routledge.

MacKinnon, C. (1989) 'Sexuality, Pornography, and Method: Pleasure under patriarchy', *Ethics*, 99(2): 314–46.

Malamuth, N. (1984) 'Aggression against Women: Cultural and individual causes', in N. Malamuth and E. Donnerstein (eds) *Pornography and Sexual Aggression*, Orlando, FL: Academic Press.

Monto, M. (2004) 'Female Prostitution, Customers, and Violence', *Violence Against Women*, 10(2): 160–88.

O'Neill, M. (2001) *Prostitution and Feminism: Towards a politics of feeling*, Cambridge: Polity Press.

Quadara, A. (2008) *Sex Workers and Sexual Assault in Australia: Prevalence, risk and safety*, ACSSA Issues 8. Melbourne: Australian Institute of Family Studies.

RhED (2002) *Power*, St Kilda, Victoria: Resourcing Health and Education. Online. Available at http://www.sexworker.org.au/uploads/documents/RHED_power.pdf (accessed 15 January 2008).

Satz, D. (1995) 'Markets in Women's Sexual Labor', *Ethics*, 106(1): 63–85.

Whittaker, D. and Hart, G. (1996) 'Research Note: Managing the risks: the social organization of indoor sex work', *Sociology of Health & Illness*, 18(3): 399–414.

Wood, E. (2000) 'Working in the Fantasy Factory: The attention hypothesis and the enacting of masculine power in strip clubs', *Journal of Contemporary Ethnography*, February 2000, 29(1): 5–31.

Zillman, D. and Bryant, J. (1989) 'Effects of Massive Exposure to Pornography', in N. Malamuth and E. Donnerstein (eds) *Pornography and Sexual Aggression*, Orlando, FL: Academic Press.

11

REGULATING ADULT WORK IN CANADA: THE ROLE OF CRIMINAL AND MUNICIPAL CODE

Mary Laing

> [T]he reason why there's different by-laws [is because] different cities like [to set] moral standards for themselves. I know that in Toronto massage parlours aren't illegal downtown, but once you get into the ... region which is north of Toronto, it's illegal to have any kind of sexual contact including a hand job ... which seems silly, if you are on one side of the street I can give you a blow job for money, on the other side of the street if my hand touches your penis, I'm breaking the law
>
> *(Interview with Participant 15)*

The quotation above is from one of the female escorts I interviewed as part of an on-going research project that began in September 2009 at Simon Fraser University in Vancouver. The research explores the complex relationship between municipal by-law and Criminal Code, and how adult workers – defined in this context as escorts, exotic dancers, body rubbers/masseuses[1] and sex business managers – experience and manage licensing and law enforcement in their everyday working lives. The quotation offers an insight into the complex regulatory landscape of Canada, and how the current municipal by-law system enables the intimate touching of bodies to be legal and licensed in some spaces but not others, depending on which municipal jurisdiction the client and the person providing adult services happen to be in. Consensual commercial sex between adults is not illegal in Canada, but the Criminal Code makes many of the activities surrounding commercial sex illegal. So, for example, it is legal for consenting adults to exchange sex for money – however, in relation to escorting, for the exchange to be legal, transactions must be done on an out-call basis only. Out-calls, which usually constitute going to a client's residence or a hotel were generally viewed by the escorts I interviewed to be less safe than illegal in-call work, which constitutes working from home or a working flat.

The Criminal Code in Canada dictates the federal laws surrounding sex work. The key prostitution laws are: communicating in public for the purpose of prostitution (section 213); the 'bawdy house' laws around brothel keeping (section 210); encouraging people to engage in prostitution for gain (section 212); and living on the avails of prostitution (section 212) (O'Doherty 2011a). The provinces in Canada also have some jurisdiction in the regulation of prostitution. Provincial law cannot 'overwrite' the Criminal Code, but provinces can enforce legal provisions, and historically provinces have had limited success in implementing injunctions against the so-called 'nuisance' of street prostitution (Barnett 2008). In addition, there are specific provincial laws that seek to regulate sexual service work in different ways. For example, in British Columbia the liquor laws dictate what practices dancers may and may not engage in whilst working in clubs, and revisions around alcohol consumption were made in April 2011[2] (O'Doherty 2011b).

However, at the municipal level, a varied geography of licensing operates, with spaces of sexual encounter including exotic dance venues, escort agencies and body rub parlours, and the workers of these businesses being subject to by-laws and the associated licensing stipulations depending on the local legal geography of the area. The municipal licensing system in Canada demarcates spaces of sexual encounter and, depending on local context, licences proscribe legal as well as occupational and personal identities to adult workers. As Hubbard (2007: 138) suggests:

> the law's spatial inscriptions are more than admonitory, shaping 'legal consciousness' as well as wider understandings of identity and practice: legal definitions of spaces such as the street, the brothel, a private club, the Internet or a licensed premise thus intersect with definitions of the prostitute, the client, the pimp and the trafficker to create a veritable legal geography evident on a variety of spatial scales.

The licensing system also reflects a moral sexual geography, not only demarcating where spaces of sexual encounter may exist in the city via zoning by-laws, but also by stipulating who can enter and work in sex businesses, and how and who they might touch. In some municipalities, by-laws explicitly define what kind of touching is acceptable and which body parts may be accessed by workers and clients if they are to remain within the law (for comparison with Australia, see Chapter 10). In theory, acts of prostitution remain illegal in licensed adult businesses. In practice, however, sexual practices and encounters are performed within a messy legal landscape. This is tricky to negotiate with sexual services being variously legal, illegal or tolerated depending on local context and relationships with the police and by-law enforcement. It is this complex entanglement of policing, health, safety and the law lived and felt by adult workers in Canada that forms the key focus of the chapter. Specifically it will explore how adult workers across Canada negotiate their (il)legal/(un)licensed status through relationships with the police, by-law enforcers and local regulatory processes more generally.

To explore these issues, the chapter will draw on 22 qualitative, thematically driven interviews[3] conducted with adult entertainers (19) and by-law officials (3) across Canada. Some of these workers operated independently, others worked with other women in pairs or as small cooperatives, some managed businesses and worked within them, one interviewee was just an adult business manager rather than an adult worker. All of the adult workers I interviewed were women, except for one. Two of the by-law officials were men and the other was a woman. The analysis will reflect key themes from across the data set holistically, but, due to the geographical disparity of the sexual–legal landscape in Canada, it was not possible to explore all of the cities discussed and the associated interview data. The data presented is therefore a snapshot of the whole data set. All of the data published in this chapter was approved by the participants before being incorporated into the analysis. The chapter is broadly split into two sections: the first looks at the relationship between adult workers and by-law, and the second between adult workers and practices of policing. Tying these together will be a conceptual exploration of how law and bodies entwine to produce an embodied legal geography of sexual commerce in Canada, which is manifest in the negotiations between adult workers, police and by-law enforcers, and the perceptions adult workers have of them.

Licensing adult work

As discussed above, by-laws and the attached licensing stipulations play a considerable role in the local regulation of adult business across Canada. Licences and the attached stipulations vary between municipalities, and businesses and workers are licensed in different ways. Some municipalities do not license adult businesses. For example, the City of Saskatoon in Saskatchewan does not license any form of adult entertainment, whilst others license some types of work but not others; Toronto licenses body rub parlours and exotic dancing but not escorting. Table 11.1 illustrates some of the different ways in which municipalities in Canada license adult work. Even though the cities listed in Table 11.1 are major metropolitan centres, it is evident they all license different aspects of the work, and also have different fee structures.

Calgary is a notable exception, charging a much lower fee. The city significantly reduced their licence fees following the trial of a Calgary fire-fighter who ran licensed escort agencies to make additional income. He was found guilty of 'two counts of living off the avails of prostitution, one count of operating a common bawdy house and one count of using a cell phone when he was prohibited by the courts' (*Calgary Herald* 2006). He escaped prison, arguing that, because he was licensed by the city, he thought he was not committing a federal offence. He believed that the licence to escort superseded any Criminal Code provisions around prostitution, and that the women providing sexual services were therefore working legally. The City of Calgary feared similar charges of profiting from the proceeds of prostitution with their considerable licence fees. These have now been significantly reduced.

The very high fees more generally are particularly noticeable. For example, the fee for a body rub parlour in the City of Vancouver municipality is $9,504.[4] This is currently the third highest licence fee the city charges. The Pacific National Exhibition Centre licence costs $15,236 and a casino or horseracing track could be licensed for $10,880. Indeed, it would be cheaper to buy a licence for an amusement park at $4,595 than for an individual body rub parlour, which is typically no bigger than a

TABLE 11.1 Examples of by-laws pertaining to adult work in Canada

City	License escorts	License escort agency	License exotic dance clubs	License exotic dancers	License body rub parlours	License body rubbers	By-law
Vancouver	Social escort licence $151	Social escort service licence $1,123	Under liquor licence	No	Body rub parlour $9,504	No	Licence by-law 4450
Toronto	No	No	Adult entertainment parlour $11,614.62	Burlesque entertainer $347.06	Body rub parlour $11,539.59	Body rub attendant $347.06	Licensing chapter 545
Ottawa	No	No	Adult entertainment parlour $2,933	No	Body rub parlour $556	No	Schedules 20 and 11. By-law 2002-189
Calgary	Date or escort $146	Date or escorting service $146	Exotic entertainment agency $146	Exotic entertainer $111	Massage centre $146	Massage practitioner $146	Dating and escort service by-law 48M2006; massage licence by-law 51M97; exotic entertainers by-law 51M97

hair salon (see Lowman 2005 for similar analysis from 1997). The expensive licence fees are, according to Vancouver Councillor Lynne Kennedy, set to hamper the opening of adult businesses in the city (cited in Gardner 2003). Yet, echoing Gardner (2003), 'if these are lawful businesses like any other, why would the city want the fees to be prohibitive?' With licence fees so high across Canada, it is possible to argue that municipalities are one of the biggest profiteers of sex business in the country.

The variation in the types of work that are licensed is also geographically specific. It was not clear from the interviews with by-law officers why this specificity exists, although it was suggested that local policing priorities, political will, policing resources, how much adult work is being done, and also the discretion of that work are all contributing factors. The wording of the by-laws differs between municipalities, with some explicitly stating that prostitution may not occur in licensed adult business and others purposely not mentioning prostitution because of the potential entanglement with Criminal Code provisions and regulating beyond the purview of the by-law. For example the Toronto Municipal Code states that body rub can include the:

> kneading, manipulating, rubbing, massaging, touching, or stimulating, by any means, of a person's body or part thereof but does not include medical or therapeutic treatment given by a person otherwise duly qualified, licenced or registered so to do under the laws of the Province of Ontario.
>
> *(Toronto Municipal Code, Chapter 5454, Licensing, 545-21)*

If interpreted literally, this could allow for legal sexual services. It is interesting to note that during fieldwork, there were 25 fully licensed body rub parlours (each paying approximately[5] £11,539.59 in fees to the City of Toronto), operating under this by-law in the municipality of Toronto.

How adult workers manage the process of licensing and their relationships with by-law enforcers was a key theme in the interview data. There has been limited previous research on licensed adult work in Canada (Lewis and Maticka-Tyndale 2000; Lowman 2005; Maticka-Tyndale and Lewis 1999; Kohm and Selwood 2004; van der Meulen and Durisin 2008), and some work in other contexts where adult businesses are licensed (e.g. see Godden 2001 and Harcourt et al. 2005 on the Australian context). The findings presented here strongly reflect the findings of Lewis and Maticka-Tyndale's (2000) research on licensing in Windsor (Ontario), which found that licences were deemed poor value for money by workers. Another key finding in both sets of research was that, because of the process and paperwork associated with purchasing a licence, participants were concerned about their personal details being associated with paperwork detailing their involvement in adult work. Through the licensing paper trail, a legalistic, occupational identity was created which in some cases led to workers having to negotiate personal identity in more specific ways. Also reflecting Maticka-Tyndale and Lewis's (1999) work were concerns over having to buy more expensive licences to work independently, as in some cases workers were expected to purchase an agency and independent licence. That said, in the participant group some workers got around this by purchasing a licence which was for a similar occupation, such as a massage practitioner licence; though this covered massage or therapy rather than any explicit form of adult work, it was considerably cheaper. Finally, in Maticka-Tyndale and Lewis (1999) it was stated that the stipulations of the by-laws were so unclear that adult workers were really 'left on their own to figure out how to conduct their work in a manner that minimised risk to health and well-being and the possibility of being charged with the Criminal Code or municipal violation' (Lewis and Maticka-Tyndale 2000: 440). Again this was reflected in the accounts of the participants in the study. That said, there were also a number of participants who never purchased licences and worked in municipalities that do license adult work. This was largely due to the lack of enforcement in these cities. In addition, and as will be discussed later, there were some participants who supported the licence process in principal, with some detailing the benefits especially in the context of legitimizing adult work. An example of how sex workers are seeking to revolutionize the licensing system is presented towards the end of the chapter.

Moving forward to consider the data itself, analysis of the interviews suggests that participants had a varied relationship not only with by-law officers, but with the process of obeying by-laws and the attached licensing stipulations in a holistic sense. Many women expressed concern over giving personal details when applying for a licence, having to reveal real names rather than the 'scene' names they might use in their work; having their real names connected to scene names was also unsettling as some licences required real names together with all other names an individual might be known by to be formally provided. Also problematic was having to hand over photographs, and going through intrusive police checks without being given detailed information on how the information would be stored, for how long it would be stored and who might have access to it. In Maticka-Tyndale and Lewis (1999) there was evidence that police officers exploited this process, accessing the details of adult workers through the paperwork trail left by the licensing process. Two escorts from Toronto commented on this:

> Well I understand why they do it basically for tax purposes ... it's really easy to under report what you make, but I personally would not work, like I would not strip and I would not work in a massage parlour because of licensing. Like I wanna be an academic, so at some point in my life people are gonna know who I am.
>
> *(Interview with Participant 15)*

> So whenever an employer says they are going to do a background check, now I always ask them what kind, and it's a little frustrating because you don't know what they are looking for, and you don't know where it's posted.
>
> *(Interview with Participant 11)*

In interviews some adult workers discussed a clear separation from their working and 'other' life: 'My family does not know what I do and if it ever came out that would not be good' (Interview with Participant 15); 'I don't want my real name associated with this' (Interview with Participant 9). Although this does not represent the experiences of all adult workers who contributed to the research, with some participants being very open about their status, the separation of the working and personal self is reflective of the broad body of literature exploring the negotiation of identity and self through sexual labour, whereby separation of working and personal self is, for some adult workers, central to work management (Brewis and Linstead 2000; O'Connell Davidson 1996; Oerton and Phoenix 2001). Thus the concern women expressed over being licensed and having to hand over personal details and photographs was problematic in the sense that, by applying for the licence, boundaries between work/self would be transgressed and result in an entanglement of sex working and non-sex working lifestyles. Through licensing, the legalistic identity of body rubber/escort/exotic dancer was attached to their identity through legal processes, despite privacy being seen as central to practices of adult work:

> Yeah it's nothing to do with finances and everything to do with privacy. And even though I am fairly confident that the police here know my first and last name, my real first and last name, they know where I live and I'm very open with them, at the same time, I don't want that on paper.
>
> *(Interview with Participant 15)*

The process of law and licensing in this context becomes entwined with sexual citizenship, notions of understanding, belonging and acceptance within society (Sanders 2009) and, in this case, the role the law plays in the construction of normative and non-normative sexualities (Stephen 2002). As Sanders (2009: 519) suggests: '[t]hose engaged in the sex industry struggle to gain sexual citizenship as stigma, marginalisation, a lack of recognised employment rights … , and criminalization means that commercial sexual behaviour is heralded as non-conformity and therefore "deviant"'. Thus in the context of regulation through licensing and by-law, it is possible to suggest that the law rewrites the bodily scripts of the people engaged in adult work. Not only are licensed workers engaged in sexual service provision in a corporeal and embodied sense, their identities as workers in the adult economy are also inscribed materially in the licences that they own. In some cities, such as Edmonton, where licences are essential due to frequent busts, the link between bodily and legalistic practice is made clear, as escorts when advertising must also display their licence number. In this sense, the licence represents a material manifestation of the links between sexual bodily practice and legal structure. It is important to state that some women are supportive of this, one agency manager suggesting that she liked the licensing system and regular busts associated with it as it kept competition low. Another participant commented on her clients liking that she was licensed: 'Yeah yeah a lot of guys like the licence because, well, they know I'm legal and don't have a criminal record' (Participant 21). In this sense, the licence communicates a sense of legal legitimacy. In a Foucauldian sense, law is powerful in its inscription because of its claims to objectivity; law is perceived as an expression of hegemony (Stephen 2002; see also Proudfoot and McCann 2008). Applying this conceptually to the data then, the licensing and by-law process was powerful due to the inscription of an implicitly sexual occupational identity upon participants. The inscription and association of a sex working identity through legalistic processes was seen as powerful and problematic by many of the women interviewed, especially in terms of how this identity could impact in the longer term. Thus even though by-laws maintain the illusion that adult workers are not engaged in the provision of sexual services for money, the stigma perpetuated through the legalistic labelling process still has the potential to impact on workers in detrimental ways. One interviewee stressed that sex workers were stigmatized simply through perceptions of law and identity:[6]

> I think most people believe that prostitution is illegal, and if something is illegal therefore it's criminal right? Therefore it's a bad thing, that's kind of the idea right. You know the thing with … like smoking weed is illegal and therefore you smoke you're a pothead you're a criminal … like that's kind of the connection that is made, whereas you drink beer its legal therefore you're not a criminal, but where the exact difference is like, it's totally arbitrary. So in that sense, in the sense that the law creates category and creates criminal behaviour in deciding what is the criminal and what isn't, I do think it contributes to stigma.
>
> *(Interview with Participant 9)*

Even for those women who did not feel the stigma of licensing in the same way, licences were deemed expensive and very poor value for money. This was especially the case when fees alone could top $2,500 for independent workers. This is evident in Vancouver where, to work independently, workers, as well as purchasing an individual licence, also need to invest in an agency licence, even if they are not running an agency per se. An escort from Edmonton spoke of similar issues in her interview:

> there was *nothing* that made me feel there was any value to getting a licence. It was a great imposition and an annoyance. I don't appreciate going through security clearance check every year. Goodness I'm 51[7] – what am I going to do that's criminal after all these years?
>
> *(Interview with Participant 25, emphasis as original)*

The cost of licences and different municipalities having different rules and regulations is especially problematic for women doing working tours. If a female escort wanted to tour five Canadian cities, crossing municipal boundaries, and at all times be operating 'legally' under a licence, the fees could easily top $10,000. Thus, not only are licences problematic in the sense that they violate personal norms of privacy and rights to anonymity, but they are prohibitive in their geographical limitations, they have the potential to curtail the mobility of women, and do not reflect mobile, fluid and dynamic working practice. One of the participants discussed how her licence impacted on where she could work and advertise:

So I still have a[n] [escort] licence number but I can advertise in the escort ads only if my ad says that I work outside the city. If I want to work inside the city then I use my licence as a massage practitioner, because I'm not an escort in the city, I'm a massage practitioner in the city, it's the same damn job! ... Pisses me off, the job includes screwing the client, so it doesn't matter what you want to call it!

(Interview with Participant 21)

It is not surprising that research has shown that those working in sex-related businesses are frequently confused about the laws pertaining to their work practice, and are often unsure as to whether they are operating legally or not (Lewis and Maticka-Tyndale 2000). In addition, interviewees complained that when the licence was purchased they were not offered any information about what is legal and what was not under the terms and conditions of the licence by the police or by-law authorities. The municipality of Edmonton does offer information leaflets to all escorts, but this only details the fines applicable if the stipulations of the licence are breached; it does not clearly state what escorting is, apart from mentioning 'introduction services' in one section (City of Edmonton 2010: 2). This leaves adult workers in a precarious legal situation, with all of the by-law officers I spoke to recognizing the link between adult work and sex work. Lowman (2003, cited in Gardner 2003) is also cited in the *Ottawa Citizen* newspaper discussing the futile denial of the link between escorting and sexual services by authorities: 'Police know this. Members of the public know this. So when the politicians say they don't know it, my general reaction is that if they're that ignorant of contemporary Canadian life, they should stand aside.' Canadian municipalities profit from the licence fees they charge whilst turning a blind eye to the fact that workers are engaged in sexual services, thus arguably negating the health and safety of men and women doing adult work. As Participant 21 suggested: 'The City knows what escorting is but they just brush it under the carpet, so they don't have to give us any protection or information.'

Requirements and demands from licensing officers are also uneven. In one interview, a Victoria (British Columbia) based massage worker told me she was informed by by-law that she had to purchase an escort licence, despite her not providing an escort service (which she defined as distinct from massage):

Yeah all of us have an escort licence there is no, there is no erotic massage and for a while I had a massage licence which is only $80 dollars and they called me and I said 'yes I have a licence I have a massage licence', they said 'no, no, you've got to come down and get an escort licence which is $250' and so but they only made me pay the difference between the $80 and the $250 you know they didn't make me have both which was nice ... quite fair.

(Interview with Participant 5)

It was perhaps due to her work being of an 'adult' nature, and the municipality not providing an erotic massage licence, that she was requested to purchase an escort licence. This participant also had good relationships with local by-law officers, describing them as 'on our side' (Participant 5). Other participants saw the main (and sometimes only) benefit of being licensed as working 'legally': 'not only do I work legally ... but I don't risk the fine. Fines for working illegally in Edmonton are IMHO [in my humble opinion] astronomical' (Interview with Participant 25; see Thompson 2010). In relation to this, and as previously mentioned, some escorts and agency owners interviewed were grateful for police busts as they kept unlicensed women (and more competition) out of the market, and relationships with by-law officers and officials (where they existed, which was with a minority of the participants) were usually fairly placid. One woman commented:

> They treated me fairly enough ... with a twinkle in their eyes usually (amused men), but fairly, some thought it was a lark (licensing) but it was their job so they did what they were supposed to do. No one was judgmental though.
>
> *(Interview with Participant 25, as original)*

In relation to this, Participant 5 commented about her local by-law officer: 'He's a nice guy, he likes – he likes flirting with the ladies'. Other benefits of licences in the literature were stated to be the maintenance of good standards on premises used for adult work, for example having hot and cold running water and basic standards of cleanliness (van der Meulen and Durisin 2008). Yet this was not reflected in the experiences of all participants, especially with reference to the exotic dance clubs, which were argued by several participants to have poor levels of cleanliness in toilets and changing areas. Additionally, having nowhere to keep food and drinks, and treacherous poles and dance floors were frequently cited by many of the dancers interviewed, and differed from club to club and area to area.

Policing adult work in Canada

The relationship between police and sexual service providers has been well documented in a number of international contexts (Matthews 2005; Lowman 1992; Shannon et al. 2008). A variety of relationships and regulatory procedures exist in practice, which may or may not follow national regulatory guidelines. While punitive policing policies operate in some contexts, under the guise of Zero Tolerance Policing (ZTP) and associated punitive tactics, in other contexts there is a significant amount of negotiation, resistance, communication and engagement between police and sex/adult workers. This can take various forms, from negotiating a space to work in exchange for intelligence (Policek 2009), operating only in demarcated areas of the city (McKeganey and Barnard 1996) or by showing resistance to policing regimes through geographical mobility, agency and the ability to adapt to changing spaces of sex work (Hubbard and Sanders 2003). Indeed this was reflected in the geography of licensed adult workspaces themselves, especially in relation to exotic dance clubs. Several of the dancers interviewed commented how in some clubs, the licensed areas are those areas connected to the sale of liquor – the bar and the club. Yet there remained other spaces in the clubs – rooms upstairs, spaces which did not fall under the liquor license, which could be used for private dances, where the purview of the by-law did not stretch. The official demarcated spaces were therefore 'stretched' by workers and management alike. Hubbard (2011: 42) describes the demarcation of space by police and other regulators as "'tidying up" the sexual city through acts of partition and boundary-making in order to manage expressions of sexuality that make police and politicians "anxious"'. Licensing and by-law are the embodiment of this process in Canada – making sexual bodies and acts less visible, keeping premises away from schools, churches and residential areas, where such expressions may be deemed offensive to middle-class sensibilities and normativities surrounding appropriate public sexual behaviours and intimacies.

The policing of sexual service work in Canada reflects more general trends of policing internationally. The majority of convictions for prostitution-related offences are for on-street working, with little attention paid to off-street work unless there are suspected links to wider criminal issues, such as underage workers or drugs (Lewis and Maticka-Tyndale 2000; Lowman 2001). The data revealed the women's experiences and perceptions of the police were varied, and dependent on the geographical area where they were working. As elsewhere, the actions of individual officers towards adult workers and their peers had a significant influence on perceptions and experiences of women working in the adult industries. One participant, for example, had a particularly poor experience with the police and would never contact them again, whereas another woman had productive positive experiences and stated she would contact them if required; this was in the same municipality. Relationships with officers were fragile and dependent on the wider political climate of the municipality. Toronto was cited by the interviewees as being one area where the working women had a productive and positive relationship with a local officer who dealt with sex industry issues in the municipality.[8] The women stated that, should they need to, they could contact the nominated person who dealt with sex work issues in confidence:

> Yeah yeah, when we had her [the liaison officer] over for a meeting she was very helpful and like telling us what the laws are ... I mean she can't give a clear there's no risk kind of thing, the [work] is still what it is. She did however sort of say well you know like we don't have the resources, there's no political will to start busting all escorts and whatever, you know, basically be careful and she kind of also repeated that the way they go about and do busts is usually because of complaints by citizens, so again you know don't piss off your neighbours and you should be fine ... don't have drugs involved and don't be involved with underage and you should be fine. But again, you know until there is a will, you know political will to bust like hookers then, you know.
>
> *(Interview with Participant 9)*

Hence, the regulation of sex business through policing is selective and geographically variable. Proudfoot and McCann (2008) discuss this in the context of liquor licence inspectors in Vancouver. Key to the argument made by Proudfoot and McCann (2008; see also Lipsky 1980) is that work completed by local bureaucrats (in the case of this chapter, police and by-law enforcement officers) requires a degree of discretion and tolerance for it to be manageable, and it is through these micro-practices and informal discourses that regulatory frameworks and relationships are developed and performed. This is reflected in the above quotation, with the police officer showing discretion, understanding and being open to developing a working relationship with sexual service providers in the city. It is an informal discursive type of regulation that, although in conflict with the Criminal Code, reflects the local regulatory politics and political will. Of course, this is all premised on who is in local government, the decision-makers in the local police department and the prevailing general attitudes towards sex for sale in the city, which make for an altogether fragile regulatory relationship.

Interviewees and evidence from Edmonton provide a different picture. As discussed earlier there are monthly busts of escorts in Edmonton, and this was deemed by some interviewees as beneficial in terms of markets and competition. Yet the fines levied against unlicensed escorts can reach thousands of dollars and, if workers cannot afford to buy the licence in the first place, it is questionable where the money will come from to pay the fine; this might lead to workers adopting more covert and dangerous working practices to earn the money. Indeed even paying the initial fee for the licence was problematic for some workers, as Participant 9, who has experience of exotic dancing in Toronto explained:

> So in many cases, if you need a licence to start working, well you don't have the money to pay for that licence, like a lot of places the licence is somewhere around 200 bucks or something like that, I think you know in many cases 200 bucks is money that you don't have and usually you need to pay rent, so and that's how pimps get in, it's like well ok I'll pay for the licence, I'll pay for your costume your whatever, like the expenses you need to start, and then you go work and you can pay me back. Er, so basically from my understanding there is a much higher rate in strip clubs of girls being pimped out in places where they need to be licensed to work.
>
> *(Interview with Participant 9)*

For unlicensed or covert workers working in Ottawa, although busts were not common, there was not the productive relationship that workers in Toronto had with police officers. A masseuse commented on this:

> I think everybody's greatest fear in the sex trade is that a cop will show up, like an undercover cop and like … obviously they're not going to say hey I'm a cop and you're not going to ask them, even if you do they're allowed to lie so … I was given lots of tips like don't take money directly out of their hand, let them put it on the table because you don't even see it, you know like.
>
> *(Interview with Participant 14)*

The fear of being busted led women doing adult work to discuss tips and tricks of the trade (which at times were unsuccessful), and ways to work out if clients were undercover cops. Tips and tricks included: knowing when and how to take money;

ensuring the clients are fully undressed before sexual contact occurs; and asking for some intimate contact prior to money being exchanged to prove sex worker/client status (see also Holt et al. 2009). Although less common in the data set, there was also the more sinister suggestion made by a few interviewees that some police officers would exploit adult workers by demanding what one worker described as a 'freebie' (see also Chapter 5):

> [I] don't know if it's true but it's kind of like, I got this through you know the grapevine, but, there were two cops actually ... they say you know if you want me to not bust you then you've got to give us a freebie you know.
>
> *(Interview with Participant 14)*

In addition, evidence from Windsor suggests that the licensing process has actually damaged any potential fruitful relationships escorts had with local police providers. In this case, escort agencies developed a relationship with policing providers, and operated openly under a licence. Soon after the relationship was established, however, the same policing providers busted the agencies for prostitution-related activities. One escort comment on this: 'this is ridiculous. How can anyone imagine that escort work is about anything but sex? How are we supposed to work?' (in Lewis and Maticka-Tyndale 2000: 443).

Hence, the entanglement of municipal and Criminal Code is evident, with localities not sanctioning commercial sex, but openly profiting from it. The recognition of by-law officers that businesses licensed as escort agencies or body rub parlours provided sexual services was explicit in the interview data: 'the body rubs were seen as you know people who were doing it for more than, it was primarily for sexual purposes' (Interview with Participant 33). The licensed premises are regularly inspected by by-law officers and the police. This was also an annoyance for many of the women I spoke to, as many paid taxes on their sex work, which in terms of the Criminal Code meant the authorities were in fact 'living on the avails of prostitution' (S.212 Criminal Code):

> Then what's also frustrating is, I still pay taxes, I pay taxes on everything I make from sex work, escorting is technically illegal but that's what is used to pay taxes, so the government is breaking the law, from what they consider the avails of prostitution.
>
> *(Interview with Participant 11)*

Lowman (2003, cited in Gardner 2003) describes the practice of turning a blind eye by local police departments and by-law officers a 'deliberate blindness, wilful blindness ... Almost all escort agencies and massage parlours are in the business of prostitution.'

So why does regulation in Canada work this way? The licence fees certainly make a great deal of money for municipalities at around $10,000 per premises for a body rub parlour licence, with some municipalities having upwards of 20 licensed parlours within their boundaries. In addition, the closure of adult business has historically led to the movement of women onto the streets, into much darker and dangerous working conditions (Ross 2010; Pitman 2002). The final sections of the chapter will therefore draw on the data presented and speculate more broadly about the policing, regulation and legal geographies of adult work in Canada before briefly offering some conclusions and recommendations for further research in this area.

Understanding the sexual legal landscape

This chapter has presented empirical data on how adult workers in Canada negotiate and experience policing and the processes of by-laws. What is clear is the disparity in work practice and engagement with police and by-law officers between workers operating in different locales. This geographical legal unevenness exists in a country context where the same criminal sanctions apply nationwide, yet local regulatory practices lead to varied experiences of sexual service work. Take, for example, the monthly busts of unlicensed escorts in Edmonton, with media reports citing that women are being fined thousands of dollars for working unlicensed (Thompson 2010). Contrast this with Toronto, where escorts do not require any sort of licence to work, and Vancouver where licences are required but by-laws are rarely enforced (see also O'Doherty 2011a). By simply crossing municipal boundaries for work, the legally defined sex worker/adult entertainer body, identity and the legal reading of the sexual practices of workers are transformed. Godden (2001: 78) describes this type of control at the municipal level as something that 'seeks to make safe: to contain the "vice" by imposing on the body a system of constraints and privations, obligations and prohibitions', thus reflecting Hubbard's notions of 'tidying up' the sexual elements of the city that transgress political and social sexual norms. Employing a Foucauldian analysis, Godden (2001: 79) explores the licensing of brothels in Queensland, arguing that licensing keeps 'bodily activity associated with prostitution within regulated, coercive spaces, while at the same time disciplining the body to ensure the potential vice of prostitution does not erupt to contaminate the wider community'. Through licensing, the commercial sexual body is separated, surveyed and contained. In addition, the managers and operators (the licensees) are defined as the 'intermediary of a regulatory technology that surveys the body at work'. Thus defining madams and escort agency managers as providing a key element of social control within licensed brothels, ensuring that workers abide by 'health criteria and community amenity standards' (Godden 2001: 84). In Canada, however, unlike Queensland, madams and managers can legally go only so far to keep their workers safe because of the criminal limits imposed on commercial sex. However, many managers go above and beyond the law in attempts to keep workers safe, although practice in this regard is variable. Some women interviewed reported very good standards of health and safety. For example, Participant 15 who worked and managed an agency in Toronto reported that she ensured that the women who worked for her agency had a driver nearby and available on the phone at all times, and that security staff were always nearby. Another worker spoke to me about a different manager who

> wouldn't acknowledge the service being offered and if we want[ed] to offer more
> services she would tell us how that it is soliciting or breaking the law but she still

makes money from us so [laughs]. Every time she would tell me something, it seemed like, it was like, she was trying to be proper but she wasn't.

(Interview with Participant 11)

The denial of the agency manager that the women working from her agency were providing sexual services in this case was potentially dangerous in terms of the health and safety (sexual and otherwise) of the women working as escorts.

Returning to the broader context, although licensing serves to segregate and separate sexual bodies in the city, in practice, transgression of stipulations, norms and regulations is common. Indeed, all those licensed workers, even those who are working 'legally' are still not technically – under the terms of their licence – able to sell sexual services. The Foucauldian arguments made by Godden (2001) around the control of sex business through local regulatory mechanisms are compelling and represent what Hubbard describes as a more 'diffuse social control' (Hubbard 2011: 71). This diffuse form of social control and indeed the disciplinary gaze exercised by police and by-law officers is lived and experienced in multiple formal and informal ways by adult workers through local regulatory processes. Indeed it is through these day-to-day encounters that we garner an understanding of the embodied legal landscape, and how policing and by-laws play out in practice and create unique micro-political landscapes of sexual regulation (see also Lipsky 1980; Proudfoot and McCann 2008). As Proudfoot and McCann, (2008: 356) suggest: 'Bureaucratic geographical imaginations draw on deeply held, social (rather than individual and personal) discourses about places as desirable, dangerous, unhealthy, problematic and so forth. These discourses order and direct policy.' Hence, the unevenness is unsurprising as local priorities are developed by different by-law and police departments, who have different tolerances, which, as described by the escort at the start of the chapter, can literally vary from street to street (see also Proudfoot and McCann 2008).

Conclusion

This chapter has described and conceptualized the complex legal geography of adult work in Canada with reference to processes of licensing and policing. Central to the arguments made have been how adult workers experience regulatory processes, the relationships between key regulators and adult workers. This chapter has painted a fairly critical picture of the licensing process. Although this critical view is certainly reflected in the wider literature, it is important to highlight a case where adult workers have used licensing to their advantage, which further demonstrates the patchy nature of regulation in Canada. In British Columbia, the British Columbia Coalition of Experiential Communities (BCCEC) has put forward proposals to the City of Vancouver for the introduction of a sex industry accreditation scheme. The accreditation scheme would work independently or as an add-on to the existing business licences. The scheme would be voluntary, and it would not be compulsory for workers to have a licence. However, for businesses seeking a sex business licence, if managers were a member of the scheme it would carry favour with the city of Vancouver when business licences were up for renewal. The BCCEC argue that accreditation has a number of important benefits for sex workers, sex businesses and the wider community including: safer places of work with minimum health and safety standards implemented; the industry would be demystified; standard ethical business practices and procedures would be implemented; there would be a procedure to lodge complaints against businesses or individuals without harming livelihoods; and the scheme would allow for greater ability to target and remove exploiters, pimps and traffickers from the sex industry (BCCEC 2011: 8–10). In addition, the licences would be available at a reduced rate, and no personal information would be held on record in municipal offices. Instead workers would take an open book exam as part of the process, and appear in person to collect the licence and present ID at this point. The accreditation scheme would therefore deal with many of the key issues faced by workers as described earlier in this chapter, and would arguably provide a more realistic and workable system which would also offer value for money by increasing industry standards (BCCEC 2011).[9] If local variations of the system were implemented nationally it could also contribute to preventing contradictory and stigmatizing manifestations of by-laws;[10] emphasizing the health and safety of workers rather than thinly veiling the practice of commercial sex ongoing within adult businesses; and also work towards preventing and perpetuating stigma in adult work whilst cities make money from exorbitant licence fees. Hence, the notion that sex, the body and the law are mutually reinforcing and relational is certainly valid and evidenced through the above data (Hubbard 2007). I would also add that law, (commercial) sex and the body are also transgressive, have agency and are bound through practice to the geographies of particular sexual spaces. Drawing on Blomley (2005) there is certainly some mileage in considering how the law and legal frameworks define certain spaces of work, like the body rub parlour or the escort agency, and also how these frameworks also demarcate what type of practice can take place where. An additional key issue highlighted by workers interviewed, but which represents a grey area in terms of research and practice, are sexual practices which do not necessarily constitute sex for money, for example erotic needle play, fetish work, phone sex and naked cleaning. Although some municipalities offer a licence for 'nude working' many do not, which again leaves workers uncertain of whether their work practice is actually lawful. As one worker commented:

> there's no way to know (how) the law applies to (kink) or the traditional dominatrix where there is no sexual contact at all, even though you know … it itself more or less a sexual service. It does not even have any sexual contact and they still have to worry about the law because it's so ambiguous.
>
> *(Interview with Participant 14)*

Another Participant commented on the ambiguous situation of fetish and domination work, and specifically expressed concerns over how this type of practice was regulated in different cities:

> Well actually when I started into domination I actually went to the city of Vancouver to check all the licence thing and there was nothing that seemed

suitable for the type of work I was doing so I didn't bother and then, and then when I heard about, that there was a dungeon busted in Toronto, under bawdy house laws got really surprised and I contacted the legal centre to find out more laws around it because … to find out what the legalities were because then at that point then Canada had decided dungeons were considered the same as prostitution.

(Interview with Participant 8)

As has been evidenced above, the law impacts on who we can touch, be intimate with and under what circumstances and contexts related to commercial adult industries. The law remains very much in our bedrooms, boudoirs and commercial sex encounters (however, in the fetish context, there is less clarity about this.) Although in some municipalities, by-law provisions might offer a licence which allows people to work in the nude, most workers interviewed spoke of an absence of law and regulation in relation to adult work which would not normatively be constructed as commercial sexual or adult services. Perhaps future research on licensing and local regulatory politics could therefore usefully address this lacuna, as well as the regulation of other 'grey' areas within the adult industries.

Acknowledgement

I would like to thank the Canadian Bureau for International Education for the award of a Commonwealth Post-Doctoral Fellowship which allowed me to carry out this piece of research.

Notes

1 The terms body rub/rubber and masseuse are used interchangeably in this chapter as body rub is the legal term and masseuse is often how the women defined themselves and their work.
2 BC Liquor laws: http://www.pssg.gov.bc.ca/lclb/docs-forms/guide-liquor-primary.pdf, pp. 31–2 (accessed 8 January 2012).
3 In total 23 interviews were completed but one participant pulled out of the project.
4 All licence fees are current as of 24 March 2011.
5 This is approximate as the 2010 fee would have been slightly less than the stated 2011 fee.
6 It is important to note that, although the majority of participants, when asked about stigma, report a negative impact, a minority of participants commented that they did not feel stigma from wider society. As with any data set there was some variation in responses.
7 It is interesting to note that this interviewee pointed out that Edmonton is 'top heavy' with older licensed escorts, with the oldest licensed escort in the city stated to have been born in the 1930s.
8 That said, one interviewee who also had experience working in the Toronto area had had a negative experience with a different police officer from the same police department.
9 See also a critique of Vancouver by-laws on-line: http://rabble.ca/babble/sex-worker-rights/proposed-municipal-bylaw-revisions-vancouver (accessed 8 January 2012).
10 For example, Ottawa's Adult Entertainment Parlour Schedule 11, sections 24 1a & b states:

The adult entertainment owner or an adult entertainment operator shall post the following notices in an area accessible to the patrons and employees, in the adult entertainment performers' dressing rooms, at all public entrances and in the washrooms: a notice to advise that physical contact is prohibited which notice shall include the telephone numbers of the Ottawa Police Service and Bylaw Services of the City of Ottawa; and a notice that sexually transmitted infections can be transmitted through unprotected physical contact.

Bibliography

Barnett, L. (2008) 'Prostitution in Canada: International obligations, federal law, and provincial and municipal jurisdiction', *Library of Parliament*, PRB 03-30E.

BCCEC (2011) *Opening the Doors: Final report*, Vancouver: BC Coalition of Experiential Communities.

Blomley, N. (2005) 'Flowers in the Bathtub: Boundary crossings at the public–private divide', *Geoforum*, 36: 281–96.

Brewis, J. and Linstead, S. (2000) '"The Worst Thing is the Screwing": Consumption and the management of identity in sex work', *Gender, Work and Organisation*, 7: 84–97.

Calgary Herald (2006) 'Ruling Raises Doubts on Escort Law', 22 February. Online. Available at http://www.canada.com/calgaryherald/news/story.html?id=7a3d644a-9bd6-445d-8109-7d9b43b0f348&k=23420 (accessed 19 April 2011).

City of Edmonton (2010) *Escort Licensing: We have information you need to know*, Edmonton: City of Edmonton.

Gardner, D. (2003) 'How Cities "License" Off-Street Hookers'. Online. Available at http://www.missingpeople.net/how_cities_'license'_off-street_hookers-june_16,_2002.htm (accessed 21 April 2011).

Godden, L. (2001) 'The Bounding of Vice: Prostitution and planning law', *Griffith Law Review*, 10: 77–98.

Harcourt, C., Egger, S. and Donovan, B. (2005) 'Sex Work and the Law', *Sexual Health*, 2: 21–128.

Holt, T., Blevins, K.R. and Kuhns, J.B. (2009) 'Examining Diffusion and Arrest Avoidance Practice among Johns', *Crime and Delinquency*, 20: 1–24.

Hubbard, P. (2007) *Regulating the Spaces of Sex Work: Assessing the impact of prostitution law: Full research report*, ESRC End of Award Report, RES-000-22-1001, Swindon: ESRC.

——(2012) *Cities and Sexualities*, London: Routledge.

Hubbard, P. and Sanders, T. (2003) 'Making Space for Sex Work: Female street prostitution and the production of urban space', *International Journal of Urban and Regional Research*, 27: 75–89.

Kohm, S.A. and Selwood, J. (2004) 'Sex Work and City Planning: Winnipeg's red light district committee and the regulation of prostitution', Working Paper 42 Winnipeg: University of Winnipeg.

Lewis, J. and Maticka-Tyndale, E. (2000) 'Licensing Sex Work: Public policy and women's lives', *Canadian Public Policy*, 36: 437–48.

Lipsky, M. (1980) *Street Level Bureaucracy: Dilemmas of the individual in public services*, New York: Russell Sage Foundation.

Lowman, J. (1992) 'Street Prostitution Control: Some Canadian reflections on the Finsbury Park experience', *British Journal of Criminology*, 32: 1–17.

——(2001) *Identifying Research Gaps in the Prostitution Literature*, Research and Statistics Division, Department of Justice: Canada.

——(2005) 'Submission to the Subcommittee on Solicitation Laws of the Standing Committee on Justice, Human Rights, Public Safety and Emergency Preparedness'. Online. Available at http://24.85.225.7/lowman_prostitution/HTML/SCJHPE/Submission_to_the%20Subcommittee_on_Solicitation%20Laws_Brief.pdf (accessed 19 April 2011).

McKeganey, N. and Barnard, M. (1996) *Sex Work on the Streets: Prostitutes and their clients*, Buckingham: Open University Press.

Maticka-Tyndale, E. and Lewis, J. (1999) *Escort Services in a Border Town: Transmission dynamics of sexually transmitted infection within and between communities*, Literature and Policy Summary, Ontario: STAR Project.

Matthews, R. (2005) 'Policing Prostitution Ten Years On', *British Journal of Criminology*, 45: 877–95.

O'Connell Davidson, J. (1996) 'Prostitution and the Contours of Control', in J. Weeks and J. Holland (eds) *Sexual Cultures: Communities, values and intimacy*, London: Macmillan.

O'Doherty, T. (2011a) 'Criminalization and Off-Street Sex work in Canada', *Canadian Journal of Criminology and Criminal Justice*, April: 217–45.

——(2011b) 'Discussion of Provincial Law in Relation to Adult Work'. E-mail. (28 July).

Oerton, S. and Phoenix, J. (2001) 'Sex/Bodywork: Discourses and practices', *Sexualities*, 4: 487–512.

Pitman, B. (2002) 'Re-mediating the Spaces of Reality Television: America's most wanted and the case of Vancouver's missing women', *Environment and Planning A*, 34: 167–84.

Policek, N. (2009) 'Policing the Truth: Sex workers as police informants', paper presented at Annual Socio-Legal Studies Association conference, Leicester: De Montfort University, 8 April.

Proudfoot, J. and McCann, E.J. (2008) 'At Street Level: Bureaucratic practice in the management of urban neighbourhood change', *Urban Geography*, 29: 348–70.

Ross, B.L. (2010) 'Sex and (Evacuation from) the City: The moral and legal regulation of sex workers in Vancouver's West End, 1975–1985', *Sexualities*, 13: 197–218.

Sanders, T. (2009) 'Controlling the "Anti Sexual" City: Sexual citizenship and the disciplining of female street sex workers', *Criminology & Criminal Justice*, 9: 507–25.

Shannon, K., Kerr, T., Allinott, S., Chettiar, J., Shoveller, J. and Tyndall, M.W. (2008) 'Social and Structural Violence and Power Relations in Mitigating HIV Risk of Drug-Using Women in Survival Sex Work', *Social Science and Medicine*, 66: 911–21.

Stephen, K. (2002) 'Sexualised Bodies', in M. Evans and E. Lee (eds) *Real Bodies,* Basingstoke: Palgrave.

Thompson, M. (2010) 'Escort Sting Nets $90K in Fines'. Online. Available at http://www.edmontonsun.com/news/edmonton/2010/06/30/14566686.html (accessed 9 May 2010).

Van der Meulen, E. and Durisin, M. (2008) 'Why Decriminalize? How Canada's municipal and federal regulations increase sex workers' vulnerability', *Project Muse*, 20: 289–311.

INDEX